WITHIN THE BOUNDARIES OF ISLAM

WITHIN THE BOUNDARIES OF ISLAM

A Study on Bid'ah

Shaykh Muḥammad al-Ghazālī

Translated and introduced by
Aslam Farouk-Alli

Islamic Book Trust
Kuala Lumpur

Published by
Islamic Book Trust
607 Mutiara Majestic
Jalan Othman
46000 Petaling Jaya
Selangor, Malaysia
www.ibtbooks.com

Islamic Book Trust is affiliated with The Other Press.

Perpustakaan Negara Malaysia   Cataloguing-in-Publication Data

Ghazali, Muhammad, 1917-1996
    Within the boundries of Islam : a study on Bid'ah / Shaykh
    Muhammad al-Ghazali ; translated and introduced by Aslam Farouk-Alli.
    ISBN 978-967-5062-66-7
    ISBN 978-967-5062-65-0 (pbk.)
    1. Heresies, Islamic.   2. Kufr (Islam).   3. Sin--Islam.   I. Title.
    297.29

Contents

Publisher's Note

What is *bid'ah* or innovation? This Islamic term has been the subject of debate for centuries among Muslim scholars, the majority of whom try to define it from their own sectarian perspectives. Some stretch their arguments too far, even linking them to a practitioner's *īmān* and *'aqīdah*.

While this is going on, innovations in various forms have continued to creep into Muslim societies, casting a shadow on the pristine purity of Islamic religious practices, some of them clearly outside the boundaries of Islam. Thus the debate has been turned into subjectively defining 'positive' and 'negative' types of *bid'ah* or innovation.

In this book, Shaykh Muḥammad al-Ghazālī addresses a 'central characteristic of Islamic thought, i.e., the constant process of deviation and correction that it is continually subjected to. The specific focus of this study is the subject of *bid'ah* which is best understood as heretical innovation in matters related to religious practice.'

The translator has successfully conveyed Shaykh al-Ghazālī's work to the English reader in the best way possible, staying true to his style of writing, which is straight to the point. The translator's own deep insight into the subject is reflected in his Introduction to the book.

This book is one of three works by Shaykh al-Ghazālī published by Islamic Book Trust, the others being *A Thematic Commentary on the Qur'an*, and *Our Beginning in Wisdom*.

It is hoped that the reader will approach this book with an open mind. Finally, it is worth noting that there is a common thread running through the text and it is therefore recommended that the book not be read in bits and pieces but as a whole, so that justice can be done to the author.

Islamic Book Trust,
Kuala Lumpur,
Dhū al-Ḥijjah 1431 /
November 2010

Glossary

This Glossary provides a list of important terminology encountered in the text. Sometimes more than one rendition is provided for a single term, as a result of the varying contexts in which a single term may appear, thereby requiring a more nuanced rendition. Most of the terms below have been indexed and are sufficiently explained in the text itself; the purpose of the Glossary is simply to ensure ease of reference.

ādāb. Etiquette or manners.
'ādāt. Matters of custom.
aḥādīth (pl. of *ḥadīth*). Prophetic saying.
aḥkām (pl. of *ḥukm*). Legal judgements, precepts or rulings.
ahl al-bayt. Followers of the household of the Prophet, i.e, the Shī'ah.
ahl al-bida'h. Heretics.
ahl al-futyā. The jurisconsults.
ahl al-ḥadīth. The followers of the Prophetic tradition; a school of thought that adopts a literalist approach to understanding Islam.
ahl al-'ibādāt. People of worship, i.e., those that heed the teachings of the jurists and not the Sufis.
ahl as-sunnah. A doctrinal school that emphasises the importance of the Prophetic tradition.
akhlāq. Behaviour, ethics.
'aqā'id (pl. of *'aqīdah)*. Islamic doctrines of faith.
asbāb an-nuzūl. Occasions of revelation.
aṣḥāb ad-dā'ī al-muṭlaq. Companions (followers) of the absolute herald.
asrār al-ḥurūf. Numerology.

asrār ash-sharī'ah. Principles of the sacred law.

barā'ah. Freedom from liability.

bid'ah. Heretical innovation in matters related to religious practice.

al-bid'ah al-iḍāfiyyah. An imitative innovation.

al-bid'ah al-ḥaqīqiyyah. An original innovation.

al-bid'ah al-murakkabah. A compound innovation.

bid'ah ḥasanah. A good or commendable Innovation.

bid'ah wājibah. An obligatory innovation.

ḍa'īf. A weak (unreliable) Prophetic tradition.

dalīl al-'aql. Reason as a source of legislation.

dhawq. Personal spiritual inclination, Spiritual Sensibility.

dhikr (pl. adhkār). Ritual recitation of incantations.

du'ā'. Supplication.

fatwā. Juristic Opinion.

fiqh. Islamic substantive law (jurisprudence).

fiṭrah. The natural dispensation of a human being.

ḥāfiẓ al-Qur'ān. A person who has memorised the Qur'an.

ḥajj. Pilgrimage.

ḥalāl. Lawful.

ḥarām. Forbidden, prohibited.

ḥasan. A Good (credible) Prophetic tradition.

ḥikmah. The science of aphorisms.

ḥudūd. The Islamic penal code.

ḥulūl. Immanence.

'ibādāt. Acts of worship.

ijmā'. Consensus.

ijtihād. Mental exertion, reasoned opinion, creative intellectual exertion.

'illah. Clear motive.

al-'illah al-manṣūṣah. Underlying textual motive.

'ilm al-kalām. Dialectic theology.

'ilm al-khilāfiyyāt. Science of disputation.

imān. Belief, faith.

'irfān. Gnosis.

isnād. Chain of transmitters of a Prophetic saying.

istihsān. Jurisitic preferance.

istiṣhāb. Presumption of continuity.

istiṣlāḥ. Welfare or well being, convention.

i'tiqād. Doctrine.

jihād. To strive, exertion in the path of religion.

kashf. Spiritual unveiling of the divine.

khawārij. The rejectionists; literally, "Those who went out." The term refers to an early Islamic sect that opposed both Imam ʿAlī and Muʿāwiyyah during the first civil war in Islam.

madhab ahl ar-raʾy wa al-qiyās. School of opinion and analogy.

madhab aẓ-ẓāhiriyyīn. The literalist school.

makrūh. Disliked, detestable.

mandūb. Recommended.

maqāmāt. Spiritual stations or levels.

maqāṣid al-āyāt. Objectives of revelation.

al-maṣlaḥah al-mursalah. Public welfare.

matn (pl. *mutūn*). The text of a Prophetic tradition (as opposed to its chain of transmitters).

mawlid. Ritual celebration of the Prophet's birthday or that of a saint.

mazār. Place of holy pilgrimage.

maʿrifah. Knowledge.

mubāḥ. Neutral.

muftī. Jurisconsult.

muqallid. Adherent to a specific school of jurisprudence.

murīd. Sufi initiate.

mushāhadah. The state of spiritual witness.

mutakallimūn. Dialectic scholars.

muwaththaq. An attested Prophetic tradition. This term is used in Shīʿah jurisprudence for a trustworthy narration, but one that is not narrated by a person from the Prophet's lineage.

muḥāsabah an-nafs. Self-accountability.

muʿāmalāt. Matters pertaining to conduct (as opposed to matters pertaining to worship).

an-nāsikh wa al-mansūkh. Abrogating and abrogated verses of the Qurʾan.

qiyās. Analogy.

al-qiyās al-jalī. Apparent analogy.

quṭb. Charismatic sufi leader.

qāḍī. Judge.

rakʿah. Prayer cycle.

ar-riyāḍah an-nafsīyyah. Spiritual exercise.

ruqā. Incantations.

ṣahābah. Companions of the Prophet.

ṣaḥīḥ. An authentic Prophetic tradition.

salafī. A term derived from the Arabic word *salaf,* which literally means predecessor, so the term *salafī* generally connotes an atavistic posture, where one looks back to the precedents of the earlier generation for guidance and inspiration.

sharī'ah. The sacred law.

shar'. The revealed law.

shirk. Associating partners with Allah.

siḥr. Magic.

sunan. Established Prophetic practices.

as-sunnan al-āḥād. Singularly narrated Prophetic traditions.

as-sunnan al-mutawātirah. Prophetic traditions narrated by a plurality of narrators.

sunnah. Prophetic practice.

sīrah. Prophetic biography.

tafsīr. Qur'anic exegesis of interpretation.

tajallī. Transfiguration, divine manifestation.

Takhrīj. Citation of *ḥadīth.*

ṭalmisāt. Talismanry.

tamā'im. Amulets.

taqlīd. Blind imitation.

taqwā. God consciousness.

ṭarīqah. Sufi brotherhood.

tawḥīd. Monotheism, union with the divine (in sufi thought).

taṣawwuf. Islamic mysticism.

tābi'īn. Companions of the companions of the Prophet.

'ulamā'. Religious scholars.

'urf. Customary practice.

uṣūl al-fiqh. Principles of source methodology in Islamic law.

walī (pl. *awliyā'*). Saint (lit. Friend of Allah).

waḥdah al-wujūd. Unity of being.

waḥdah ash-shuhūd. Unity of witness.

wilāyah. To pay allegiance to a saint.

wuḍū'. Ablution.

wājib. Obligatory.

zakāh. Almsgiving.

Translator's Preface

Translation is an elusive practice that is regarded by some as more difficult than writing.[1] In addition to meeting the challenges of rendering an accurate account, the translator must also strive to attain a level of fluency and aesthetic composure that meets the minimum requirements of the target language. Sensitive translators have therefore for a long time been fairly disinclined towards literal translation. With this in mind, a contemporary translation theorist convincingly argues that the process is more firmly grasped when approached from the point of view of negotiation, where the translator mediates between the original text and the destination text.[2]

Moreover, since all languages are culturally specific, any attempt to provide a literal translation runs the risk of offending both the original work and the translation itself. Our translation theorist illustrates this point very effectively by reflecting upon the English expression, *you're pulling my leg*. He explains that rendering such an idiom in Italian can only be achieved by "substituting an English leg with an Italian nose," since a literal translation would be absolutely unusual in Italian.[3] This example succinctly demonstrates that it is only by sometimes being *literally unfaithful* that a translator succeeds in being truly faithful to the source text.[4]

Two examples from this book make the same point. In his introduction, Shaykh al-Ghazālī uses the term *asrār ash-sharī'ah*, which may be literally rendered as *Secrets of the Sacred Law*. However, this expression is more accurately rendered as *Principles of the Sacred Law*, not only because it is being used in reference to the science of Islamic Jurisprudence, but also because of the provenance of the term itself.

Islamic Jurisprudence is one of the most rational of Islamic sciences and the literal translation lends a mythological import to an expression that carries no such connotation. The term carries no such indication in the Arabic lexicon in this context as well. Any prudent student of Islamic legal philosophy understands that the expression reflects the epistemological posture of Islamic Jurisprudence, where revelation is given primary consideration over all other sources of law. On this basis, even the principles and objectives of the Sacred Law are extracted from revelation. Therefore, in the Arabic idiom, the expression *asrār ash-sharī'ah* recognises the derivative status of the principles of the Sacred Law and is not intended to suggest something of a magical nature. Rendering the expression as *Secrets of the Sacred Law* would not only be incorrect, but misleading as well.

The second example relates to the translation of the title of this book: *Laysa min al-Islām* literally translates as *Not of Islam*. However, this translation is not only cumbersome in English but also lacks the nuanced import of the Arabic title, which strongly suggests limitations. As such, I have chosen to render the title as: *Within the Boundaries of Islam—A Study on Bid'ah*. This in my opinion far more accurately captures the import of the Arabic title.[5]

In spite of sometimes indulging in extra-judicious license, I have striven to produce a translation that is equally faithful to the meaning of the original Arabic text as well as to the lexical and syntactic requirements of the English language. This has not been an easy task and, as always, it is ultimately the reader who will pass final judgement. Some clarification on certain aspects of the translation is necessary, so as to justify the liberties exercised in the process.

With regards to the rendition of the Arabic definitive article "al" (*the*) I have chosen to avoid the standardized, morphologically-fixed form and have accommodated the pronunciation conventions dictated by the occurrence of sun and moon letters in the Arabic alphabet. Where it precedes a sun letter, the "l" is elided and replaced with the first letter of the next word, to indicate the correct pronunciation. For example, the transliteration for the Arabic expression "The Sun" would be rendered as *ash-shams* and not *al-shams*.

The citation of sources has also posed a challenge because Shaykh al-Ghazālī draws on material from various sources without providing full reference details. He writes with the urgency of an activist more concerned with making a point and changing the world than with providing meticulous citation, which would be more suited to a narrow intellectual audience and not the general reader that al-Ghazālī wants to address. In deference to his method, I have chosen to confine myself to the citations he provides and not to attempt to provide citations for other works he refers to. Furthermore, he sometimes quotes from English sources, providing his own Arabic rendition. In such instances I have simply translated these passages back into English. Although these passages cannot be regarded as direct quotes, care has been taken to ensure that authorial intent was clearly conveyed.

The present work is replete with Qur'anic verses and Prophetic traditions. I have relied upon the work of Muhammad Taqī-ud-Dīn al-Hilālī and Muhammad Muhsin Khān[6] for the translation of the Qur'anic verses but have, at times, made certain changes to suit my own preferences. All translations of *aḥādīth* (Prophetic Sayings) are my own.

The citation (*takhrīj*) of *ḥadīth* sources in this work deserves special mention. Shaykh al-Ghazālī was not in the habit of providing full *ḥadīth* citations for the prophetic sayings that he utilized. This does not, however, suggest that his citations are random, or that they do not pay attention to the authenticity of the material in question. Al-Ghazālī followed a very specific methodology of authentication, even though he does not explain it in this particular work. If he found that a particular prophetic tradition was in total agreement with the Qur'an or with an authentic *ḥadīth*, he would have no problem quoting it, even if some scholars of *ḥadīth* regard it as weak or incredible. This is not the place for a lengthy discussion on the subject and the interested reader can refer to the introduction of the English translation of al-Ghazālī's *Fiqh as-Sīrah*[7] for elaboration on his *takhrīj* methodology.

Nonetheless, I have striven to reference as many of the *aḥādīth* that appear in the book as possible, in the hope that this will be of added benefit to the reader interested in exploring the original sources in further detail. Wherever possible, I have provided the source collection, the relevant book (or chapter), and the *ḥadīth* number. In tracing the *ḥadīth* material back to its sources, I have benefited tremendously from two Arabic websites that have archived a tremendous amount of source material, and the interested reader is advised to explore them further. These are *www.al-islam.com* and *www.dorar.net*. I also owe a debt of gratitude to Muḥammad al-Hindī and Jamāl Sa'īd, for their assistance in tracing a few of the sources I had difficulty in locating.

All writing is context-bound and this book is no exception. Al-Ghazālī produced this work in the late 1950s and it sometimes relates events that are specific to that time and which might no longer be relevant, important or even familiar to the contemporary reader. Certain liberty has been exercised in such cases and the text has been edited accordingly, excluding such material. However, this has only been done in instances where such sections were not part of the central argument. In some instances, these edits are indicated in translator's footnotes with the necessary elaboration.

I have also included an introductory chapter that provides additional insight into the author's personal background and the socio-political context that informed his work. Such introductions are useful but may not be deemed essential by all readers. The reader is welcome to skip over the Introduction and move straight on to the translation itself.

Many debts have been incurred in the process of completing this work and many valuable lessons have been learnt. The greatest debt is owed to members of my immediate family: my wife Nadia and our children Umar, Hamza, Haytham and Hawwa, who more than anyone else, carried the burden of my absence as I sacrificed time with them to complete this work. My in-laws, Rashieda and Abdul Razak Ismail, provided great support. I benefited tremendously from the input I received on the translation from the many people who read parts of it at various stages, but mostly from Nadia, who read it at least twice. Basheer Nafi read and commented on the Translator's Introduction and also drew my attention to a few very useful reference works. Ibrahim Abu-Rabi' (who I have never had the pleasure to meet in person yet) graciously responded to my queries on al-Ghazālī via email. S. Parvez Manzoor read a translation of the conclusion and made some insightful suggestions that I was happy to include. Nadia Ahmed (*nee* Gani), provided assistance very early on in the process by word processing the initial chapters, which were handwritten. Na'eem Jeenah undertook the final copyedit and his superb efforts have made the text a far more pleasurable read. Murshid Davids spared no effort in trying to find a suitable publisher for this work, which would not have seen the light of day without his efforts and commitment. I would also like to express my immense gratitude to the Islamic Book Trust for agreeing to publish this book, especially to Abdar Rahman Koya and his team, for their diligence, easy manner and equal commitment to academic excellence and aesthetics.

Parts of this book were submitted as a thesis in fulfilment of an M.A. in Arabic from the University of South Africa (UNISA). I am grateful to UNISA for permission to publish the relevant sections, and to Professor Yousuf Dadoo, who supervised the original thesis. His input has contributed tremendously to improving the standard of this work.

The lessons that were learnt in the process of completing this book cannot be quantified, and the people that have added to my knowledge cannot be easily recalled. I therefore dedicate this effort to all my teachers, starting with my parents, Naseem and Farooq Alli Gani, the first and finest: *Rabbi irḥamhumā kamā rabbayānī ṣaghīrā* (Qur'an 17: 24).

Aslam Farouk-Alli
Damascus
7 Ramaḍān 1430 /
29 August 2009

Notes
1. Muḥammad ʿInānī (2004), *Fann at-Tarjamah* (Cairo: ash-Sharikah al-Miṣriyyah al-ʿĀlamiyyah li an-Nashr).
2. Umberto Eco (2003), *Mouse or Rat? Translation as Negotiation* (London: Weidenfeld & Nicolson), p. 6.
3. ibid., p. 5.
4. ibid.
5. Such license is not unprecedented. Shaykh al-Ghazālī's first book to be translated into English was entitled *Min hunā Naʿlam* (lit. *From Here we Learn*), but was rendered as *Our Beginning in Wisdom* (translated by Ismāʿīl Rājī al-Fārūqī, Octogan Press, 1953). His second book to be translated into English carried the Arabic title *Fann adh-Dhikr wa ad-Duʿāʾ ʿind Khātim al-Anbiyāʾ* (lit. *The Art of Remembrance and Supplication [as practiced by the] Seal of the Prophets*); this was however rendered as *Remembrance and Prayer— The Way of the Prophet Muhammad* (translated by Yusuf Talal De Lorenzo, The Islamic Foundation, 1986). The Indonesian translation of this book carries the title: *Not From the Teachings of Islam*; see: Shaykh Muḥammad al-Ghazālī (1995), *Bukan dari Ajaran Islam*. Translated by Suranto Solo (CV: Pustaka Mantiq).
6. *Interpretation of the Meanings of the Noble Qurʾān in the English Language*, (Riyadh: Dar-us-Salam).
7. *Fiqh-U-Seerah—Understanding the Life of the Prophet Muhammad* (Riyadh: International Islamic Publishing House, 1997).

Shaykh Muḥammad al-Ghazālī:
His Life and Work

Shaykh Muḥammad al-Ghazālī (b. 1917) died in Riyadh, Saudi Arabia, on 9 March 1996. He collapsed at the podium while delivering a lecture on Islam and the West, at a conference deliberating over Samuel Huntington's now infamous "clash of civilisations"[1] thesis. His death was mourned throughout the Muslim world and beyond. An obituary in *The New York Times*[2] bore strong testament to the far-reaching impact of al-Ghazālī's ideas and activism.

Al-Ghazālī lived an eventful life, regularly suffering censure, blacklisting, imprisonment and exile. He was a person of prodigious energy and intellect, and left behind a written legacy that included over seventy books,[3] ranging from erudite commentaries on the teachings of Islam and their application in the modern world to spiritual works enjoining personal conviction and practice.

Having held teaching posts in universities in Makkah, Qatar and Algeria, al-Ghazālī was also a devoted public intellectual, preaching in Mosques, appearing on radio and television, engaging in open debates and, towards the end of his life, even finding time to write two weekly newspaper columns in separate publications. He inspired an entire generation of scholars and activists and when death came knocking, it found him engrossed in the singular pursuit he had dedicated his entire life to: serving the cause of Islam.

While his legacy unquestionably attests to the fact that he was a man of unique genius, al-Ghazālī was also the product of a specific context. He was born into a world in which the vestiges of the Ottoman Empire were just about to be effaced, where a triumphant Europe majestically straddled conquered Arab and Muslim lands with shackles firmly in hand.

The socio-political context[4]

The decline of the Ottoman Empire had a tremendous impact on Islam and the Muslim world. For the Arab peoples who lived within its domains, its dismemberment not only marked the end of an Empire, but also the end of a political, social and religious order that had shaped their patterns of public behaviour for 400 years.[5] It also resulted in a subversion of the role that the *'ulamā'* (religious scholars) had played within the state bureaucracy.

The relationship between the political authority and the *'ulamā'* class had been a tense one from the time of the establishment of the first Islamic dynasty under the Ummayads (661-750), when the clearest separation between the two first became apparent. After the rule of the first four caliphs after the Prophet Muḥammad (the so-called Rightly-Guided Caliphs), the "official" Islam of the state became more concerned with legitimising the status quo than with ensuring the preservation of the fundamental tenets of the religion. With the onset of dynastic Islam, the *'ulamā'* class distanced itself from the politics of the state and claimed for itself the responsibility of being the preservers of the religion. These piety-minded representatives, as they were referred to by Marshall G.S. Hodgson, made their greatest contribution in the safeguarding of Islamic doctrine and the development of Islamic substantive law (*fiqh*).[6]

Nevertheless, the state often needed the support of the *'ulamā'* to extend its legitimacy over society. The scholars were thus co-opted into the bureaucracy, holding posts as *qāḍīs* (judges), teachers, *muftīs* (jurisconsults), guardians of religious endowments, market inspectors and scribes.[7] In spite of this, there was always a segment within the *'ulamā'* class that refused to be co-opted and who chose to maintain a critical posture vis-à-vis the state. This gave them the freedom to speak in defence of their religious convictions, free from any compulsion to defend practices or teachings endorsed by the ruling authorities. Although such individuals were often persecuted by the state for their rulings and for their refusal to be co-opted, they remained important dissenting voices and while they may not have been very influential in their immediate environment, they left significant legacies that served to sustain those that followed in their footsteps. As a result, there was always some inspiration for reform-minded scholars seeking to challenge the status quo over the centuries. The ideas of such dissident *'ulamā'* formed the fabric of a reformist tradition that remained intact throughout Islamic history, even if it was not always in ascension.

The rise of the bureaucratised Islamic empires of the fifteenth and sixteenth centuries resulted in the incorporation of a large section of the *'ulamā'* class into the state machinery.[8] Although this granted these *'ulamā'* a certain degree of influence, they were adversely affected by the sweeping transformation brought about by the attempts of the Ottoman Empire to modernise, especially in the late nineteenth and beginning of the twentieth century. Modern education, modern court systems based on foreign legal procedures and laws, and modern economic practices all contributed to the traditional *'ulamā'* losing much of their economic and cultural capital as individuals educated in modern institutions and influenced by new ideas began impacting upon society.[9] With the onset of modernity, the traditional Islam of the old *'ulamā'* class thus had to bear the twin burdens of coping with a rapidly changing world transforming before its very eyes and the loss of the central authority that gave it its legitimacy and strength.

The onset of modernity also marked the emergence of a modern Muslim intelligentsia not exclusively dominated and influenced by the *'ulamā'* class but influenced also by the Islamic reformist tradition and by Western modernity. Nevertheless, being deeply rooted in Arab and Muslim society and culture, these Islamic intellectuals self-consciously rejected Western imperialism and its accompanying secular baggage. Reform-minded Muslim intellectuals therefore had also to face a double challenge if they hoped to reconcile their faith with the challenges of the modern world: they would have to engage in an internal dialogue with their own rich past so as to draw upon the essential elements that defined authentic Islam, while simultaneously engaging in an external cross-cultural dialogue so as to understand and confront the challenges of a new and different reality that drew its inspiration exclusively from the West.[10] This was obviously not a universal trend and some Arab intellectuals chose to make a complete break with their Arab and Islamic roots, calling for a total embrace of Western modernity and secularism. Muḥammad al-Ghazālī thus opened his eyes to a world in the grip of a painful transformation.

Shaykh Muḥammad al-Ghazālī: the early years[11]

Muḥammad al-Ghazālī Aḥmad as-Saqqā was born on 22 September 1917 in the village of Naklā al-'Inab in the Egyptian province of Buhayrah, into a well-known family of traders who were devout Muslims. His father, Aḥmad as-Saqqā, was a *ḥāfiẓ al-Qur'ān* (i.e., a person who had memorised the Qur'an) and was regarded as a pious man with Sufi leanings. He named his son Muḥammad al-Ghazālī in the hope that he would follow in the footsteps of the great 12th century reformer, Abū Ḥāmid al-Ghazālī. "Al-Ghazālī" is not the family surname as many people erroneously believe, but an aspirational appendage to the baby Muḥammad's first name. He would nonetheless attain fame as Muḥammad al-Ghazālī, prompting his student and long-time friend, Shaykh Yūsuf al-Qaraḍāwī, to comment that the father's hopes had not been in vain as the 20th century al-Ghazālī carried the spirit of the 12th century al-Ghazālī.[12]

Al-Ghazālī's primary education entailed memorising the Qur'an, just as his father had done, and he completed the memorisation of the entire scripture by the age of ten. It was the beginning of a permanent and strong attachment to the Qur'an. He later recalled that he would regularly practise its recitation: as he strolled through the streets of his village, during his daily prayers, before he slept and in periods of solitude. He even remembered reading it from memory in its entirety during his incarceration. The Qur'an was to have a formative influence upon the young al-Ghazālī, being a faithful companion in the solitude of his early years and a wellspring of inspiration and guidance in later life.

After completing the memorisation of the Qur'an, the boy was enrolled at the Alexandra Religious Institute for primary and secondary education. In order to enable him to continue his studies, al-Ghazālī's father was forced to move to Alexandria with him. He therefore sold the little shop in the village—by which the family earned its living—and bought a bookstore in Alexandria. The bookstore sold stationery, translated novels, school books, academic books, works of poetry and classical religious texts; it played an extremely important role in the cultural enrichment of the boy. The young al-Ghazālī was a veracious reader and his father encouraged him, guiding his reading by choosing appropriate titles for him. Much later on, al-Ghazālī fondly recalled this formative period and paid tribute to his father, who was "the hero of this phase…who sold all of his possessions to enable his son to gain an education that enabled him to serve Islam."[13]

Al-Ghazālī left for Cairo in 1937, after having completed his primary and secondary education in Alexandria, registering as a student at the College of Religious Sciences at the al-Azhar University, one of the oldest centres of learning in the Islamic

World. Al-Ghazālī completed his undergraduate studies in 1941, but continued studying, specialising in Islamic Guidance and Propagation, and receiving a Master's degree in 1943. He also married while a student at al-Azhar, and was blessed with nine children over the coming years.

Al-Ghazālī's intellectual mentors

The movement of intellectual inquiry that sought to rediscover the intellectual principles of Islam and to explain their application to the changing world of the twentieth century was most powerfully represented in Egypt by the reformist Shaykh of al-Azhar, Muḥammad 'Abduh (1849-1905), and his Syrian student Muḥammad Rashīd Riḍā (1865-1935).[14] Both men had been deeply influenced by the pan-Islamist activism and thought of Jamāl ad-Dīn al-Afghānī (1839-1897), who had left an indelible impression upon the entire Islamic world in the last quarter of the nineteenth century.[15] Shaykh al-Ghazālī acknowledged the impact of al-Afghānī, 'Abduh and Riḍā on his thought, and regarded himself as a student of the *al-Manār*[16] school of 'Abduh and Riḍā.[17] Speaking about the three men in an interview in March 1995, al-Ghazālī explained his abiding attachment to them even though he himself was at an advanced stage in his intellectual career: "What I like most about Sayyid Jamāl al-Dīn al-Afghānī is his revolutionary fervour against authoritarianism (*istibdād*) and about Muḥammad 'Abduh is his deep comprehension of the wisdom of Islam and his espousal of a conscious Muslim intelligentsia, and about Rashīd Riḍā is his combination of the teachings of the classical Salafiyyah of Ibn Taymiyyah and Ibn Qayyim al-Jawziyyah and the modern rational Salafiyyah of Jamāl al-Dīn al-Afghānī and Muḥammad 'Abduh."[18]

Al-Ghazālī was also directly influenced by some of his reform-minded teachers at al-Azhar. A thematic study of the Qur'an undertaken by Shaykh Muḥammad 'Abdullah Drāz (1894-1958)[19] left a deep impression on al-Ghazālī[20] and he would later produce his own thematic study of the Holy Book.[21] He was taught Qur'anic Sciences by Shaykh 'Abd al-'Aẓīm az-Zarqānī[22] and the science of Qur'anic interpretation (*tafsīr*) by Shaykh al-Azhar Maḥmūd Shaltūt (1893-1963),[23] another towering figure in twentieth century reformist thought.[24]

However, it was Imam Ḥasan al-Bannā (1906-1949), founder of the Muslim Brotherhood (al-Ikhwān al-Muslimūn),[25] who literally changed al-Ghazālī's life. The Brotherhood was founded in Ismā'īliyyah in 1928 and grew dramatically in the 1930s.[26] By the end of the decade, it had 500 branches throughout Egypt and a membership numbering tens of thousands. The program of the Brotherhood was a mixture of the traditional and the innovative. It was traditional in that al-Bannā believed that the social and political regeneration of Egypt was intimately tied to the restoration of Islam as a guiding force in national life. Consequently, he called for the reimplementation of the *sharī'ah*, arguing that the ills from which Egypt suffered could be traced to the replacement of Qur'anic principles by secular legal and political institutions.

Al-Bannā's insistence on the restoration of the *sharī'ah* did not imply a simplistic return to the past. Like Muḥammad 'Abduh before him, al-Bannā sought to find a way for Muslims to take advantage of the technological advances of the twentieth century without feeling that they were compromising their commitment to Islamic values. He argued that the *sharī'ah* was originally formulated to meet a specific set of historical circumstances and was thus a product of informed human reasoning. In his view, the restored *sharī'ah* would be subject to interpretation and would hence be fully compatible with the needs of modern society. Although al-Bannā's political proposals lacked specificity, they were still characterised by a powerful vision in which he called for an Islamic order (rather than an Islamic state) that—precisely because of its Islamic basis—would ensure social justice, economic well-being, and political harmony.

It is therefore not surprising that social justice, economic well-being and political harmony later also emerged as major themes in the writings of al-Ghazālī. It was, however, the deep understanding of the morality of Islam that immediately attracted the young al-Ghazālī to al-Bannā. Al-Ghazālī himself relates his first encounter with the Imam:

> [My first encounter with him] was during my student days at the Alexandria Institute. I had the habit of frequenting the 'Abd ar-Raḥmān ibn Hurmuz *masjid*, where I would revise my lessons. One day, a young man that I did not know stood up and spoke a few words of advice to the people, explaining the prophetic statement: "Be conscious of Allah wherever you may be and follow a bad deed with one that is good, to wipe it out, and engage people by displaying good character."[27] His words were extremely moving and went straight to the heart. From that very moment, I strengthened my relationship with him and my activities in the field of Islamic service continued with this great man until he was martyred in 1949.[28]

Al-Ghazālī became a regular contributor to the *al-Ikhwān al-Muslimūn* Journal founded by al-Bannā. His writings left a deep impression on his many readers as well as on al-Bannā.[29] After his graduation in 1943, al-Ghazālī held several *masjid* posts entailing preaching and administrative duties, but he remained seized with the plight of Muslims. From this point onward, he began earnestly to apply his mind and to write about the challenges facing Muslim society. However, the beginning of his intellectual career as a writer and thinker is linked to the appearance of his first book in 1947.[30]

Al-Ghazālī's Salafī reform agenda[31]

Al-Ghazālī's intellectual project is founded upon five core elements, or central pivots, that form the basis of his thought.[32] For al-Ghazālī:

1. The Qur'an is the primary source of Guidance;

2. The sunnah (Prophetic practice) is the secondary source and serves to clarify the Qur'anic message;

3. Lessons need to be drawn from human history in general and from Islamic history specifically, especially from the life of the Prophet;

4. One has to be well-versed in human cultural behaviour and practice, both general and religious, in order to develop an understanding of one's context; and

5. One has to be in touch with existential reality, of both Muslims and non-Muslims, local and international, so as to be able develop an understanding of events.

The above might be described as a Salafī[33] orientation, a description to which al-Ghazālī was not averse. He, in fact, embraced it readily but also clarified what he understood by the term. For al-Ghazālī, Salafiyyah was an intellectual and emotional leaning that was linked to the best of generations and that had a deeply ingrained fidelity to the Qur'an and Prophetic Tradition; it musters the material and intellectual efforts of Muslims in the service of Allah's guidance, without any bias towards colour or ethnicity.[34]

It must, however, be acknowledged that the term Salafī is not without controversy in the current political climate and is intimately associated with the term *wahhābī* in the popular imagination. This attitude is prevalent in both Muslim and non-Muslim contexts. In the latter, *salafī* and *wahhābī* are terms that are used interchangeably to describe Usama bin Laden's al-Qa'ida brand of Islam that shows intolerance towards any view that contradicts it. Within the Muslim community, the discourse on Salafiyyah and Wahhābiyyah is more nuanced but the tendency to use the terms synonymously is, nevertheless, still prevalent. Al-Ghazālī's self-proclaimed affiliation to the Salafī School is all the more interesting when one considers his vociferous opposition and infamous clashes with scholars who associate themselves with the teachings of Muḥammad ibn 'Abd al-Wahhāb (1703-1793), the eponym of the Wahhābī school.[35] It is therefore necessary to briefly point out two major trends within the Salafī School.

Basheer Nafi points out that it is not easy to determine the exact historical moment that gave birth to the term *salafī*, but its conception can be traced back to the beginnings of the ninth century, with the emergence of the *ahl as-sunnah*, the doctrinal school established by Aḥmad ibn Ḥanbal (780-855) that re-emphasized the importance of the Prophetic tradition and marked a clear departure from the Ash'arī school of thought, which was deeply steeped in dialectic theology.[36]

Ibn Taymiyyah, the 14th century Ḥanbalī reformist, was a central link in the development of the Salafī School, but it was only in the second half of the eighteenth century and the beginning of the nineteenth that one saw the emergence of a self-conscious Salafī ideology.[37] This had been preceded by renewed interest in the teachings of Ibn Taymiyyah in the two holy sanctuaries of Makkah and Madīnah in the seventeenth and eighteenth centuries, where scholars like Ibrāhīm ibn Ḥasan al-Kūrānī (1616-1689) and Muḥammad Ḥayāh as-Sindī (d. 1750) played important roles in spreading his teachings.[38] as-Sindī created renewed interest in the methodology of the scholars of *Ḥadīth* and also made a strong impression upon a young student from Najd by the name of Muḥammad ibn 'Abd al-Wahhāb (1703-1793) who, in turn, became the pole-bearer for this methodology in the Arabian Peninsula.[39]

By the late eighteenth century, Salafī thought split into two major trends, the first upholding the methodology of the *ahl al-ḥadīth* and the second being representative of a reformist methodology that was far more dynamic and which was rooted in four principles, namely: the promotion of *tawḥīd* (monotheism), reliance upon the Qur'an and Sunnah, emphasizing the role of the intellect, and the renewal of *ijtihād* (creative intellectual exertion). Shaykh Muḥammad al-Ghazālī was a proponent of the latter reformist trend.

The main reason for al-Ghazālī's clash with upholders of the *ahl al-ḥadīth* trend was that they took the prophetic sayings as the main source for their vision of Islam, extracting a literalist understanding that ignored the rich critical jurisprudential methodology of Islam, which had developed in response to the contextual challenges encountered by Muslims throughout the ages. Therefore, al-Ghazālī points out that:

Scholars who study the Sunnah have laid down five preconditions for the acceptability of *hadiths* of the Prophet: three concerning the *isnād* and two the text itself

- The *isnād* must be comprised of transmitters with good memories who are precise in respect of what they hear and then report it accurately.
- As well as having an intelligent grasp of the text, they must also have unimpeachable morals and a conscience which fears Allah and refrains from any temptation to adulterate it.
- These two qualities must be applied to everyone of those who make up the chain of transmitters. If any chain is lacking in one transmitter or one of the men in the chain is unsure, then the *hadith* is less than sound.

When the *isnād* has been found to be acceptable on this basis, then we examine the text transmitted by it. i.e., the text of the *hadith* itself.

- It must not be aberrant
- It must not have a fault which renders it unacceptable.

Aberration arises when the text concerned contradicts a reliable transmission from a more reliable transmitter. When those with expertise see such an impairing fault in the *hadith*, that moves them to reject it.[40]

Al-Ghazālī consequently emphasized the importance of critiquing the import of the prophetic sayings and not simply limiting critique to the chain of narrators, thereby presenting a vision of Islam firmly rooted in its doctrinal teachings and moral objectives.[41]

Over and above this methodology, al-Ghazālī's work concentrated on three overlapping spheres within which he constantly shifted and which are reflected in his writings, all of which fall into one of these spheres. First, he showed tremendous concern with the Muslim context, i.e., the conditions within which Muslims found themselves. He therefore assessed the challenges that Muslims face due to their socio-economic conditions, their intellectual underdevelopment and their political subjugation. As a result, some of his earlier books bore titles such as *Islam and the Economic Condition* and *Islam and Socialist Methodologies*.[42]

Al-Ghazālī's second area of focus also relates to the Muslim context, but is more specifically concerned with the role of Islam in society. This category of work not only engages the problems that Muslims face but also seeks solutions within an Islamic frame of reference. Most of al-Ghazālī's writings in this regard were influenced by his political activism. When he was released from prison in 1949 he published *Islam and Political Authoritarianism*. After his disillusionment with Nasser's Free Officers' revolution in 1952—which al-Ghazālī had fervently supported—he wrote a series of books that explored what Islam had to offer to society. These included titles such as *The Struggle of Religion* and *Islam and the Red [Communist] Onslaught*.[43]

The above titles should not be taken to suggest that al-Ghazālī had cast exclusive blame for the poor state in which Muslims found themselves at external factors. Indeed, the third trope in his thought is exclusively concerned with Muslim Self-Critique. In his reading of Islamic intellectual history, it is the Muslim political elites and the *'ulamā'* who support them who came in for the harshest criticism.[44] Al-Ghazālī believed that after the collapse of the Rightly-Guided Caliphate, Islam manifested in two opposing trends: the first was *Official Islam*, which was the preserve of the political elite and which failed to come to grips with the essence of Islam. It was merely concerned with protecting the status quo. In contrast, *Islam of the Masses* was the expression of the majority, which made it a viable social and religious force.

Al-Ghazālī believed that Islam has survived because of the masses, who were in need of the kind of intelligentsia that would be able to create a new consciousness. Al-Ghazālī contributed to fulfilling such a role in Egypt during Anwar Sadat's reign. He took the initiative—with strong voluntary support from the public—to revitalize the 'Amr ibn al-Āṣ Mosque, the first ever mosque built in Egypt and undoubtedly its largest, after neglect had left it in a poor state. The Friday Prayer in this mosque, which was led by al-Ghazālī and followed by hundreds of thousands of Cairenes, was transformed into a weekly event that reflected the depth of the Islamic revivalist movement of the 1970's.[45]

Al-Ghazālī further believed that this new consciousness could only be initiated after a process of self-critique.[46] In this regard, he was of the opinion that the most dangerous phenomenon facing Islam was corrupt religiosity, and he believed that the only way to remedy deviant religious practice was to engage the intellectual and spiritual blemishes that caused this calamity. As such, many of his books battled against these practices, whether institutional or popular.[47] Our present work fits into this category, with al-Ghazālī addressing both institutional and popular practices which he believed needed revision in light of the authentic teachings of Islam.

Al-Ghazālī's legacy

Shaykh al-Ghazālī's legacy remains extremely relevant at the contemporary juncture of Islamic intellectual development, and his Salafī reformist agenda still inspires Islamists all over the world. While some scholars prematurely pronounced the failure of political Islam,[48] developments in many Muslim countries suggest otherwise. The introduction of democratic practices and representative political systems of governance has given the upper hand to Islamists. Unfortunately, this drew them into a fierce battle with the hegemonic global political order—led by the United States, and made them targets in the US' "war on terror", which increasingly appears to be no more than a euphemism for a war against an Islamic worldview that grows all the more assertive.

In this tense atmosphere, al-Ghazālī's legacy provides many important lessons. Perhaps the most important is that Islamic reformation begins with the self, where the individual's struggle against corrupt religious practice is as important as the struggle against corrupt political elites and the *'ulamā'* that grant them legitimacy.

The present study

In this book, al-Ghazālī addresses a central characteristic of Islamic thought, i.e., the constant process of deviation and correction that it is continually subjected to. The specific focus of this study is the subject of *bid'ah*, which is best understood as heretical innovation in matters related to religious practice.[49] His book is therefore part of the genre of correction in contemporary Islamic revivalist thought.[50] al-Ghazālī places much emphasis upon the historical dimensions of continuity and change, touched upon by Ibn Taymiyyah[51] very early on, and more recently by Nāṣir 'Abd al-Karīm al-'Aql.[52] He therefore relates *bid'ah* to the ebb and flow of the discourse on authentic Islamic thought. In so doing, he relies heavily on the work of renowned Arab Historian, 'Abd ar-Raḥmān ibn Khaldūn,[53] reminding us that the quest for Islamic authenticity requires constant reaffirmation. This approach is much broader than studies that view *bid'ah* within the parochial frame of religious praxis,[54] source methodology,[55] sectarian concerns,[56] or from the strict point of view of Islamic doctrine.[57]

Although the term *bid'ah* is frequently encountered in the sayings of the Prophet Muḥammad (ṣ), it only became an established legal category with the emergence of the early schools of Islamic Jurisprudence. However, the term was not utilised uniformly and manifested in two distinct paradigms, which can be traced back to two opposing positions held by Imam Mālik ibn Anas (d. 795), founder of the Mālikī School of Thought, and Imam Muḥammad ibn Idrīs ash-Shāfiʿī (d. 820), founder of the Shāfiʿī School.[58] Mālik's approach is best described as a *Normative Paradigm*, and represents continuity with the Prophetic *aḥādīth* that view *bidʿah* as a negative concept, or something contrary to the Sunnah.[59] According to this paradigm, the central problem with *bidʿah* is that it represents a misguided attempt to gain closeness to Allah by means that Allah did not legislate.[60]

Ash-Shāfiʿī's approach to *bidʿah* is best formulated as a *Descriptive Paradigm*, because even though he was extremely devoted to asserting the Prophet's sunnah as the most authoritative source of law after the Qur'an, he did establish a basis for allowing new practices by distinguishing between positive and negative types of innovation,[61] thereby opening a space for what popularly became known as *bidʿah ḥasanah* (a good innovation). This descriptive approach was later refined and *bidʿah* came to be evaluated according to the five ethical categories of Islamic Jurisprudence: *wājib* (obligatory), *mandūb* (recommended), *mubāḥ* (neutral), *makrūh* (disliked) and *ḥarām* (forbidden).[62]

The most important landmark in the study of *bidʿah* in the classical age is undoubtedly the work of Abū Isḥāq ash-Shāṭibī, the fourteenth century Mālikī Jurist.[63] Ash-Shāṭibī's book, *al-Iʿtiṣām* (The Refuge),[64] represents the culmination of several centuries of juristic writing against *bidʿah* and its most sophisticated articulation.[65] This work became extremely influential in the modern period, primarily due to the influence of Muḥammad ʿAbduh.[66] ʿAbduh was a great admirer of ash-Shāṭibī's work and promoted it vigorously amongst his students.[67] Therefore, it comes as no surprise that it should be ʿAbduh's principle disciple, Muḥammad Rashīd Riḍā, who undertook the task of editing and publishing the first edition of *al-Iʿtiṣām*.[68]

Ash-Shāṭibī's study on *bidʿah* influenced all of ʿAbduh's disciples thereafter and this influence is manifestly reflected in al-Ghazālī's text as well. As such, there is a clearly discernable lineage of scholars stretching from 'Abduh, to Riḍā, to Shaykh 'Alī Maḥfūẓ,[69] to al-Bannā,[70] to Maḥmūd Shaltūt (who is quoted at length in this particular work), to al-Ghazālī (in this present study), all of whom locate *bid'ah* firmly within the reformist tradition.

Like ash-Shāṭibī and his illustrious predecessors, Shaykh al-Ghazālī also advocates the *Normative Paradigm* when dealing with the question of *bid'ah*. In this study, al-Ghazālī condemns innovation in doctrine and worship, but affirms the place of reason and public welfare in matters of social morality, while insisting that they should work within the limits imposed by the moral principles of Islam.[71]

Moreover, by locating the question of *bid'ah* within a broader historical context, exploring the boundaries of authenticity, continuity and change, al-Ghazālī consciously adopts an atavistic (Salafī) posture that affirms the virtue of judging Islamic thought and practice through the lens of the Qur'an and Sunnah (Prophetic Practice). This position is very much a central pillar of the modern Islamic revivalist movement.

Chapter 1 provides an outline of the goals and methodology of Islamic Law, thus anchoring the study within the framework of the *sharī'ah*, and providing the benchmark by which religious practice is judged later in the book. Chapter 2 provides a brief excursus into the ebb and flow of Islamic thought and the various foreign elements that influenced its expansion and contraction. Al-Ghazālī draws extensively on the work of Ibn Khaldūn in this chapter. Chapter 3 discusses the issue of innovation in religion (*bid'ah*) and is more theory-based.[72] The chapter presents a succinct account of the views of Abū Isḥāq ash-Shāṭibī, one of the most important classical scholars ever to write on the topic. These first three chapters form the theoretical basis of the book.

In Chapters 4 to 6, al-Ghazālī shifts his focus to corrupt religious practices, discussing the provenance of distorted beliefs, acts of worship and customary practices pertaining to religious expression.[73] These chapters are framed within the context in which al-Ghazālī was writing, that of Egyptian society of the 1950s and 1960s, and his reflections are therefore sometimes bound by this context. However, it is equally important to note that most of the beliefs and practices that come under discussion are still prevalent in Muslim communities all over the world, even if they take a somewhat different form than that described. Al-Ghazālī judges these practices in light of the theoretical discussion he presents in the first part of the book and his responses, from the vantage point of the authentic teachings of Islam, would therefore be equally valid to similar practices inspired by the same motivations. Chapter 4 discusses heretical innovations pertaining to doctrine, Chapter 5 discusses heretical innovations pertaining to acts of worship and Chapter 6 discusses heretical innovations pertaining to customary practices.

The book concludes with a touching reflection on the importance of embracing normative Islamic practice, even if one has to "walk the solitary path" as a result. Interestingly, al-Ghazālī draws inspiration in his conclusion from a famous spiritual tract written by Ibn Qayyim al-Jawziyyah,[74] a student of Ibn Taymiyyah. In so doing, al-Ghazālī is able to emphasize the importance of a Sufi core in the reformist tradition, but a core that is stripped of the foreign accretions that have corrupted popular Sufi movements. In this regard, he is no different from Ibn Taymiyyah, who also maintained the importance of this core by what he referred to as *at-Taṣawwuf as-Sunnī*, i.e., a regime of Islamic spirituality and aesthetics based on the teachings of the Qur'an and Sunnah.[75]

Notes

1.　Huntington's thesis was originally lly argued in an article of the same title in the journal *Foreign Affairs* in the summer issue of 1993 and was subsequently expanded upon and published as a book; see Samuel P.Huntington (1996), *The Clash of Civilizations and the Remaking of the World Order* (New York: Simon & Schuster Paperbacks).

2. Douglas Jehl (1996), "Mohammed al-Ghazali, 78, An Egyptian Cleric and Scholar." In *The New York Times*, March 14.

3. Shaykh al-Qaraḍāwī said that Shaykh al-Ghazālī wrote more than 60 books, while Jehl (op. cit.) claimed that he wrote over 90 books. However, 70-odd is the figure provided by al-Ghazālī himself. I am indebted to Ibrahim Abu-Rabi' for this figure (personal correspondence), which was stated to him by al-Ghazālī himself in an interview. For further details see Yūsuf al-Qaraḍāwī, (1997), *ash-Shaykh al-Ghazālī Kamā 'Araftuhu: Riḥlah Niṣf Qarn* (al-Manṣūrah: Dār al-Wafā), p. 60. For an extensive bibliography of al-Ghazālī's work, see Fatḥī Malkāwī, (ed.) (1996), *al-'Aṭā' al-Fikrī li al-Shaykh Muḥammad al-Ghazālī* (Amman: al-Ma'had al-'Ālamī li al-Fikr al-Islāmī), pp. 228-260.

4. For a detailed account of the history of the region see William L. Cleveland (1994), *A History of the Modern Middle East.* (Boulder, Colorado: Westview Press). This section draws on Cleveland's study.

5. Cleveland (1994), *A History of the Modern Middle East*, p. 157.

6. Marshall G. S. Hodgson (1974), *The Venture of Islam: Conscience and History in a World Civilisation (3 vols.)* (Chicago: University of Chicago Press), vol. 1, p. 238.

7. Suha Taji-Farouki, and Basheer M. Nafi (eds.) (2004), *Islamic Thought in the Twentieth Century* (London: I. B. Tauris), p. 6.

8. ibid.

9. ibid., pp. 6-7.

10. Roxanne L. Euben (2002). "Contingent Borders, Syncretic Perspectives: Globalization, Political Theory and Islamizing Knowledge." In *International Studies Review*, 4(1), p. 246.

11. The best account of al-Ghazālī's life is his autobiography: Muḥammad al-Ghazālī (2006), *Mudhakkarāt ash-Shaykh Muḥammad al-Ghazālī* (al-Jazā'ir: Dār ar-Rashād). A brief account of al-Ghazālī's early life and upbringing appears on his website: www.alghazaly.org. For useful biographical details see also 'Abdullah. Al-'Aqīl (1998), "ad-Dā'iyyah al-Mujaddid Muḥammad al-Ghazālī," in *al-Mujtama'*, vol. 1296, 21/4/1998, pp. 46-48; al-Qaraḍāwī (1997), *ash-Shaykh al-Ghazālī Kamā 'Araftuhu*; 'Abd al-Ḥalīm 'Aways (2000), *ash-Shaykh Muḥammad al-Ghazālī—Tārīkhuhu wa Juhūduhu wa Ārā'uhu* (Damascus: Dār al-Qalam). This section draws on all these sources.

12. Al-Qaraḍāwī (1997), *ash-Shaykh al-Ghazālī Kamā 'Araftuhu*, p. 186.

13. Al-Ghazālī (2006), *Mudhakkirāt*, p. 238.

14. Cleveland (1994), *A History of the Modern Middle East*, pp. 113-124.

15. ibid., p. 118.

16. Named after the influential *al-Manār* Journal established by Riḍā.

17. Al-Qaraḍāwī (1997), *ash-Shaykh al-Ghazālī Kamā ʿAraftuhu*, p. 258.

18. Ibrahim M. Abu-Rabiʿ(2004), *Contemporary Arab Thought: Studies in Post-1967 Arab Intellectual History* (London: Pluto Press), p. 430, fn. 1.

19. See: Muḥammad ʿAbdullah Drāz (2001), *The Qur'an: An Eternal Challenge.* Translated by Adil Salahi (Leicester: The Islamic Foundation).

20. Al-Qaraḍāwī (1997), *ash-Shaykh al-Ghazālī Kamā ʿAraftuhu*, p. 110.

21. This specific work has appeared in English in an abridged and full text edition. See Muḥammad al-Ghazālī (1996), *Journey Through the Qur'an: The Content and Contexts of the Surahs (Abridged Translation of al-Tafsir al-Mawdu'i li suwar al-Qur'an al-Karim)*, abridged by AbdalHaqq Bewley and translated by Aisha Bewley (London: Dar al-Taqwa); Muḥammad al-Ghazālī (2000), *A Thematic Commentary on the Qur'an*, translated by Ashur A. Shamis (Herndon, Virginia: The International Institute of Islamic Thought).

22. Az-Zarqānī is the author of *Manāhil al-ʿIrfān fī ʿUlūm al-Qur'ān*, an influential modern study on the sciences of the Qur'an that has become a standard reference text on the subject.

23. For a detailed study of Shaltūt in English, see Kate Zebiri (1993), *Mahmud Shaltut and Islamic Modernism* (Oxford: Clarendon Press).

24. Al-Qaraḍāwī (1997), *ash-Shaykh al-Ghazālī Kamā ʿAraftuhu*, p. 30.

25. For detailed studies on the Brotherhood see Richard P. Mitchell (1969), *The Society of the Muslim Brothers* (London: Oxford University Press); Brynjar Lia (1998), *The Society of the Muslim Brothers in Egypt* (Reading: Ithaca Press).

26. The brief outline on the Muslim Brotherhood and al-Bannā hereunder is extracted from Cleveland (1994), *A History of the Modern Middle East*, p. 187.

27. *Musnad Aḥmad*, ḥadīth no. 20392.

28. For more details, see *www.alghazaly.com*.

29. Al-ʿAqīl (1998), "ad-Dāʿiyyah al-Mujadid Muḥammad al-Ghazālī", p. 48.

30. Abu-Rabiʿ (2004), *Contemporary Arab Thought*, p. 223.

31. This section draws primarily on: al-Qaraḍāwī (1997), *ash-Shaykh al-Ghazālī Kamā ʿAraftuhu*; ʿAways (2000), *ash-Shaykh Muḥammad al-Ghazālī*; Abu-Rabiʿ (2004), *Contemporary Arab Thought*, pp. 223-255. Abu-Rabiʿ undoubtedly presents the best account of al-Ghazālī's thought available in English, devoting two full chapters to his work. For a narrower focus on specific aspects of al-Ghazālī's work, see: Maḥfūẓ ʿAzzām (1992), *ash-Shaykh Muḥammad al-Ghazālī: Ṣuwar min Ḥayāh Mujāhid ʿAẓīm, Dirāsah Ḥawl al-ʿAqīdah al-Islāmiyyah*

fī Fiqh ash-Shaykh al-Ghazālī (Cairo: Dār aṣ-Ṣaḥwah), which examines the place of Islamic doctrine in al-Ghazālī's thought. See also: Muḥammad Waqī'ullah (1996), "Malāmiḥ al-Fikr as-Siyāsī li ash-Shaykh al-Ghazālī." In *Majallah Islāmiyyah al-Ma'rifah*, no. 7. Ramaḍān, which examines his political thought. Nūr ad-Dīn ibn Rabīḥ I'zīz's (2010), *al-Wasaṭiyyah wa al-I'tidāl fī al-Manhāj ad-Da'awī 'ind ash-Shaykh Muḥammad al-Ghazālī* (Damascus: Dār al-Fikr), examines al-Ghazālī's methodology of balance and moderation in his approach to inviting people to Islam.

32. Al-Qaraḍāwī (1997), *ash-Shaykh al-Ghazālī Kamā 'Araftuhu*, pp. 79-80.

33. The Arabic word *salaf* literally means predecessor and the term *salafī* generally connotes an atavistic posture, where one looks back to the precedents of the earlier generation for guidance and inspiration.

34. Al-Qaraḍāwī (1997), *ash-Shaykh al-Ghazālī Kamā 'Araftuhu*, p. 82.

35. These clashes are documented in scores of articles and several books by al-Ghazālī, starting in the early 1970s and culminating in a major onslaught in: Muḥammad al-Ghazālī (1989), *as-Sunnah an-Nabawiyyah bayna ahl al-Fiqh wa ahl al-Ḥadīth*. (Cairo: Dār ash-Shurūq). Daniel Brown (1996), *Rethinking Tradition in Modern Islamic Thought*. (Cambridge: Cambridge University Press), pp. 108-132, provides a useful English summary of this debate; al-Ghazālī's full study is now also available in English, see: Muhammad al-Ghazali (2009), *The Sunna of the Prophet: the People of Fiqh versus the People of Hadith*. Translated by Aisha Bewley (London: Dar Al Taqwa).

36. Basheer M. Nafi (n.d.), "ash-Shaykh Yūsuf al-Qaraḍāwī: al-Iṣlāhiyyah al-Jadīdah fī Ṭawr Jadīd" *Unpublished Manuscript*, pp. 7-10.

37. For insight into the rise of Salafi Thought in 19th century Damascus, see: Itzchak Weismann (2001) *Taste of Modernity: Sufism, Salafiyya, and Arabism in Late Ottoman Damascus* (Leiden: Brill).For insight into the work and ideas of two important scholars that played a role in the *salafi* revival in this period see: Basheer M. Nafi (2002), "Abu al-Thana' al-Alusi: An Alim, Ottoman Mufti, and Exegete of the Qur'an" in *International Journal of Middle Eastern Studies*, 34 (3), pp. 465-494; Basheer M. Nafi (2009), "Salafism Revived: Nu'mān al-Alūsī and the Trial of the Two Ahmads" in *Die Welt des Islams*, 49, pp. 49-97.

38. For further elaboration on the life and works of these two important scholars see: Basheer M. Nafi (2002), "Tasawwuf and Reform in Pre-Modern Islamic Culture: In Search of Ibrahim al-Kurani," in *Die Welt des Islams*, 42 (3), pp. 307-355; Basheer M. Nafi (2004), "The Rise of Islamic Reformist Thought and its Challenge to Traditional

Islam," in *Islamic Thought in the Twentieth Century*, edited by Suha Taji-Farouki and Basheer M. Nafi (London: I. B Tauris), pp. 28-60; John O. Voll (1974), "Muhammad Hayya al-Sindi and Muhammad ibn 'Abd al-Wahhab: An Analysis of an Intellectual Group in Eighteenth Century Medina" in *BSOAS*, 38 (1), pp. 32-39; Basheer M. Nafi (2006), "A Teacher of Ibn 'Abd al-Wahhab: Muhammad Hayat al-Sindi and the Revival of *Ashab al-Hadith's* Methodology." In *Islamic Law and Society*, 13 (2), pp. 239-241.

39. For more on the Wahhābī mission in the Arabian Peninsula (later Saudi Arabia) see: David Commins (2006), *The Wahhabi Mission and Saudi Arabia* (London: I. B. Tauris); Madawi al-Rashid (2002), *A History of Saudi Arabia* (Cambridge: Cambridge University Press).

40. Al-Ghazali (2009), *The Sunna of the Prophet.* Translated by Aisha Bewley, pp. 9-10.

41. Nafi (n.d.), "ash-Shaykh Yūsuf al-Qaraḍāwī: al-Iṣlāḥiyyah al-Jadīdah fī Ṭawr Jadīd, p. 14.

42. Al-Qaraḍāwī (1997), *ash-Shaykh al-Ghazālī Kamā 'Araftuhu*, p. 11-14.

43. ibid., p. 47.

44. Abu-Rabi' (2004), *Contemporary Arab Thought*, pp. 228-229.

45. Bashīr M. Nāfi (2010), *al-Islāmiyyūn* (Beirut: Dār al-'Arabiyyah li al-'Ulūm), pp. 107-108.

46. Abu-Rabi' (2004), *Contemporary Arab Thought*, p. 230.

47. Al-Qaraḍāwī (1997), *ash-Shaykh al-Ghazālī Kamā 'Araftuhu*, p. 58.

48. In this regard, see, for example: Olivier Roy (1994), *The Failure of Political Islam* (Cambridge: Harvard University Press), which passes rather premature judgement on the demise of Political Islam. For a more sober, historically grounded assessment, which argues that Political Islam is still very much in ascendance, see: Nāfi (2010), *al-Islāmiyyūn*.

49. Two important scholarly articles provide an excellent review of writings on *bid'ah* in the classical period; see: Vardit Rispler (1991), "Toward a New Understanding of the Term *bid'a*" in *Der Islam*, 68 (2), pp.320-328; Maribel Fierro (1992), "The treatises against innovations (*kutub al-bida'*)" in *Der Islam*, 69 (2), pp.204-246. In addition to these articles, three recent unpublished theses also explore the subject from interesting contemporary perspectives; see: Ahmad Haris (1998), *Innovation and Tradition in Islam: A Study on Bid'ah as an Interpretation of the Religion in the Indonesian Experience* (Temple University: PhD Thesis); Asep Saepudin Jahar (1999), *Abu Ishaq al-Shatibi's Reformulation of the Concept of Bid'a: A Study of his I'tisam* (McGill University: M.A. Thesis); Raquel M.

Ukeles (2006), *Innovation or Deviation: Exploring the Boundaries of Islamic Devotional Law* (Harvard University: PhD Thesis).

50. For an interesting reflection on *ijtihād* and *bidʿah* as central concepts in the process of continuity and change in Islamic thought see: Umar F. Abd-Allah (2007), "Creativity, Innovation and Heresy in Islam," in *Voices of Islam (Volume 5): Voices of Change*, General Editor Vincent J. Cornell, Volume Editor Omid Safi (Westport, Connecticut; London: Praeger), p 15. Abd-Allah calls for an authentic and sophisticated understanding of *bidʿah* as a control mechanism and *ijtihād* as an inducement for creativity.

51. Taqī ad-Dīn Aḥmad ibn ʿAbd al-Ḥalīm ibn Taymiyyah (1996), *Iqtiḍāʾ aṣ-Ṣirāṭ al-Mustaqīm Mukhālafah Aṣḥāb al-Jaḥīm* (Beirut: Dār al-Kitāb al-ʿArabī).

52. Nāṣir ʿAbd al-Karīm al-ʿAql (1996a), *Muqaddamāt fī al-Ahwāʾa wa al-Iftirāq wa al-Bidaʿ* (Riyadh: Dār al-Waṭan); (1996b), *al-Ahwāʾa wa al-Iftirāq wa al-Bidaʿ ʿibr Tārīkh al-Islām* (Riyadh: Dār al-Waṭan); (1996c), *Manāhij Ahl al-Ahwāʾ wa al-Iftirāq wa al-Bidaʿ wa Uṣūlihim wa Simātihim* (Riyadh: Dār al-Waṭan).

53. ʿAbd ar-Raḥmān ibn Khaldūn (n.d.), *al-Muqaddimah* (Cairo: al-Matbaʿah al-Amīriyyah).

54. See: al-ʿIzz Ibn ʿAbd as-Salām (n.d.), *Qawāʿid al-Aḥkām fī Maṣāliḥ al-Anām* (Beirut: Dār al-Maʿrifah); ʿAbd ar-Raḥmān ibn Ismāʿīl ibn Ibrāhīm Abū Shāmah (2007), *al-Bāʿith ʿalā Inkār al-Bidaʿ wa al-Ḥawādith* (Cairo: Maktabah al-Qurʾān); al-Sayyid Muḥammad ibn ʿAlawī al-Mālikī al-Ḥasanī (n.d.), *Regarding the Celebration of the Prophet's Birth*, Translated by a Group of Ulama (MJC) and Edited by Shaykh Fakhruddin Owaisi Al Madani (Cape Town: MJC; IFEC-SA); Al-Sayyid Muḥammad ibn ʿAlawī al-Mālikī al-Ḥasanī (1996), *az-Ziyārah an-Nabawiyyah bayn ash-Sharʿiyyah wa al-Bidʿiyyah* (Makkah: Self Published); Nuh Ha Mim Keller (1999), *The Concept of Bidʿa in the Islamic Sharīʿa* (Bartlow, Cambridge: The Muslim Academic Trust); Muḥammad ibn ʿAbd as-Salām ibn ʿAbdullah an-Nāṣirī (2003), *al-Mazāyā fīmā Aḥdath min al-Bidaʿ bi Umm az-Zawāyā* (Beirut: Dār al-Kutub al-ʿIlamiyyah); Vardit Rispler-Chaim (1995), "The 20th Century Treatment of an Old Bidʿa: *Laylat Al-Niṣf min Shaʿbān*" in *Der Islam*, 72 (1), pp.38-97; Tawfīq Yūsuf al-Wāʿī (1984), *al-Bidʿah wa al-Maṣāliḥ al-Mursalah Bayānuhā Taʾṣīluhā, Aqwāl al-ʿUlamā fīhā* (Kuwait: Maktabah Dār at-Turāth).

55. See: ʿĀyid ibn ʿAbdullah al-Qarnī (2003), *al-Bidʿah wa Atharuhā fī ad-Dirāyah wa ar-Riwāyah* (Beirut: Dār Ibn Ḥazm).

56. See: Jaʿfar Muḥammad ʿAlī al-Bāqirī (1996), *al-Bidʿah—Dirāsah Mawḍūʿiyyah li Mafhūm al-Bidʿah wa Taṭbīqātihā ʿala Ḍawʾ Manhaj Ahl al-Bayt.* (Qom: Rābiṭah ath-Thaqāfah wa al-ʿAlāqāt al-

Islāmiyyah); Aḥmad al-Kātib (2007), *as-Sunnah wa ash-Shīʿah Waḥdah ad-Dīn, Khilāf as-Sīyāsah wa at-Ṭāʾrīkh* (Lebanon: Arab Scientific Publishers); Liyakat A. Takim (2000), "From Bidʿa to Sunna: The Wilāya of ʿAlī in the Shīʿī Adhān" in *Journal of the American Oriental Society*, 120 (2), Apr. – Jun., pp. 166 – 177.

57. See: Abū al-Ḥasan al-Ashʿarī (n.d.), *Kitāb al-Lumaʿ fī ar-Radd ʿala Ahl az-Zaygh wa al-Bidaʿ* (Cairo: al-Maktabah al-Azhariyyah li an-Nashr); Aḥmad Ibn Ḥajar al-Haytamī (1996), *aṣ-Ṣawāʿiq al-Muḥriqah fī ar-Radd ʿalā ahl al-Bidaʿ wa az-Zandaqah* (Cairo: Maktabah al-Qāhirah); Abū al-Faraj ʿAbd ar-Raḥmān al-Jawzī (2004), *Talbīs Iblīs* (Beirut: Dār al-Kutub al-ʿIlmiyyah); Muḥammad Ḥāmid an-Nāṣir (1995), *Bidaʿ al-Iʿtiqād wa Akhṭāruhā ʿalā al-Mujtamaʾāt al-Muʿāṣirah* (Jeddah: Maktabah as-Suwādī); Abū al-Fatḥ Muḥammad ibn ʿAbd al-Karīm ash-Shahristānī (1998), *al-Milal wa an-Niḥal* (Beirut: Muʾassasah al-Kutub ath-Thaqāfiyyah).

58. Ukeles (2006), *Innovation or Deviation*, p. 91.

59. ibid., pp. 152-199, for a detailed account of the *Normative Paradigm* and the scholars that support it.

60. ibid., p. 196.

61. ibid., pp. 93-94, and pp. 120-152, for a detailed account of the *Descriptive Paradigm* and the scholars that advocate it.

62. This categorisation was formulated by the influential Shāfiʿī Jurist, al-ʿIzz ibn ʿAbd as-Salām, see: (n.d.) *Qawāʿid al-Aḥkām fī Maṣālih al-Anām* (Beirut: Dār al-Maʿrifah).

63. For more on ash-Shāṭibī in English see: Muhammad Khalid Masud (1977), *Islamic Legal Philosophy: A Study of Abū Isḥāq al-Shāṭibī's Life and Thought* (Islamabad: Islamic Research Institute); Jahar (1999), *Abu Ishaq al-Shatibi's Reformulation of the Concept of Bidʿa*. Two informative Arabic sources are also worth noting; these are: Aḥmad ar-Raysūnī (1995), *Naẓariyyah al-Maqāṣid ʿInd al-Imām ash-Shāṭibī* (Herndon, Virginia: International Institute of Islamic Thought); ʿAbd ar-Raḥmān Ādam ʿAlī (1998), *Al-Imām ash-Shāṭibī: ʿAqīdatuhu wa Mawqifuhu min al-Bidʿ wa Ahlihā* (Riyadh: Maktabah ar-Rushd). The latter source includes informative details on ash-Shāṭibī and the historical context within which he worked and lived.

64. See: Abū Isḥāq ash-Shāṭibī (n.d.), *al-Itiṣām* (Beirut: Dār al-Fikr). This book has appeared in many editions by various publishers, all of which draw on Rashīd Riḍā's first edition, which was published in 1913. In addition to the full length text, several abridged versions of the book have also been published over the years. One of the earliest abridgements is: Muḥammad Aḥmad al-ʿAdawī (1921), *Ṭarīq al-Wuṣūl ilā Ibṭāl al-Bidaʿ bi ʿIlm al-Uṣūl*. This same text was reprinted

as: Muḥammad Aḥmad al-ʿAdawī (1985), *Uṣūl al-Bidaʿ wa as-Sunan* (Beirut: al-Maktab al-Islāmī); Shaykh al-Ghazālī makes reference to this work in the present study. The most recent abridgement of the text is: Abū Isḥāq ash-Shāṭibī (1997), *Mukhtaṣar al-ʿItiṣām*. Abridged and Edited by ʿAlawī ibn ʿAbd al-Qādir as-Saqqāf (Kingdom of Saudia Arabia: Dār al-Hijrah li an-Nashr wa at-Tawzīʾ).

65. Ukeles (2006), *Innovation or Deviation*, p. 107.

66. Rachel Ukeles argues that modern scholarly interest in ash-Shāṭibī can be traced back to the writings of Muḥammad Rashīd Riḍā; see: Ukeles (2006), *Innovation or Deviation*, p. 299, fn. 1. However, it was in fact ʿAbduh who exposed Riḍā and his other disciples to the work of ash-Shāṭibī.

67. Shaykh ʿAdullāh Drāz, a student of ʿAbduh's (and whose son Muḥammad was one of al-Ghazālī's mentors), states as much in his introduction to ash-Shāṭibī's (1997) *magnum opus* on Islamic Legal theory. See: Abū Isḥāq ash-Shāṭibī (1994), *al-Muwāfiqāt fī Uṣūl ash-Sharīʿah* (Beirut: Dār al-Maʿrifah).

68. For more details see: Muḥammad Rashīd Riḍā (1911), "at-Taʿrīf bi Kitāb al-ʿItiṣām" in *al-Manār*, 17(10), pp. 745-749.

69. ʿAlī Maḥfūẓ (2001), *al-Ibdāʿ fī Maḍār al-Ibtidāʿ* (Beirut: Dār al-Kutb al-ʿIlmiyyah).

70. Ḥasan al-Bannā (1989), *Sharḥ al-Uṣūl al-ʿIshrīn* (Cairo: Dār ʿImār li an-Nashr wa at-Tawzīʾ).

71. Albert Hourani (1970), *Arabic Thought in the Liberal Age, 1798-1939* (Cambridge: Cambridge University Press), p. 370.

72. In the original Arabic text, the chapter on Islamic thought appears as chapter 3, while the chapter on *bidʿah* appears as chapter 2. I have however swapped these two chapters, allowing for a much smoother progression into the central focus of the book, which is the topic of *bidʿah*.

73. The most important classical scholar to explore corrupt religious practices is Ibn al-Ḥājj, also a Mālikī. See: Muḥammad ibn Muḥammad ibn al-Ḥājj (1995), *al-Madkhal ilā Tanmiyyah al-Aʿmāl bi Taḥsīn an-Niyyāt wa at-Tanbīh ʿalā baʿḍ al-Bidaʿ wa al-ʿAwāʾid allatī Intahalat wa Bayān Shanāʾihā*. Edited by Tawfīq Ḥamdān (Beirut: Dār al-Kutb al-ʿIlmiyyah). Al-Ghazālī quotes him in this book as well.

74. Abū ʿAbdullah ibn Abī Bakr ibn Ayyūb ibn Qayyim al-Jawziyyah (n.d.), *Madārij as-Sālikīn Bayna Manāzil Iyyāka Naʿbudu wa Iyyāka Nastaʿīn* (Beirut: Dār al-Kitāb al-ʿArabī).

75. Nafi (2004), "The Rise of Islamic Reformist Thought and its Challenge to Traditional Islam," p. 31.

Introduction

This book encompasses inquiries in the field of jurisprudence (*fiqh*). Custom dictates that this subject be studied at specialist institutions by students of religion. I have decided to project a more general character upon the subject, to bring it within the reach of the majority of readers and to free it, as far as possible, from technical terminology. I have faithfully observed the meticulous transmission of absolute facts, even though I may slightly overstep the bounds in expression and presentation.

The great lack of understanding that exists amongst contemporary readers has been the incentive for this study. Today's readers peruse a wealth of subjects in everyday life: on nutrition, medicine, economics, philosophy, and literature. Books and newspapers have managed to bring within the reach of ordinary readers matters that have been the preserve of specialists. We might ask why, then, has the lay reader not been as fortunate as far as deep Islamic knowledge is concerned? For how long will our readers remain impoverished of understanding religious judgements that are predominated by legal rules?

This book is not intended as an exposition of the principles of the Sacred Law (*sharī'ah*). It is, rather, a warning that draws attention to the strange additions that have attached themselves to the *sharī'ah* and which are, most definitely, not part of it.

The persistence of these innovations requires of me, first, to draw a general map of the essence of Islam and to lay down sound guidelines pertaining to the facets of belief (*'aqā'id*), worship (*'ibādāt*) and customs (*'ādāt*). The extraction of the fundamental core of these additions, which clash with the essence of Islam, also requires me to delve somewhat into the study of the Principles of Source Methodology in Islamic Law (*uṣūl al-fiqh*).

The lay person should not be taken aback by this approach and should strive to embrace it so that he may come to know his religion well and learn to separate religious superstition from true understanding. In recent times, more people have gained literacy in fields that have conventionally been monopolized by specialists. The widening of cultural horizons and the lifting of impediments to education have made this easy for anyone that has the will to learn.

We want to draw Muslims closer to the various disciplines of knowledge that have previously been inaccessible, but which should have been in widespread circulation. This liberal approach is the best way to serve Islam and to strengthen its followers. Let us elevate the general level of understanding and push forward the renaissance!

This book may anger rigid readers who are not grounded in the religious sciences. It reflects the efforts of luminaries that have struggled for a long time to awaken the Islamic intellect but have since passed on without having achieved much success. If there may be any anger directed at us as a consequence of this effort, so be it. We only do justice to the truth so that the individual may act upon it, even if the majority of Muslims are unable to.

Muḥammad al-Ghazālī

1

Islamic Law—Goals and Methodology

Tolerance and love

The laws and obligations that Allah has determined for his servants are founded upon an all-encompassing Mercy, in a manner that does not overburden or lead to partiality. A father may be harsh to his children out of ignorance. He may even treat them unfairly, as human nature sometimes tarnishes his judgement with self-centeredness and poor intent. As for the Lord of all creation, He only legislates that which brings upon His servants pure goodness and ensures their absolute wellbeing. Allah's Compassion for humankind is coupled with complete Self-sufficiency, with no dependence upon them for anything. His Guidance is an all-encompassing circle that safeguards their livelihoods and uplifts their standing.

Humankind began as a breath from Allah's Own Spirit. Guarding this honourable lineage and preserving this elevated bond are the secrets that control human behaviour, protecting us from contemptibility, obligating upon us piety, and, in the end, qualifying us for the Garden whose expanse is that of the Heavens and the Earth.

Allah wants humankind to represent Him on His earth and He places thereupon well-established scholars that make it a graceful resting place for discovering Him and for the implementation of His order. Discovering Allah and implementing His order is a path that leads to guidance that benefits humankind and is the first and last support for the wellbeing of human beings. If human beings were left to their own desires, they would stoop to the lowest depths, living far beyond Allah's laws in a pit darkened by savagery, uncertainty, and oppression.

In the words of Ibn Qayyim: "The *sharī'ah* (Sacred Law) is based upon wisdom and the wellbeing of Allah's servants in this world and the hereafter. It encompasses complete justice, mercy, and wellbeing in its entirety. Any issue that moves away from justice to tyranny or from mercy to that which is opposed to it, or from wellbeing to harm, or from wisdom to futility is not part of the *sharī'ah*, even if it has been imposed upon it by means of interpretation. This *sharī'ah* is Allah's justice towards His servants, His mercy amongst His creation, His shadow upon this earth of His, and His wisdom, indicative of His existence and the truthfulness of His messengers."

The truth of the matter is that humankind's impression of Allah's law is in need of substantial correction. Most people regard it as a blaze of anger and are stung by its severity and frightened by its grimness. There is a perception that the principles and divisions of the law are somewhat obscure. It is, therefore, sometimes perceived to challenge rationality and is met with a fear equal to that of disbelief. This is a huge mistake. The religion of Islam is a breath of Allah's Mercy and should be met with the cheerfulness with which any grace is embraced. The ideas of short-sighted puritans, who only approach religious truths fleetingly should be left aside and ignored.

Islam is truth and beauty. Take heed of the words of Allah, the Most High: "These are the verses of the Qur'an and (it is) a clear Book; a guide and glad tidings for the believers" (27:1-2).

Guidance cannot be accompanied by falsehood, nor glad tidings by disgrace. As The Great and Almighty says: "And We have sent down to you the Book (Qur'an) as an exposition of everything, a guidance, a mercy, and glad tidings for those who have submitted themselves (to Allah as Muslims)" (16:89).

Allah has conveyed all religions along this clear, passionate pattern: "…for indeed he has brought it (this Qur'an) down to your heart by Allah's permission, confirming what came before it and [as] guidance and glad tidings for the believers" (2:97).

The ease and compassion that the *sharī'ah* encompasses is needed by people just as one who is ill needs medication, or as the downtrodden require mercy. The compassion, solace and blessing that are particularized by the general nature of prophethood are explained by Allah: "And We have sent you (O Muḥammad) not but as a mercy for all creation" (21:107).

Allah explains the major objectives of the Qur'an and the resultant bliss of those that pursue them: "And We send down from the Qur'an that which is a healing and a mercy to those who believe and it increases the wrongdoers nothing but loss" (17:82).

No blind imitation *(taqlīd)*

Islam has elevated humanist objectives, some of which we will point out here. The liberation of the intellect is the foundation of respectable faith and acceptable belief. Very few people are endowed with free minds, constantly in motion, unburdened by inherited errors. Consider fast trains that cover great distances while their passengers remain seated in their compartments not taking a single step. Blind imitation *(taqlīd)* is like this; it transports its followers to opinions and teachings that they would not have embraced had they not been born with them. Blind imitation travels great distances with its followers, whether they are conscious or in a stupor, until it settles with them at its intended end. In this way they excitedly re-affirm the morals and beliefs of their predecessors as if they are a result of their own intellectual endeavour or thought: "When it is said to them: 'Follow what Allah has sent down.' They say: 'Nay! We shall follow what we found our fathers following.' Even though their fathers did not understand anything nor were they guided" (2:170).

Many generations were misguided by this rigidity, which serves only to fossilize the intellect and appease one's sentiments. It transforms people into dumb brutes that pay no attention when called because they are restricted by that which does not unite and repudiate that which they are ignorant of: "And the example of those who reject faith is as that of him who shouts out to that which hears nothing but calls and cries. (They are) deaf, dumb, and blind, so they do not understand" (2:171).

True scholars of Islam, in contrast, find no benefit in embracing *taqlīd*. The human intellect is obligated to explore the horizons of the heavens and the earth, searching and studying, so that it may know Allah and the world. If it fails to do so, then it is certainly negligent of its primary function. Everything borne of the liberated intellect, whether plausible or not within easy reach, every means that leads to the liberation of the intellect, whether difficult or docile, is of the foundations of Islam and of its objectives. The novice reader might be surprised to realise that the prevalent axiom of Islamic Jurisprudence is that "the intellect (*'aql*) is the basis for tradition (*naql*) (whose sources are the Qur'an and authentic *aḥādīth* (Prophetic Traditions))" and that the teachings constructed by revelation stand upon the foundation of plain reason and sound thinking.

The sublimity of Islam

Islam strives to bring about the reformation of the self and the creation of a refined conscience that is motivated by God-Consciousness (*taqwā*), both in private and openly. The venting of personal biases that are concealed within one's heart cannot be prevented by any action whatsoever and some manifestations of human behaviour cannot be controlled. It is thus futile to confront visible action, attempting to formulate it in a specific mould, or to force upon these actions limited boundaries while neglecting their sources and ulterior motives. For this reason the Prophet (ṣ) said:

"God-Consciousness is here, God-Consciousness is here, God-Consciousness is here," pointing to his chest.[1]

The truth is that it is impossible to establish an uprighteous civilization if it is based upon hearts that are ill. That which cannot uphold the conscience or purify intentions will not subdue the unruliness and excesses of humankind. Humankind's make-up is layered with physical and hidden drives that, when they manifest themselves, act as fuel for exhausting endeavours in life. Even though these drives may be concealed or controlled, they sprinkle upon life a carelessness that warrants removal. "And how many a town (population) have We destroyed, which were thankless for its means of livelihood! And those are their dwellings which have not been inhabited after them except a little. And verily, We have been the inheritors" (28:58).

It is no wonder, therefore, that Islam encompasses a detailed body of beliefs (*'aqā'id*), rituals of worship (*'ibādāt*), Laws (*aḥkām*), and etiquette (*ādāb*) that subdue this evil and transform this vehemence into that which is far more earnest. The Qur'an and Prophetic Tradition (Sunnah) contain thousands of guidelines for attaining this noble objective. The spirit is definitely in need of foundational and definitive depictions that are synonymous with Allah's religion.

In my opinion, nothing rivals (or even equates) Islamic education (with the Qur'an and Sunnah as its sources) in instilling nobility and terminating lowliness and depravity. In fact, as a result of this education, the Islamic nation remained for centuries the closest to civility, collaboration and mutual love, even though the politics of governance in its communities may have become unsettled and disturbing. To the neutral researcher, a comparison between common Muslims and the communities of Jews and Christians during the Middle Ages clearly demonstrates the positive effect of Islam in impressing upon its followers the characteristics of guidance, God-Consciousness and courtesy; characteristics that no other influence comes close to instilling within its followers. When the Muslims were defeated by the Crusaders of the Middle Ages due to the material and intellectual weakness of the Muslims, they were still far more outstanding than their opponents as far as conduct was concerned. In the words of a western writer: "The Crusaders committed atrocious crimes and acts, causing the world around them to tremble in fear and horror. They would kill children in the arms of their mothers and then throw their severed limbs in the air. These onslaughts brought together not only fanatics that believed in the sanctity of their cause, but also individuals engrossed in immorality, forgetting The Holy Land, going along and participating in riotous demonstrations, from disgracing their opponents to plunder and murder. These atrocities left behind the scandalous traces of their actions wherever they went."

Muslims, on the other hand, did not lose their judiciousness in the face of these repulsive events, but remained of an elevated character, described by another western writer as follows: "Many of the Christians that left Jerusalem after its conquest by Ṣalāḥ ad-Dīn, travelled to Antioch. The leader of the Crusaders there, Bohemond, not only refused to shelter them but went on to plunder their wealth as well. In contrast, these afflicted people were met with honour and compassion in whatever parts of the Muslim land they treaded upon."[2] This contrast shows one the level of spiritual development imprinted upon Muslims that made them, while in the worst of conditions, tread along the path of honour and God-Consciousness.

Overwhelming the self by depravity exposes it to a dangerous pitfall, advancing it and all that are linked to it to a bleak destiny. As Rousseau recalls in *Emile*: "I have always observed that young men, corrupted in early youth and addicted to women and debauchery, are inhuman and cruel; their passionate temperament makes them impatient, vindictive, and angry; their imagination fixed on one object only, refuses all others; mercy and pity are alike unknown to them; they would have sacrificed father, mother, the whole world, to the least of their pleasures."[3] Rousseau's statement is a truthful description of those that forget Allah and renounce their religion, becoming tainted by the darkness of disbelief and anarchy. "No! But on their hearts is the covering (of sins and evil deeds) which they used to earn. No! Surely they (evildoers) will be veiled from seeing their Lord that Day. Then, verily they will indeed enter and taste the burning flame of Hell" (83:14-16).

To the level of which human beings are deprived of the truth, so too are they deprived of elements of faith. To the level of which they lack reverence for Allah, so too are they inclined to vain desires and jesting with things of honour, even if they may affiliate to one of the divinely ordained religions. The capacity that Islam places in the hearts of the believers has left within them a great inherited legacy, safeguarding them against contemptibility and assisting them to shun evil. It saddens us, however, to admit that the Muslims of the last century have lost a lot of the characteristics of genuine religious devotion and spiritual wholeness that Muslims enjoyed in the past, which has gradually begun to fade away.

The recompense is a reality

One of the goals of Islam is to reinforce the idea of the Hereafter, recognizing it as a reality beyond any doubt. Preparing for one's transition to the afterlife is a sign of guidance and evidence of sound judgement. Inhabitants of Cairo are aware that there is a country out there called America, which one is able to travel to when given the opportunity. Similarly, one should be aware that there is another world out there, which we will be going to without a doubt, where one will live for eternity. Humankind is so preoccupied with its present state that it does not consider that which is beyond. Its attention is so deeply devoted to the seen-world that it almost renounces the unseen-world. Even though it sees death transgressing upon life by the hour, wearing away its good fortune and encroaching upon its flow, it remains deluded and oblivious.

In this regard, al-Ḥasan said: "I have not seen a truth more resembling of falsehood than death." It is no wonder that Islam continuously portrays images of Paradise and Hell in the hereafter, with elaborate descriptions, so that every living being may feel that his firmly established future is not upon the face of this earth. Even so, it is absurd to regard the reality of the Hereafter as an exhortation to bear the oppressions of tyranny in tranquillity and inactivity. Islam, with its detailed description of the joys of Paradise and the pain of Hell, makes clear that death in the struggle against tyrants is the shortest route to the highest garden of Paradise and that tolerating the disgrace of oppression causes one to slip towards the Hell-fire, the worst of abodes.

Also, the physical nature of reward and punishment is a reality and is not imaginary or metaphorical. Indeed, humankind is a creation far more magnificent than angels and devils. Their sensitivity to happiness and misery is shared by their bodies and souls equally. This applies in this world, so why should they go beyond this natural capacity in the hereafter? In the view of Islam, human beings are a creation fashioned from an essence and a physical matrix that is not separated. There is no room for dividing our nature into matter that has no connection with the soul, or a soul having no connection with matter. The efforts of philosophy in this realm do not concern us, nor do they exert any influence in matters of religion. There are youths who hush down the voices of desire within them if these voices draw them to what is forbidden, opening their ears to whispers of faith that urge purity and virtuousness. Is it not fair that they attain complete compensation as a reward, or a compensation that profits from this abstinence? Why do some look down upon the worth of such compensation, which entices these youths to practice chastity (along with many other incentives) when the following has been revealed in this regard: "And (there will be) fair females with wide, lovely eyes (as wives for the pious), like unto preserved pearls. A reward for what they used to do. No false, vain talk will they hear therein, nor any sinful speech, but only greetings of peace" (56:22-26).

Indeed, the Hereafter is a reality and the destined reward in it is material as well as spiritual because humankind is composed of matter as well as spirit. Islamic society is founded upon constant preparedness for the abode in the Hereafter and obligates its adherents to order their daily lives on this basis.

Brotherhood and equality

One of the goals of Islam is the strengthening and consolidation of bonds between different races, between the first and the last, the close and the distant, to establish a brotherhood that is not biased towards state, nor partial towards tribe, nor renouncing of colour; a brotherhood that ignores all lineages except the lineage of Adam and rejects all preferences except the preference of ability and integrity; which looks at all servants of Allah heeding only their behaviour and talents, paying no attention at all to the differences in faces or languages or origins; a brotherhood that prompted the Prophet (ṣ) to say to his people: "If you are commanded by a maimed, black slave that leads you with Allah's Book, then listen and obey."[4]

This brotherhood, inculcated by Islam and spread amongst its people, has no equivalent anywhere in the world. Yes, the maligning of ancestry and slandering of lineage does occur. Is there not always someone who falls into sin? However, such maligning and slander does not affect the established principle, neither in its legislation nor in its implementation. For extended periods in Islamic History, even "slaves" were able to be kings, accumulating everything they desired but managing, in the shade of brotherhood, to maintain equality between all types of people and to establish states united in solidarity and authority.

Look at al-Mutanabbī, the arrogant Arab Poet, abandoning the court of Sayf ad-Dawlah in the Levant, going to Kāfūr, the ruler of Egypt, asking for his assistance and praising him in verse:

Those who ask Kāfūr are free of need from any other
Just as one at the ocean has no need for a water-carrier.

Kāfūr realized that the Poet had high expectations, but did not entrust him with the governance of a principality or even a village. He, instead, sufficed by rewarding him with ordinary gifts. Al-Mutanabbī responded by urging him to show more generosity:

Father of Musk, is there in a cup
any honour that I may attain;
for I am in need,
while you are still drinking

Kāfūr refused to respond to the ambitions of the Poet, who came to him singing praises of wealth and honour. For this, al-Mutanabbī slanders him:

Who taught this castrated Negro how to pay rewards,
His white fathers or His black forefathers?
Never buy a slave without buying a whip as well
for indeed slaves are unfortunate and defiled.

Al-Mutanabbī's response is the curse of a strained man, a rejected beggar, and does not reflect the traditions of a nation or the politics of a state. Before this period and after, loyalists were able to ascend to the highest positions without being restricted by colour, lineage or nationality.

It is frightening and humiliating to relate what has taken place recently in the modern world, where western civilization has reached its climax and sent forth its ripest harvests. In his book *Color and Conscience: The Irrepressible Conflict*, Buell Gordon Gallagher notes that: "Slavery as ownership of chattel is gone: as a caste system, it remains. Its purpose is to keep nonwhites in a position that, in one way or another, is inferior or subordinate to that of whites."[5] It is painful to see how even the laws of murder were discounted by Whites when applied to their own race in cases related to Black victims. Unjust legislation and oppressive legal procedures are severe afflictions that have no authority and have not been sanctioned by Allah.[6]

There is a vast difference between the wretched slaves of modern civilization and their predecessors, who attained honour in the Land of Islam and were not afflicted, with the passing of time, with some of the afflictions of their Black brothers at the hands of Whites in the modern world.

Equality between all categories of people in the light of sincere brotherhood and the outlawing of colour differentiation, along with shared principles of unity, made the Egyptians a model for the blossoming of unity in the Nile Valley. People there are not concerned about Black or White. One even sees a White man standing in prayer behind a Black imam. The imam's knowledge and character are the only traits that qualify him to stand in the prayer niche, leading the congregation. This is a consequence of the influence of Islam and the maturation of its inherited teachings.

Punishment (*al-ḥudūd*)

One of the goals of Islam is the reinforcing of good and the restraining of vices in all sectors of society by training individuals to do good and to reject evil by their own initiative. Islam strongly rejects moral transgressions and the implementation of severe punishments upon perpetrators is not an innovation but is also a characteristic of earlier religions. Allah, the Glorious and Sublime, is indeed vigilant over humankind, which had prompted Him to send forth prophets with a message that dispels doubt from amongst His servants.

The harshness that characterizes the punishments for stealing and adultery are not the only means to protect honour and wealth or to induce people to respect the honour and possessions of others. The safeguarding of general rights is primarily based upon faith, worship and character. Even the harshest punishments do not seriously serve to elevate a nation whose conscience has been shaken and whose system of belief has been disturbed. Crime begins like disease, causing manifest changes to the body and activating invisible germs. Its danger then worsens until it becomes life-threatening, invoking fear in the healthy as well as the afflicted. The afflicted fear for their own lives and the healthy fear the consequences of infection. This is a result of disobedience and the continual transgression of the boundaries of Allah.

Minor transgressions are not an alarming characteristic of human nature. In an immaculate society minor errors shrivel and vanish, just as pollutants vanish in an environment that enjoys good weather and rejuvenating winds. But the very same minor transgressions, in an environment that welcomes and reinforces them, devising excuses for their occurrence, transforms them into crime and insolence. Islam is strongly committed to the expulsion of wrong when it has been exposed. The lashing and capital punishment that it enforces—or threatens to enforce—is for the sake of maintaining a decent general environment in which evil does not develop from offensive traces of insanity into outright forbidden sin.

A fact that we feel free to state is that the controversy between Islam and human-made political ideologies is not based upon the principle of implementing Divinely-Ordained punishments, but rather upon other principles.

Are free sexual relationships—that arise from unrestricted interaction—forbidden? Is the animalistic intercourse between young males and females a crime that should be prohibited and should the paths that lead to it be blocked? Is drunkenness a deficiency that lowers the honour of a person and makes him an outlaw, like one who abuses opium or hashish, for example? Indeed, much controversy centres on these issues. Salvation of the community from these tokens of immorality may not require the implementation of some of these frightening punishments inasmuch as Islamic Ideology requires deeming some things permissible and others forbidden.

Propagation of grace

One of the primary goals of Islam is to correct the egocentrism with which the human being is born, to make his outlook more liberal and his conduct more uplifting so that he may understand that existence was not founded only for him and that he does not exist alone.

When a person senses his own rights he becomes aware of the rights of others and is saved from the stupidity of greed, insolence, arrogance and vanity. The Noble Qur'an drives one to this realization when it requires us to show benevolence to the orphan. And who knows? Perhaps we will leave progeny that will be in need of mercy and equity. Will it then please us to abandon these orphans? "And let those (executors and guardians) have the same fear in their minds as they would have for their own, if they had left weak offspring behind. So let them be conscious of Allah and speak right words" (4:9).

Egocentrism is like a fire, increasing in intensity when fuel is added to it. People are intoxicated by the graces granted to them—like the fulfilment of desires and incessant wealth—and they forget Allah's rights over that which He has granted them, i.e., the portion of their wealth reserved for His less fortunate servants, dispensed by *zakāh* (almsgiving). This intoxicating egocentrism causes them to refuse others, resulting in degeneration on this earth and the severing of close links with people.

The Prophet (*s*) warned against this infested breeding ground, saying: "Indeed, that which I fear most for your sake is that which Allah brings forth for you of the blessings of the earth." When asked what the blessings of the earth were, he said: "The wealth of this world." A man then asked him: "Does good come with evil?" The Prophet (*s*) remained silent for a long time, until it was thought that revelation was descending upon him. He then wiped his brow and asked: "Where is the questioner?" "Here", he replied. The Prophet (ṣ) said: "It does not come except with good! Indeed, this wealth is a beautiful meadow. Indeed, everything that grows in spring shrivels out unsuccessfully or is harvested, except that which is consumed of the meadow. It is eaten by livestock who then ruminate on it and finally excrete it. It thus returns to fertilize and is once again consumed. Verily this wealth is a beautiful meadow. He who partakes of it justly and spends of it justly is the best of those who are righteous. And he who partakes of it unjustly is like one who eats and is not satisfied."[7]

Amongst the grazing livestock are animals that are lured by the moist spring-meadow—their insides having shrivelled in the dry season—and approach it like desirous gluttons. It is their ignorant nature that causes them to over-indulge upon this easy food-source, eating, devouring, seeking more, and accumulating. They proceed in this way, filling their stomachs until nothing remains in front of them. How many creatures destroy themselves simply because they have food close at hand? How many people are astounded by the wealth of this world, their eyes and hearts enchanted by it, their hands stretched forth towards it, whetting their appetites, accumulating it until they have more than enough? But their egocentrism presses them to accumulate more, until they finally meet the fate of the over-indulgent creatures and are destroyed. To be satiated by the world in this foolish manner is indeed a manifest loss. The hoarding of wealth is like holding food in the stomach: any surplus that is suppressed for too long changes into a lethal poison. This prophetic parable exemplifies a moderate lifestyle.

Consider livestock that maintain moderation in their grazing, ruminating what they eat and eliminating whatever remains from their bodies, as opposed to animals that reach the butcher, fattened by their own gluttony. The butcher benefits from their meat because it has become impractical to derive benefit from their existence. Do you not see that this wealth was confiscated because its owner held it back? Because of their clinging to their wealth it was taken away from them and given not to one complaining of indigestion but rather to one complaining of starvation. This is how one who is lured by the wealth of this world is treated; his excess wealth is confiscated while he still retains superfluity of speech. The principle established by the Prophet (ṣ) is thus: "Indeed this wealth is a beautiful pasture; he who indulges in it justly is blessed by it; and the one who hordes it, taking whatever pleases him of Allah's and His Prophet's wealth, will only partake of the fire on the Day of Retribution."[8]

The formidable campaign that Islam wages against stinginess, hard-heartedness and greed has no rival in any other philosophy. Plain generosity thus becomes a trait of Muslims, which Allah alludes to as follows: "Those who spend their wealth (in Allah's cause) by night and day, in secret and in public, they shall have their reward with their Lord. On them shall be no fear, nor shall they grieve" (2:274).

In the darkest of times, this trait fulfilled its merciful function, healing the wounded and softening calamity and harm, doing for the masses what in our time not even general or National Socialism can achieve.

What do people imagine when considering the Mamluk Era in Egypt? What do they say when they compare the level of social welfare services in this era with that in England or in Russia? For the sake of historical record we invite responses to this inquiry, demonstrated in the *Qalāwūn Hospital Endowment Document*, which states: "This mental hospital was established for the treatment of sick Muslims—male and female, rich or poor—in Cairo and its precincts, those resident and newcomers, for people of all nationalities, for the treatment of all sicknesses and afflictions. Young and old may enter, alone or in groups. Poverty-stricken patients, male and female, may stay for the period of their treatment and spend only that which is intended for their treatment. The only differentiation that will be made is between those coming from afar and those living nearby and between those resident and those who are not, without any stipulations being imposed for any form of compensation.

"The administrator of this endowment will spend of its proceeds according to the needs of the patients, fulfilling their bedding needs, seeing to it that every patient's needs are fulfilled according to his condition and the requirements of his illness. He will deal justly with all of them, in obedience and heedfulness to Allah. He will exert all his efforts to fulfil their needs as they are his subjects and every administrator is responsible for his subjects. The hospital's kitchen will undertake to prepare both chicken and meat for the patients. Every patient will be served in his own platter, not sharing it with another; his food will also be brought to him covered. Every patient's nutritional needs will be fulfilled in this way for all meals, morning and evening.

"The administrator will also spend of the proceeds of this endowment for the remuneration of the Muslim doctors that attend to the patients, whether on a rotational basis or together. The doctors will monitor the patients' conditions and write down their nutritional requirements, etc. in a file. The doctors will also remain resident at the hospital, whether on a rotational basis or together, every night. They are also expected to undertake the treatment of their patients with kindness and consideration.

"If someone is sick in his home, then the administrator may spend upon the patient's needs, for medicine and food, etc., taking into consideration the availability of funds, etc...."

The *Qalāwūn Hospital Endowment Document*, permeated with the Islamic Spirit, was written seven centuries ago. At this time, Europe was a continent that knew only the law of "survival of the fittest". Have the most developed Socialist parties presented a system more refined and more charitable than this one for the ill and calamity-stricken?

This is the secret behind why Muslims find their religion completely sufficient, and why they turn away from other ideologies. In my opinion, the disappearance of an Islamic orientation in the West is the only reason why Leftist inclinations and principles have flourished and spread.

Jihād

One of the goals of Islam is to combat dictatorial regimes and misdirected sedition until freedom of conscience and intellect is firmly established on earth, so that no truth may be degraded and no belief neglected. This is genuine *jihād*. *Jihād* is a deterrent against terrorism, remedying its ferocious might and eradicating its authority. The use of force for tyranny and aggression is terrorism. The seizing of this force to ensure the safety of people, to implement justice, and allay fear, is *jihād*. Colonialist attacks upon the lands of the East for the sake of plunder and the enslavement of its people is terrorism. Fighting against such attacks with whatever may come to hand is *jihād*.

Productive *jihād* converts sound scientific theories and individual methods into established realities, general practices and systematic programs. It creates a generation that embraces an idea, so that it may be exploited by coming generations.

As such, Islam gives tremendous importance to *jihād* because of the great desired benefit derived from it and because of the wide circle it creates for the establishment of truth. Without a doubt, one who heads out for *jihād* receives a greater reward from Allah than one who dedicates himself to his individual obligations, even if he had to spend his entire life fasting by day and worshipping by night. Aḥmad narrates that the Prophet (ṣ) said: "Every nation has its form of asceticism, and for this nation it is *jihād* in the path of Allah."[9]

It is also narrated that a man came to Abū Saʿīd al-Khudrī, asking for advice. He replied: "I had asked Allah's Messenger the same question before you. I advise you to be heedful of Allah because it is the pinnacle of everything, and also to go out in *jihād*, as it is the asceticism of Islam. Also remember Allah and read the

Qur'an as it is a remembrance for you in the Hereafter and a light for you in this world."[10]

The state which Islam establishes bears no link with oppression upon earth and has no place for singing the praises of personalities or for the realization of vain desires. It is a means for the attainment of some of the objectives we have just mentioned, the rest of which we have explained in some of our other works.

The Qur'an and then the Sunnah (prophetic tradition)

The primary source for the study of Islam is the Noble Qur'an. The position of the Qur'an in relation to the other sources is comparable to the roots of a tree in relation to its branches and fruit. As is stated in a *ḥadīth*: "The superiority of Allah's words over all other words is like the superiority of Allah over His creation."[11]

In the general administration of any organization, fundamental constitutions make up the foundation; then comes administrative, criminal, personal, and business laws; then bulletins and resolutions, and explanatory notes, etc. Constitutions are required to group together critical principles of legislation, administration and implementation, to encompass issues that have to be recorded, leaving no room for contrasting hypotheses. Issues that are not addressed in the constitution will be addressed by drawing on the constitutional sanctity and therefore cannot possibly contradict it in word or in spirit. If this disparity does arise, then it is automatically nullified.

And, so too is Allah's book. It is the central pivot of Islam, the source of its laws, the constitution that prioritizes Islamic ethics, orientation, advice, and legislation. Included in it are the foundational principles of Islam, and it portrays a general picture of that which pleases Allah as far as His servants are concerned, in matters of their livelihood, orientation of their thoughts and behavioural characteristics. Unfortunately, Muslims do not show enough esteem for the Noble Book. They do not attach their sights or their perception to its meanings and goals as is required. Great attention should not be paid to its melodious recitation or to the temporary effect one sees upon some individuals as a result; neither points to anything of great significance.

The Qur'an is indeed the primary source of guidance for humankind. The guidance sent forth from Allah embodies calculated principles of truth and guarantees for success. The verses of the Qur'an are like milestones leading to the Straight Path, just as the horizons of the cosmos point to the secrets of knowledge and the repositories of power and creation. If humankind were only to realize this, they would stop in front of every chapter, in fact every letter, seeking certainty and ascertaining how to strengthen their links with the Lord of all creation. Indeed, the Word of Allah is above all words. It is thus obligatory to receive the Qur'an with hospitable awareness, seriousness, and a spirit of inquiry. The Qur'an undoubtedly carries the greatest of benefits for humankind and one is therefore astonished by people who grant preference to other laws, holding them above the laws and words of Allah: "Allah! None has the right to be worshipped but He. Surely, He will gather you together on the Day of Resurrection about which there is no doubt. And who is truer in statement than Allah?" (4:87).

One of the signs of sincere belief in Allah is devotion to reflecting upon His Book, seeking from it benefits that are indispensable, and extracting its wholesome fruits for the short and long term. It is impossible for one who believes in the Noble Qur'an to give credence to some other proof over the Qur'an or to equate some outside orientation to its guidance. The Qur'an overrides all else and is never overridden; it stands in judgement over all other proofs and is not judged by any outside criterion; this would be alien to the religion of Allah.

The relationship of the Sunnah (Prophetic Tradition), *qiyās* (Analogy), *istiṣlāḥ* (Convention), etc. to the Qur'an is comparable to the relationship of branches to roots or members of a group to the leader. The Prophet (ṣ) conveys from Allah, making clear that which He has desired, completing the finer details of the legislation, the portions which a general constitution does not usually delve into. The Qur'an, for example, discusses business transactions—the most common of transactions—mentioning only a small number of laws, not exceeding the number of fingers on the hand. The Sunnah, in contrast, contains hundreds of *aḥādīth* (prophetic sayings) explaining further and going into extensive detail. The Sunnah—in addition to this legislative framework—covers a very wide field and we are required to reflect lengthily upon it as well.

Let us suppose that an organization were to appear before us with a clear system of order contained in a specific book, and it wanted to popularize itself and strove to control the politics of its society. What would it do? It would, in all probability, issue a newspaper to express its status and establish it as a platform for promoting its opinions, using it to attract the masses. This newspaper, speaking on behalf of the organization and expressing its official opinions and viewpoints, without a doubt, occupies an important position. Every now and then, that which it circulates draws criticism to the organization as it is regarded as an in-depth exposition of the organization's position.

The function of the official newspaper of an organization is to portray its judgements on current incidents, to exploit opportunities, to recommend its programs and to commend its reforms. It illustrates—in accordance with the times and the people—the principles that it projects. It may address a student in a manner different from a worker, or it may take a foreigner to task on issues that it would not address a citizen on. Some people may understand the organization incorrectly, so it would elaborate by explaining its position, thereby refuting the notions contradicting it, thus defending its position. This change and explanation follows the change in conditions and people; the requirements of different circumstances call for suitable guidelines. There is no place for sowing dissension by claiming variance or contradiction between the positions of the organization and what is circulated in its official newspaper.

This is—by way of an exaggeration in expression—the function of the Sunnah in relation to the Qur'an. The Prophet (ṣ) spent 23 years speaking to his community, his conduct made manifest to friends and opponents alike, just as his perseverance in his function of guiding humankind was known to all. It is not important to only know what he said, but how, when, and to whom. All these factors assist us tremendously in understanding the Sunnah correctly.

Examples of the principle

Ibn 'Abbās narrates that a man came to the Prophet (ṣ) and said: "O Messenger of Allah, which action is most loved by Allah?" The Prophet (ṣ) replied: "The present and the departing." He said: "And what are the present and the departing?" The Prophet (ṣ) replied: "The one who recites the Qur'an from beginning to end. Every time he stops, he departs [i.e. resumes recitation]."[12]

'Abdullah ibn Mas'ūd narrates: "I asked the Prophet (ṣ) which action is most loved by Allah? He said: 'The prayer at its appointed time.' I then said, 'then which (action)?' He said: 'Obedience to one's parents.' I then said, 'then which?' He said: '*Jihād* in the path of Allah.'" Ibn Mas'ūd then said: "He spoke to me about these actions and if I had continued to ask him, he would have continued answering."[13]

Abū Hurayrah relates that Abū Dharr asked the Messenger of Allah (ṣ): "Which is the best action?" He replied: "Belief in Allah and His Messenger." It was then asked: "And what after?" He said: "*Jihād* in the path of Allah." It was then asked: "And what after?" He said: "The hajj (Pilgrimage) correctly performed."[14]

Abū Mūsā al-Ash'arī narrates that the Messenger of Allah (ṣ) was asked which act of Islam was the best. He said: "He who safeguards Muslims from his tongue and hand."[15]

'Abdullah ibn 'Umar relates that a man asked the Messenger of Allah (ṣ) which aspect of Islam was the best. He replied: "To share your food with and to greet with the salutation of peace someone that you know and someone that you do not know."[16]

What is significant about there being these various answers to the same question? It indicates that the pronouncements of the Messenger of Allah (ṣ) addressed the conditions of the people he was speaking to, and he therefore stressed aspects of worship or behaviour that he deemed most suitable for the individual, or what he considered to be their most pressing need. He remained silent on other aspects, not out of neglect but because the Qur'an itself or other traditions carried the burden of explaining them.

Furthermore, those who benefited from these answers were in no way to regard any one *hadīth* as the entire faith. It is also a mistake to be ignorant of the circumstances in which the *hadīth* was recalled as this context throws tremendous light upon its intent. Just as attention is paid to the conditions of the one being addressed in any of the traditions, so too are the general conditions of the group also considered. For example, when the disbelievers crave for our lands, occupying them with their savagery, *jihād*—in these circumstances—is better than the pilgrimage. In the face of severe crises and poverty, charity is better than the voluntary prayer. When the shortcomings of our community in the fields of crafts and industry become apparent, preoccupation with chemistry and steel-works is more liked by Allah than ploughing the earth and tending to goats. Understanding of the Qur'an is not complete without knowledge of the Sunnah and the Sunnah cannot be correctly understood without knowledge of the context within which the prophetic guidance was directed.

If we are not completely acquainted with the timeframes, places, and situations in which these *ahādīth* were set, we may find that they are part of a group of other traditions whose framework is known, thus making up for this deficiency. One is faced with many narrations of varying meaning, making it difficult to giving priority in classification and arrangement, and in placing every *ḥadīth* vis-à-vis the conditions that concur with it. There are books available on "occasions of *aḥādīth*,"[17] in the same style as "occasions of revelation" studies found in books of *tafsīr* (Qur'anic Interpretation). These works are very important for serving the study of the Sunnah and to repel attacks against it.

What we have recollected concerning the understanding of the Sunnah and its relationship to the Qur'an is nothing new. This knowledge was possessed by the early scholars, which led them to the correct understanding of the realities of this religion.

The function of the Sunnah

When citing from the Qur'an or Sunnah on a specific topic, I came to notice that many *aḥādīth* corresponded in intention and objective to the intentions and objectives encompassed by the Qur'an itself. In many instances the *ḥadīth* would reinforce the meaning of the Qur'anic verse or provide a similar meaning relating to the verse, thereby taking on the same orientation, even if it may seem to the naked eye that the relationship between the *ḥadīth* and the verse is a distant one.

The Prophet (ṣ), for example, says: "O Allah! There is none that can prevent that which You bestow, and there is none that can bestow that which You prevent."[18] This meaning is no different from the following statement of Allah, the Most High and Honoured: "Whatever of mercy (i.e., good) Allah may grant to Humankind, none can withhold it, and whatever He may withhold, none can grant it thereafter. And He is the All-Mighty, the Wise" (35:2).

Examples of this type are indeed many. For example, the Messenger (ṣ) "prohibited the use of gold and silver utensils for eating and drinking, and prohibited the wearing of silk, and to sit upon it (use it to cover chairs, etc)."[19] This ruling enforced by the Sunnah is drawn from the Qur'anic prohibition of opulence and lavishness, which regards the opulent and the lavish as enemies of all reform, as opponents of all prophets, and as a factor that leads to the collapse of all nations: "And We did not send a warner to a township, but those who were given the worldly wealth and luxuries among them said: 'We believe not in the (message) with which you have been sent'" (34:34).

The prohibition of using graveyards as places of prayer—which was enforced by the Sunnah[20]—is in reality a definitive protection of *tawḥīd* (Allah's Oneness), a concept from which Christians deviated by taking as places of worship the graves of their saints; even the Makkan idolaters referred to this practice as evidence to oppose the Messenger (ṣ). Allah relates that they said: "We have not heard (the like) of this among the people of these later days. This is nothing but an invention!" (38:7).

The Sunnah takes the position of reinforcing the objectives of the Qur'an, whether explicit or implicit. It also explains its general aspects and clarifies its ambiguities. The Sunnah commands a high status in the eyes of Muslims and its position as an evidentiary source for legislation is well known. There are *sunan* (traditions) that specify general rulings of the Qur'an, as in the verse: "Allah commands you as regards your children's (inheritance); to the male, a portion equal to that of two females" (4:11). The Sunnah clarifies that a child that murders (his parents) gets no portion of inheritance.

In the verse: "Forbidden to you (for food) are: dead animals, blood" (5:3), the Sunnah clarifies that there are two allowable categories within these prohibitions. The Prophet (ṣ) said: "Made allowable for us are two categories of dead animals and two categories of blood: Fish and locusts and liver and spleen."[21]

Concerning the verse in which Allah, the Most High and Honourable states: "Cut off the hand of the thief, male and female" (5:38), the Sunnah clarifies that not the hand of every thief is to be cut off. The hand is not cut off if the item stolen is not in excess of a specific value; it is also not cut off in the case of the hunger-stricken searching for food, or in the case of one who was robbed and then retrieves his stolen property. And if the hand is to be cut off, then it must be the right hand and at the point of the wrist-joint as is stipulated by the Sunnah.[22]

The Sunnah is also a source of rulings that make easier some of the requirements that the Noble Book commands. For example, the Qur'an commands that the feet be washed when performing *wuḍū'* (ablution), regarding it as one of the pillars of *wuḍū'*. The cleaning of the feet is therefore a necessary requirement for the prayer, i.e., for it to be regarded as having been fulfilled correctly. The Messenger of Allah (ṣ) however specified that if one had worn socks or leather socks after having cleaned his feet, then it was not necessary to wash the feet every time one performed the *wuḍū'*. It is sufficient to just wipe the top of the foot, over the sock or shoe, as an indication of the pillar of *wuḍū'* that has been exempted.[23]

Whatever the Messenger (ṣ) constituted and commanded is not an act of vain desire or a subjective inclination on his part: "Your companion (Muḥammad) has neither gone astray nor has he erred. Nor does he speak of (his own) desire" (53:2-3). It is Allah's directive to him, a directive that conforms to the primary principle of Islam: tolerance and ease, as long as it does not contradict the teachings of the Qur'an. We are thus able to say that there is no Sunnah that contradicts any Qur'anic ruling; it is in fact impossible to find a *ḥadīth* that contradicts a specific Qur'anic ruling or its general principles for that matter.

Any single *ḥadīth* cannot simply be chosen for the sake of drawing evidence. We are required to choose several *aḥādīth* that have been narrated concerning a topic, and then to add the corresponding verses of the Noble Book, never ignoring this connection. Simply to draw conclusions randomly using any *ḥadīth* that may be in sight, ignoring the circumstances under which it was narrated and the extent of its application, would be no less than misguidance. Muslims suffered the consequences of such misguidance in the past and are experiencing its harm in the present as well. I will now present a series of *aḥādīth*, arranged chronologically, so that the reader may be able to picture the blunders that a Muslim might commit if he were to isolate the first *hadīth*, or any of them from the series, intending to implement it while ignoring the others:

1. "Whosoever bears testimony that there is none worthy of worship except Allah and that Muḥammad is His messenger, Allah makes it forbidden for him (to enter) the Fire."[24]

2. "Three (things) dismantle Islam and the principles of the religion. Islam is based upon these three, and whosoever leaves one of them has committed disbelief, making the spilling of his blood allowable. These are: bearing testimony that there is none worthy of worship except Allah, the prescribed prayers and fasting in the month of Ramaḍān."[25]

3. "I swear by three things—that Allah will not make one who has a share in Islam like one who has no share in it—and the parts of Islam are three: the prayer, fasting, and *zakāh* (alms-giving)."[26]

4. "Islam is founded upon five things: bearing testimony that none is worthy of worship except Allah, performing of the prayer, giving *zakāh* (alms), the pilgrimage and fasting in the month of Ramaḍān."[27]

5. "And by He in whose Hands is my soul, there is no slave that performs three things: the five obligatory prayers, fasting in the month of Ramaḍān and abstaining from the seven major sins, that shall not find the doors of Paradise open for him."[28]

6. "Islam consists of eight parts: belief is a part, the prayer is a part, *zakāh* (alms-giving) is a part, fasting is a part, the pilgrimage is a part, enjoining what is good is a part, forbidding what is evil is a part, *jihād* in Allah's path is a part. He who has none of these parts has attained failure."[29]

It is self-evident that the first *hadīth* was uttered before the implementation of the obligatory acts, the second before the legislation of *zakāh* (alms-giving), and the third before the obligation of the hajj (pilgrimage).

In this way, the Sunnah serves the objectives which the Qur'an makes clear. It is the Qur'an alone which occupies the primary position in portraying the realities of the religion completely and in enumerating its established principles under various conditions and timeframes.

It is also self-evident that the first *ḥadīth* cannot be refuted by any of the other *aḥādīth* and that it cannot refute verses of the Qur'an in any aspect of legislation. This should be known by those whose minds are not at ease as far as understanding Islam is concerned and who think that the reason for this is contradiction within the texts. In reality, it is only due to the ignorance that fills their heads. The earlier scholars of Islam—the honoured Imams (founders of the various jurisprudential schools)—possessed unerring theories in methods of deduction, in addition to their magnificent understanding of the Qur'an and Sunnah. Anyone who follows the history of Islamic legislation in its Golden Era knows this. We have only explained a small portion of what they had resolved.

The validity of the Sunnah

If it is correctly proven that the Messenger of Allah (ṣ) had commanded or forbidden something then obedience to his command is obligatory and it is likened to obedience to Allah. A Believer is not allowed to overstep the commands of the Messenger (ṣ) in any ruling: "He who obeys the Messenger (Muḥammad), has indeed obeyed Allah" (4:80).

"It is not for a believer, man or woman, when Allah and His Messenger have decreed a matter, that they should have any option in their decision. And whoever disobeys Allah and His Messenger has indeed strayed in plain error" (33:36).

Muslims are in full agreement concerning the position of the Sunnah and regard it as the second source of Islam after the Noble Qur'an. The *sunan* (narrated traditions) vary in authenticity and intent. But this is not the place for this discussion. Sound intellectual criteria have been established for this purpose, and one can refer to this body of knowledge if required. The observant critic is required to discuss any *ḥadīth* from two perspectives—its *matn* (body, content, or text) and its *sanad* (chain of narrators). He may only refute a *ḥadīth* on the basis of established academic considerations. The technical sphere for this subject is very well articulated, and earlier scholars have delved into it in tremendous detail, leaving behind an enormous legacy.

Unfortunately some short-sighted individuals—who have no foothold in the field of Islamic knowledge—attack the Sunnah with their foolishness and reject it altogether. Some individuals hastily reject any *ḥadīth* that is related to them simply because it does not impress them or because they do not understand it. To reject the Sunnah in protest that the Qur'an encompasses everything is an innovation of immense danger. Allah, the Honoured and the Most High, had left the responsibility of presenting and clarifying the practical traditions to the Messenger (ṣ). This has been verified unanimously, just like the unanimous verification of the Qur'an, so how can one possibly reject it. In fact, how can one reject the Sunnah and accept the Qur'an in the same breath? Indeed, rejection of the unanimously declared practical traditions (*as-sunan al-mutawātirah*) places one outside the fold of Islam. Rejection—simply based on vain desire—of the singularly-narrated traditions (*as-sunan al-āḥād*) is a transgression of fearful ramifications. We are obligated to study the Sunnah very carefully and to seek benefit from its rulings, ethics, and advice. Inclination towards its rejection is both unjust and unreasonable.

I have closely followed a group of those who reject the Sunnah and have not found in any of their views anything that warrants intellectual respect. They say: "The predecessors gave importance to the chain of narrators and confined their efforts to measuring the worth of these narrators. They did not place emphasis upon the text itself or exert any notable effort in examining the text." This is incorrect, as emphasizing the chain of narrators is not a self-serving purpose; the intention behind it is, in fact, to judge the text itself. Also, the authentication of *aḥādīth* is not based upon the uprighteousness of its narrators only; how they harmonize with the clearly-established facts of the religion is also a factor which is considered. Any unnatural irregularity or dubious intent contained therein qualifies them for exclusion from the framework of authentic *aḥādīth*. It is not permitted to make vain accusations of falsity towards any *ḥadīth*, especially if it has an authentic chain of narrators. This can only be done by submission to respected technical principles. These were the criteria that the earlier scholars imposed upon themselves and which we regard as absolutely necessary to adhere to.

Some in this group mention the *ḥadīth*: "The Black Seed is a healing for all diseases except poisoning."[30] One might say that practical reality gives us reason to reject this *ḥadīth*, even if al-Bukhārī regards it as authentic. It becomes apparent that the understanding of "all diseases" is what is problematic to people. This is an unfounded understanding because if this was the intention of the Messenger (ṣ), there would be no place for all the other *aḥādīth* that describe cures for various afflictions. In reality, "all diseases" only implies some fever-invoking sicknesses. This is similar to the verse in the Noble Qur'an which describes the wind that was sent to the people of 'Ād as "destroying everything by the command of its Lord" (46:25). "Everything" in this context is limited to only the dwellings of this transgressing tribe. If a Muslim had to die unaware of this *ḥadīth*, it would not reduce his faith by even an atom's weight.

Indeed, both Abū Bakr and 'Umar were unaware of the following authentic *ḥadīth*, where the Messenger of Allah (ṣ) said: "I have been commanded to fight against the people—i.e., idolaters of the Arabian Peninsula—until they bear testimony that there is none worthy of worship except Allah and that Muḥammad is the messenger of Allah, and that they establish the prayer and give alms. If they do that then their wealth and blood are safeguarded from me, except with regards to the laws of Islam; and (after this) their reckoning is upon Allah."[31]

The *ḥadīth* which 'Umar and Abū Bakr had memorized did not contain "establish the prayer and give alms." If 'Umar had been aware of this additional statement he would not have protested against Abū Bakr for fighting against those who refused to give alms. And if Abū Bakr had been aware of this addition he would not have deduced his position by analogy and citation from the Qur'an. However, their understanding of the Noble Book and their sound deductions from the Sunnah was more than sufficient and they were thus not disadvantaged in any way by not knowing certain narrations.

But to slander, in such random fashion, the *isnād* (chains of narration) and *mūtūn* (texts) of *aḥādīth*, as some people do, does not serve to outlaw any specific *ḥadīth* but rather acts to outlaw the entire Sunnah and places the rulings derived from it in a position of contempt and suspicion. This, as well as being a denial of plain facts, exposes the whole of Islam to alienation. The recorded collections of the Sunnah are historical documents of the most accurate nature known to this world. We are even able to say that the historical value of certain sacred books of other communities have been increased because they include accounts recorded by our scholars, these scholars having judged some of these works as weak and others as fabricated.

The Sunnah encompasses many rulings because of the tremendous accumulation of detail. Rulings are but shackles that are placed upon the behaviour of people. A shackle has to be placed in a suitable place, to which it conforms, so that there is no reason for complaint or repudiation. Complaints will only arise through misuse of these shackles because—in this instance—it serves to shut doors that should be open, to narrow boundaries that should be wider, and to impede movements that should be allowed to go in stride, without any harm. The greatest harm done to the Sunnah is when a specific *ḥadīth* that was intended for implementation in a specific framework has its context distorted by short-sighted people who generalize it.

Perhaps a fear of exposing Islam to foolish understandings of the Sunnah best describes what al-Ḥārith al-Aʿwar conveys in the following narration. He said: "I went to the *masjid*, and noticed that people were speculating about *aḥādīth* (Prophetic sayings). So I went to ʿAlī and said to him: 'O Leader of the Believers, do you not notice how the people speculate upon *aḥādīth*?' He said: 'Is that what they are doing?' I replied: 'Yes.' He then said: 'I had heard the Messenger of Allah saying: "Indeed, there will be turmoil!", so I asked: "What is the solution to it, O Messenger of Allah?" He said: "Allah's Book! In it is news of what was before you and news of what will be after you, and judgement for that which occurs amongst you; it is a resolution and not a thing of jest. The tyrant that turns away from it is destroyed by Allah, he who seeks guidance in anything other than it is misled by Allah; it is Allah's firm rope and (a guide to) the Straight Path. It is that which cannot be deviated by vanity nor obscured by tongues; scholars never grow weary of it nor is it worn out by attempts to refute it and its wonders are unending. It is that which even the jinn could not abstain from upon hearing it and they thus said: 'Verily! We have heard a wonderful recital (this Qur'an)! It guides to the Right Path' (72:1-2). He who quotes it speaks the truth, and he who acts upon it is rewarded, and he who judges by it is always just, and he who invites to it guides to the Straight Path." Cling to it (the Qur'an) O Aʿwar.'"[32]

Scholars of *ḥadīth* regard the narrations of al-Ḥārith al-Aʿwar as weak, but the text of this *ḥadīth* encompasses very valuable truths. It must also be noted that ʿAlī is not rejecting the Sunnah; knowing that its rulings and narrations are innumerable, he would never do that. What he is dismissing is that it should be engaged by dimwits who inadvertently turn night into day. He rejects as well the diminishing of effort and attention on the part of the community in engaging the Qur'an, thereby neglecting a fundamental cornerstone and the firmest of pillars. The only sound methodology is to direct all concerns to Allah's Book and then to rely upon *aḥādīth* of Allah's Messenger (ṣ) in understanding the Qur'an, conveying its guidance, and implementing its rulings.

Acceptable differences in understanding the Sunnah

If a government that is stable perpetrates an injustice, does one try to enforce change by using force? There are many narrated traditions concerning this matter, which justify lengthy consideration. One who traces the opinions of our scholars on this matter finds that the majority dislike conflict and try to delay it by passing judgements that allow an armed struggle only if certain very strict stipulations are met, under conditions very difficult to fulfil. Perhaps the reason behind this apprehension is that Muslims faced tremendous turmoil at the onset of their history, where revolting against the leadership was sought even for the most trivial reason and where short-sighted individuals were given the right to govern under conditions of which they had no understanding. This caused the politics of the state to be toyed with by the ordinary masses and placed the blood of the virtuous Caliphs within the reach of the mobs.

The effects of this heedless revolt against the government left behind turmoil within the state mechanism. The effort exerted by its leaders to quell uprisings is one of the most important causes for the termination of Islamic expansion. This distraction also caused Muslims to fail in the fulfilment of their greater mission. It also caused differences of opinion regarding transgressions and errors perpetrated by the rulers. Abū Ḥāmid al-Ghazālī expressed his opinion concerning a ruler that perpetrates a wrongdoing in the following words: "Enforcing change by the use of force by any subject against his ruler is not an option because this only serves to stir up turmoil and arouse evil, leading to greater danger." Al-Ghazālī allowed repudiation of the ruler in one's own mind, or criticizing him verbally, only if it does not develop into general upheaval that would harm the state more than it would harm the individual. Pessimism in this regard reached such a stage that some legal scholars even began regarding perseverance in the face of the injustice of the ruler as a branch of faith! This is an unhealthy opinion and its unconditional acceptance served as a pretence for paralyzing the nation in the face of any injustice, until the immorality of rulers in the lands of Islam reached a point that was intolerable.

Expressing an advisory or legal opinion supporting rebellion against a ruler or submission to him requires sound vision. Reality is always misplaced between excessiveness and negligence. The pristine Sunnah encompasses a multitude of teachings which lay out the relationship of the Muslims with the ruler, and indicating when he should be opposed and when he should be supported. Approaching the relevant *aḥādīth* narrated on this topic requires a balanced orientation; ignoring these *aḥādīth* altogether would be better than implementing them foolishly.

Suppose that you gave your servant a bunch of keys for the rooms of a house and he hastily tried to open the door with the first key that came to hand. If he was unsuccessful, he would go to another door using another key that was also not suitable and then move on to another door once again trying an unsuitable key. He would return to you at the end without having opened a single door and may even inform you that the keys are incorrect. There is no fault with the keys; the fault is in the way in which they had been used. If the keys were entrusted to a knowledgeable, skilful person, he would have no problem in placing every key in the correct position, turning it, and opening the door. In the same manner, a suitable *ḥadīth* requires that it be placed in a similarly suitable context.

Indeed, the ruler and the subject are equally constrained by the boundaries set by Allah and there is nothing that is made exclusively permissible to one and prohibited to the other. The ruler that violates the trust of the position bestowed upon him stands, without a doubt, in disobedience before Allah. To be rid of him is more befitting to the religion of Allah and to the religion of humankind together. If it is possible to eliminate him with only slight damage, then abstaining from doing so is certainly a crime. But if addressing the injustice leads to turmoil far greater than the injustice itself, then leaving things as they are becomes the primary consideration. It is possible to arrange the relevant *aḥādīth* on this topic in a manner that would repel any apparent contradictions between them.

It is not always allowable to hold an unjust ruler in contempt, nor is it acceptable in all circumstances to attack and expel him from his position. Some scholars rely upon the general spirit of Islam and its many teachings to oppose oppression and to stand up to tyrants, rejecting *aḥādīth* that promote reconciliation, or regarding them as abrogated. They thus obligate the Muslim not to submit to tyranny and to deal with the ruler if his transgression becomes apparent so that he is restrained from incurring the anger of Allah, no matter what suffering one would have to endure to achieve this.

We will quote the opinion of Ibn Ḥazm, who argues and defends this position. We will also comment upon it in terms of what we regard to be closest to the truth and to the laws of Islam. No matter what our position may be, Ibn Ḥazm is a free-thinking scholar entitled to his understanding and methodology. In quoting his opinion, we are more concerned with exposing the wide intellectual freedom, detailed consideration in understanding the Sunnah, and good assessment of the related narrations that our jurists possessed.

Ibn Ḥazm says, criticizing those advocating submission to the ruler, even if he is unjust:

> The group mentioned draw evidence, firstly, from *aḥādīth* wherein the Prophet was asked: 'Must we fight them, O Allah's Messenger?' He said: 'No. (Are they not of those) who pray.'[33] And in another narration: 'Except if you see suggestions of disbelief of which you have proof from Allah.'[34] And in another

narration, the Prophet responded: 'Patient perseverance is obligatory even if our backs are struck and our wealth is taken.' And another: 'And if you fear being dazzled by the glare of the sword, then pull your garment over your face and say: "Verily, I intend to let you draw my sin as well as yours onto yourself, then you will be one of the dwellers of the Fire, and that is the recompense of the wrong-doers" (5:29).'[35] And in yet another narration: 'Be the slave of Allah who is slayed, and not the slave of Allah who slays.'[36] Allah, the Most High, also says: 'And recite to them, in truth, the story of the two sons of Adam; when each offered a sacrifice (to Allah), it was accepted from the one but not from the other. (5:27).'"

None of the above *aḥādīth* holds any evidence for them in this matter when investigated one by one from the perspective of the chain of narrators and of their import. This is demonstrated in our book: *al-Īṣāl ilā Fahm Maʿrifah al-Khiṣāl (The Conduit to Understanding Information on the Attributes)*. We will quote some parts from it here—if Allah wills—and we seek help from Allah, the Most High:

As far as the Prophet's command to patiently persevere in the face of one's wealth being taken and back being struck is concerned, this is—without doubt—only in the case of the ruler doing so rightfully. In this instance there is no doubt that we should obligate patience upon ourselves, even if the subject refuses to do so. Even if a ruler is obligated to implement capital punishment he cannot decline, as he would then be showing disobedience and transgression of Allah's laws. But if this were to be done unjustly, then we seek Allah's protection for the one who thinks that the Prophet (ṣ) could have commanded perseverance in such an instance. Proof of this is found where Allah, the Most Honoured and High, states: "Help you one another in virtue, righteousness and piety; but do not help one another in sin and transgression" (5:2).

We know that the statements of Allah's Messenger (ṣ) do not contradict those of his Lord. Allah, the Most Honoured and High, states: "Nor does he (Muḥammad) speak of (his own) desire. It is only an inspiration that is inspired (to him)" (53:3-4).

And again in another verse: "Had it been from other than Allah, they would surely have found therein much contradiction" (4:82).

It is therefore correct to hold that everything that Allah's Messenger (ṣ) states is inspired by Allah, the Most Honoured and High, containing no variance, contradiction or deficiency. If this is so, then without a doubt, every Muslim should know that to take the wealth of a Muslim or non-Muslim unjustly, or to punish him unjustly, is a sin and a transgression and is strictly prohibited. Allah's Messenger (ṣ) has stated that: "Verily your blood, wealth, and honour are all sanctified."[37] There is, thus, no doubt or variance concerning this on the part of any Muslim. It is oppressive to take the wealth of a Muslim or to punish him unjustly, and he is justified in trying to stop this by any means possible. If he does not do so then he is effectively helping in the promotion of sin and transgression, which is strictly prohibited, as stated in the Qur'an.

As far as the remaining *aḥādīth* and the story of the two sons of Adam are concerned, they serve as no form of proof whatsoever. The story of the two sons of Adam relates to a different code of law, unlike our law-code. Allah, the Most High and Honoured, states: "To each among you, we have prescribed a law and a clear way" (5:48).

As far as the *aḥādīth* are concerned, it has been correctly established that Allah's Messenger (ṣ) has stated: "If any of you see an injustice, then he should change it with his hand if he is able to do so, and if he is unable, then with his tongue, and if he is unable to do even this then with his heart, and this is the weakest form of faith, behind which no traces of faith are to be found."[38]

Allah's Messenger (ṣ) also stated: "There is no obedience to transgression, only obedience to obedience. You should only show obedience and compliance to one who does not order transgression. If one is ordered to transgress then he should show neither obedience nor compliance."[39]

And he (ṣ) also said: "One killed protecting his wealth is a martyr. He who is slain protecting his religion is a martyr, and one slain in the face of oppression is a martyr."[40]

The Prophet (ṣ) also said: "You shall indeed enjoin what is good and you shall indeed forbid what is unjust, or else Allah shall bring upon you of His punishment."[41]

All these narrations stand clearly in opposition to the ones previously quoted. It can thus only be that one of these groups abrogates the other; nothing else. We are therefore obligated to establish which group of narrations is abrogated and which group remains. We established that the *aḥādīth* that prohibit fighting conform to customary principles at the beginning of Islam while the other narrations were pronounced after the principle of fighting had been added to the Law-Code. Therefore, it is clear, that the meanings of the former *aḥādīth* were abrogated and their application lifted as soon as the Prophet (ṣ) began making the latter pronouncements. It is absurd, and also strictly prohibited, to use that which has been abrogated and ignore that which abrogates, or to use that which is doubtful above that which is certain.

In response to Ibn Ḥazm, we hold that it is not correct for him to advocate abrogation as this is only allowable when one is not able to reconcile between *aḥādīth* that are thought to be contradictory. In this case reconciliation is possible.

Correcting an injustice at all levels does not necessarily imply general rebellion or fighting to the death to protect one's rights. The position that al-Ghazālī holds is closer to the truth in that armed sedition bears terrifying consequences. To make this an allowable option for any discontented individual is not a position advocated by any objective or valid legal system. The first group of *aḥādīth* is valid—in our opinion—and one is obligated to implement them when placed in the position of choosing between the lesser of two evils. The perseverance of an individual in the face of oppression directed towards him is of a lesser consequence to his livelihood and religion than the actions of individuals that cause turmoil that could result in the collapse of the state at the hands of its enemies. There are circumstances that obligate opposition, just as there are circumstances that obligate reconciliation, and the *aḥādīth* reported are applicable to both instances easily and correctly. Concerning the *aḥādīth* that Ibn Ḥazm regards as abrogated, we find that he has no evidence—from a historical perspective—to prove that the abrogating *aḥādīth* were in fact stated after the ones abrogated. In fact, the Prophet (ṣ) had stated some of these *aḥādīth* towards the end of his life and it does not therefore make sense to regard them as abrogated.

Ibn Ḥazm states:

Another proof is the statement of Allah, the Most High: "And if two parties or groups among the believers fall to fighting, then make peace between them both, but if one of them rebels against the other, then fight you (all) against the one which rebels till it complies with the command of Allah" (49:9). No Muslim disagrees that this verse—which obligates fighting against the rebellious party—is valid and not abrogated. It is correct to hold that it is the deciding factor in light of the earlier *aḥādīth*. Whatever *aḥādīth* are, therefore, in accordance with this verse are to be regarded as abrogating and thus established and whatever is opposed to it is regarded as abrogated and thus inapplicable.

Some individuals regard this verse and the *aḥādīth* mentioned as being applicable to criminals and not to the governing authority. This, without a doubt, is incorrect as it is a mere claim without any supporting evidence, which therefore does not prevent one from insinuating that these *aḥādīth* are only applicable to certain people and within a certain time-frame. Insinuation without proof holds no basis and to make insinuations against the Qur'an and Sunnah is sinful as it is equivalent to speaking about Allah with ignorance.

It is reported from Allah's Messenger (ṣ) that someone had inquired about one who asks for wealth that he is not entitled to. The Prophet (ṣ) said: "Do not give it to him." He was then asked: "And what if he attacks me?" He said: "Then defend yourself." He then asked: "And what if I kill him?" The Prophet (ṣ) replied: "He will enter the fire." He then asked: "And what if he kills me?" He (ṣ) said: "Then you will enter paradise"[42] or something to this effect.

It is also correctly proven that the Prophet (ṣ) said: "A Muslim is the brother of a Muslim. He does not endanger him nor oppress him."[43] The Prophet (ṣ) also said concerning *zakāh*: "Who asks of it in accordance with its stipulations should be given and who asks of it beyond its stipulations should not be given."[44] This is a well established report narrated from Anas ibn Mālik, from Abū Bakr, from Allah's Messenger (ṣ). It refutes the interpretation of the *aḥādīth* concerning fighting over wealth to be restricted to criminals only as criminals do not ask for *zakāh* (alms tax); the governing authority does so. The Prophet (ṣ) restricted (the reasons for the) refusal to give *zakāh* only to instances that contradict that which he had ordered. If only the defenders of justice could unite, they would then not be challenged by the perpetrators of falsehood ... We seek only Allah's help and success.

Ibn Ḥazm concludes: "It is obligatory to inform the Imam (political authority) of the occurrence of injustice (even if it is on a small scale) so that he may prohibit it. If he declines to do so and retracts the truth, submitting to the authority of some person or group, then he should be punished with the punishments implemented for adultery, slander and drinking, but he should not be discharged from his position. He still remains Imam as before. But if he refuses to implement any of these obligations—in his capacity as Imam—and is not willing to compromise, then he should be dismissed and replaced by one who will lead with the truth, as Allah, the Most High, states: 'Help you one another in virtue, righteousness, and piety; but do not help one another in sin and transgression. And fear Allah. Verily, Allah is severe in punishment' (5:2). It is not allowable, in any instance, to squander the obligations of the legislation ... and success is only from Allah."

We are in full agreement with Ibn Ḥazm as to the necessity of protecting the legislative process of Islam and to see to its implementation with care and accuracy. We may, however, differ as to what may be the most successful way of implementing this. Is it necessary to dismiss a ruler that perpetrates sins—as is held by Ibn Ḥazm—without exception? Or, expressing this differently, is it correct to dismiss him—if his poor political practices warrants this—no matter what harm and turmoil this may result in? This matter definitely requires wisdom and a balanced outlook. The nation does not have to tolerate oppressive revolutions, but it also does not have to accept injustice and the degradation of its concerns.

Qiyās (analogy)

The Qur'an and the Sunnah are the first and last sources in matters of *'aqā'id* (belief) and *'ibādāt* (worship). No person or authority has any right to add anything to the established system of belief or practices of worship that have come to us from Allah and His Prophet (ṣ). They are finite and bounded.

The matter is somewhat different with regards to *al-mu'āmalāt* (conduct), because Islamic jurisprudential rulings stretch beyond verses of the Qur'an and *aḥādīth*, encompassing other legislative sources that Islam points us to and places in our hands so that we may be able to face new and different realities and developments in life with the passing of time. At the forefront of these sources is *qiyās* (Analogy), which is employed by the majority of jurists to extract rulings that are not mentioned by the Lawgiver.

Qiyās is defined as the transfer of a ruling on a particular issue, for which a text provided by the Lawgiver is known, to another and similar issue, because the two issues are linked by the same underlying cause.

An example of the use of *qiyās* is the following. The Prophet (ṣ) stated: "A person is not permitted to propose marriage to a woman that his brother [in faith] has proposed to, or to make a bid to purchase that which his brother is busy buying."[45] On this basis, we are able to draw the analogy that a person cannot try to hire that which his brother is trying to hire because of the similarity between these issues. In all such instances there would be a transgression upon the rights of the other.

Another example is that of intoxicating drink. Both the Qur'an and the Sunnah prohibit intoxicating drinks. Therefore, by analogy, any substance that affects the mind in the same way that alcohol does is prohibited. The cause or reason for prohibition is that all these substances share the common characteristic of being intoxicating.

The majority of jurists are of the opinion that *qiyās* is a valid means of deducing rulings, and that its outcomes are acceptable. They quote various proofs, both textual and logical, in support of this position. We will present a summary of the most important proofs.

1. In the Qur'an, Allah, the Most Honourable and High, states: "(And) if you differ in anything amongst yourselves, refer it to Allah and His Messenger, if you believe in Allah and the Last Day. That is better and more suitable for final determination" (4:59). Referring differences to Allah's Book and His Messenger's Sunnah is appropriate for the application of the general principles of legislation just as it is appropriate for the implementation of specific rulings. It also sanctions the transference of a ruling from one situation to another, similar one. *Qiyās* does not generate an altogether new ruling, but, rather, implements the Lawgiver's rulings in situations that are of a similar nature.

2. Allah, the Most Honoured and High, says: "then take admonition, O you with eyes (to see)" (59:2), after narrating to us the destruction of the wrongdoers. He also says: "Indeed, in their stories is a lesson for people of understanding" (12:111). The evidential perspective of these verses suggests that Allah is saying: "draw analogies for yourselves from these people; if you were to do what they have done then your fate will be exactly the same as theirs." Professor 'Abd al-Wahhāb Khallāf states: "One cannot say that this is only related to physical laws and is specific only to worldly aspects. The implication of the verses is that Allah's order is consistent in all of His creation. His grace and retribution and all of His laws lead to these premises and causes are due to the reasons occasioned by them. *Qiyās* is no more than a progression along Allah's

established tradition, regulating the cause with its reason, in any situation in which it may be found."[46]

3. When the one who rejects resurrection says: "Who will give life to these bones when they have rotted away and become dust?" (36:78), Allah, the Most High, invalidates his suspicion with a deduction based upon analogy and thus says to His Prophet (ṣ): "Say: (O Muḥammad) "He will give life to them who created them for the first time! And He is the All-Knower of creation" (36:79). Allah thus bases the analogy of the possibility of resurrection upon the occurrence of creation.

4. It is reported in the Sunnah that when Allah's Messenger (ṣ) sent Muʿādh ibn Jabal to Yemen, he asked him how he would pass judgement if required to do so. Muʿādh replied that he would judge by Allah's Book, and if he did not find the necessary ruling in it, then with the Prophet's Sunnah; if he still did not find the necessary ruling there, he would exercise his own discretion, without resorting to subjectivity. The Prophet (ṣ) then patted him on the chest—glad with his response—and said: "Praise be to Allah who has guided the Messenger of Allah's Messenger to that which pleases Allah's Messenger."[47]

Qiyās is not regarded as an example of exercising one's opinion by reason, i.e., inquiry by scrutinizing the reality. Professor Khallāf says: "It is firmly established in authentic *sunan* (Prophetic traditions) that Allah's Messenger (ṣ)—in many instances where he did not receive revelation—would deduce a ruling by means of *qiyās*. The Prophet's action in this general matter is therefore regarded as a means of legislation for his followers. There is no evidence suggesting that this was specific to the Prophet (ṣ) alone."

It is reported that a young woman said to Allah's Messenger (ṣ): "My father is an old man upon whom the obligation of the hajj (pilgrimage) has become incumbent, but he is not able to fulfil it. If I had to do it on his behalf, would he benefit?" He (ṣ) said: "If there was a debt upon your father, would he benefit by you fulfilling it?" She replied that he would. The Prophet (ṣ) then said: "The debt owed to Allah is more deserving of being fulfilled."[48]

It is reported that 'Umar asked the Prophet (ṣ) about kissing while one was fasting i.e., kissing that did not cause one to ejaculate. The Prophet (ṣ) responded by saying: "What if you gargle your mouth while fasting?" 'Umar responded that there was no harm in it. The Prophet (ṣ) then said: "That is enough (for you to know)."[49] The Prophet (ṣ) thus drew an analogy between kissing that does not cause ejaculation and the gargling by a fasting person, in that it does not invalidate his fast.

It is also reported that a man from the tribe of Fazārah rejected his newly-born son because the baby was dark in complexion. The Prophet (ṣ) asked him: "Do you have camels?" After hearing his affirmative reply, the Prophet (ṣ) asked him what their colours were. He said that they were red. The Prophet (ṣ) then asked whether there were any brownish ones among them. He replied that there were, and to this the Prophet (ṣ) responded by asking him how that could be possible. He replied that perhaps it was an extraction caused by the camel's lineage. The Prophet (ṣ) then said: "And this—i.e., his dark-complexioned son—may perhaps be an extraction of his lineage."[50]

5. The actions of the Prophet's companions indicate that they also made deductions using *qiyās* and that they also reinforced its rulings and conducted their affairs in its light. Indeed, after the demise of the Prophet (ṣ), the first Caliph was nominated to the position of governance by an excellent example of *qiyās*. Because he had been chosen by the Prophet (ṣ) to lead the prayers during the Prophet's period of illness, the companions were prompted to say: "The Prophet (ṣ) is pleased to let him lead us in matters of our religion, should we not be pleased to let him lead us in our worldly matters?" They thus drew an analogy between governing the state and leading the prayer.

'Alī is reported to have said: "The truth is known by the standards set by those who possess knowledge."

During the reign of 'Umar ibn al-Khaṭṭāb, Abū Mūsā al-Ash'arī had said: "Concerning understanding that which is brought forward and for which a ruling is not found in the Qur'an or the Sunnah, analogy between matters is used, judging by similar examples and then relying upon that which would be most pleasing to Allah and closest to the truth, as seems apparent to you."

The sphere of *qiyās*

The logic of the intellect and our instinct obliges us to respect *qiyās* in the deduction of the law. How can one disregard a matter in which harm is clearly apparent and then consider another matter proven to encompass this very same harm? Another consideration is that the incidents in which the Lawgiver has specifically expressed a judgement are restricted, so should the law be restricted as well to only these few incidents, or should the wisdom behind these judgements be identified so that it may bring benefit to a much wider sphere? Notwithstanding, *qiyās* is only used in the field of *mu'āmalāt* (conduct) and with regards to issues where it is possible for the intellect to identify causes and to declare an opinion. As far as *'ibādāt* (acts of worship) are concerned, it is the text alone that is to be resorted to. There is thus no expression of opinion with regards to that which is monopolized by the Lawgiver alone, through His Wisdom. Therefore, questions such as the number of cycles in prayer, or the days appointed for fasting, or the number of circumambulations of the Ka'bah, or the types of atonements, or the shares of *zakāh*, or the punishments for adultery and slander, or the stoning of the *jamr* (a ritual of the pilgrimage), etc; all are determined by Allah alone.

Abū Ḥāmid al-Ghazālī states in his book *Iḥyā' 'Ulūm ad-Dīn* (*The Revival of the Religious Sciences*):

> The pilgrim should undertake the stoning of the *jamr* with the intention of showing compliance to an order, portraying

servitude and bondage, invoking within him clear imitation, without any consideration for the self or the intellect in this matter. His intention should then be to try and imitate Ibrāhīm when the Devil (may Allah curse him) exposed himself to him at that particular place. In this way he is able to draw relevance to his pilgrimage, or else he invalidates it (by not performing this ritual) through showing disobedience. Allah's command to stone the Devil is so that he may be expelled and his expectations may be destroyed. If one argues that Satan had exposed himself to Ibrāhīm, who had seen him and therefore stoned him, but that Satan has not exposed himself to me, then know that these thoughts are from Satan and it is he who has cast them into your heart to weaken your desire to perform the stoning ritual, making you imagine that there is no benefit in it and that it is similar to a game, and questioning why you should occupy yourself with it. Expel him from within you in earnest and prepare yourself for the stoning ritual in defiance of him. Know that although it is apparent that you are stoning a barrier, you are in reality stoning the face of Satan and dealing him the deathblow. One cannot show defiance to Satan except by acting out the orders of Allah, the Glorious and Sublime, out of awe for Him and simply because it is His command, without any consideration for one's self.

Qiyās is only resorted to in the absence of a text and is not used if a text from the Qur'an or Sunnah on a relevant matter is available. Another point that facilitates our understanding is that the scope and form of acts of worship are restricted and do not change with time. In fact, any addition—or subtraction for that matter—is a transgression that is to be completely rejected. Jurists thus adopted the practice of restricting acts of worship within the framework in which they had been established. They, therefore, regarded any introduced changes as *bid'ah* (a reprehensible heretical innovation) that could not have been introduced except by one prone to excess.

As far as conduct is concerned, the ruling is exactly the opposite. General principles and derivations served to fulfil their necessary function for people of every era, thereby shaping that which they required in the fields of legislation, legal opinions and implementation. By this process, Islamic jurisprudence expanded and grew, giving rise to various orientations, schools of thought and opinions. The bond between these new horizons in Islamic jurisprudence and the reality of Islam is like the bond between a tree and its living roots, or like the bond between consumable commodities and the production mechanism. If we were to imagine that a printing press grew bigger because it had printed thousands of books, it would then be correct to say that Islam has added to its origins, or has expanded with time because its jurisprudence has increased in volume since the era of the Prophet (ṣ) and his companions. This is the kind of doubt cast upon Islam by Orientalists, with the bigoted roots of the Crusader era still growing strongly within their depths. They, unfortunately, do not recognize Islam as having been revealed from the heavens, but rather regard it as an earthly effort with limited beginnings that developed over time. Any man that enters the field of research freely and is of the opinion that Christianity and Judaism are religions but that Islam is a fabrication is the biggest liar in all of creation, even if he is supposedly promoting intellectual freedom and neutrality.

Dr Muḥammad Yūsuf Mūsā has exposed this false theory directed at Islamic jurisprudence in a thesis on the jurisprudence of the companions and their followers. He refutes Orientalist insinuations as follows: "The Orientalists have their theories on the reasons and extent of this development, but they add to it things that do not concern the matter, thereby differing with our theories, i.e., theories of Muslim scholars. They regard Islam as something that is always open to development, even, for example, acts of worship and matters related to it. Even Ignaz Goldziher, a renowned Orientalist with a firm foothold in the field of Islamic Studies, regards the development of jurisprudence—which began immediately after the Prophet's era—to be based upon pressing needs that are faced in everyday life. He says, "Islam, in all its relationships, did not come into being as a complete system." That is what he insinuates! May Allah disgrace him! This is certainly farfetched for a religion whose book confirms, in many verses, that the Prophet (ṣ) is Allah's Messenger to all of creation, and to all of humankind, with no differentiation between Arab and non-Arab, or between White and Black! As such, the Prophet (ṣ) was truly the seal of the prophets, just as his message is the final of all of Allah's messages and is thus valid for the entire world, encompassing all nations and valid for all time to come.

'Ibādāt (acts of worship) and *mu'āmalāt* (conduct)

We are obligated to ponder the following assertion made by Goldziher: "Islamic Jurisprudence—in aspects that are related to both religion and the world—has submitted to codification." Does he mean that the conventions of development have affected acts of worship, as they have undoubtedly affected matters of conduct? We believe that this is exactly what he means when speaking about the development of jurisprudence as a general development that affects both religious and worldly matters. He brushes aside the truth as well as historical fact when asserting that "acts of worship were also subjected to development". Acts of worship, in all their different manifestations, have not changed since the era of the Prophet (ṣ) right up until today. This is because the Law—i.e., the Qur'an and the Sunnah together—had specified all the required rituals, leaving no room for *ijtihād* (exertion of opinion), which is the only path that leads to development. The difference in opinion amongst Jurists concerning certain actions and formats is due to different understandings of the Qur'an or is based upon differing reports from the Prophet (ṣ).

In another place, Goldziher says: "People in Egypt, Persia and the Levant reconciled their customs, practices and different cultures with the new laws. In brief, Islamic Jurisprudence, whether with regards to religion or worldly matters, had submitted to codification. The Qur'an itself served as a source of only a few laws and it is not possible that these laws could encompass all the unanticipated dealings that came forth after the various conquests. It was restricted to the conditions of the unsophisticated Arabs and specifically directed at them but was, as a result, insufficient for this new situation."

Discussion of this theory

His contentions that Islam "did not come to this world in a perfected manner," and that "the Qur'an was restricted to the conditions of the unsophisticated Arabs and specifically directed at them" is totally incorrect. Indeed, Islam came to this world in a perfected manner, including aspects of both livelihood and the hereafter, including all-encompassing laws pertaining to matters of religion and livelihood. (History bears testimony to what we are saying, although the framework of our research does not allow substantiation.) These were, however, expressed as principles and norms, as is the requirement of all general laws and comprehensive systems. In other words, it is comprised of universalities, leaving the finer details and specifics to those responsible for its comprehension and implementation, relying always upon the inspiration of the Islamic spirit and the objectives of the law. This divine law is therefore always suitable for application in all conditions, if we study it deeply and know how to be guided by it and are able to deduce from it that which is not explicitly stated. As such, the insinuation that the Qur'an is restricted to the conditions of "the unsophisticated Arabs" alone is proven to be untenable.

There is no harm in jurists differing on the understanding of a particular text, or in questioning the authenticity of any *ḥadīth*. This sphere is wide enough for the exercising of their opinions. Nevertheless, the comprehensiveness of the Qur'an and the Prophetic Sunnah—on all rulings concerning acts of worship, and what we regard as "personal affairs", was finalized in detail, and with restrictions, leaving no objective unaddressed. The non-comprehensiveness of the Qur'an regarding rules of conduct and the insufficiency of what is reported from the Prophet (ṣ) on this matter bears important meaning and is of great significance. In our opinion, this points to a restriction upon all that concerns acts of worship and the like, to that which is reported in the two sacred sources of the *sharīʿah* i.e., the Qur'an and Sunnah. This is indispensable when we realize that the rules governing devotional acts of worship lay outside the sphere of human understanding. It is therefore absolutely necessary to refer to these two sources because they sufficiently address these aspects.

Conduct is concerned with worldly matters and its rulings conform to occurrences and relationships that continually arise and change. It was in reference to this that the Prophet (ṣ) said: "You are most knowledgeable concerning matters of your world."[51] This translates as permission for us to exercise our opinions concerning worldly matters, as long as we do so in the light of the Qur'an and the Sunnah, bearing in mind the Qur'anic verse that states that the Prophet (ṣ) does not speak out of vain desire.[52]

We have recollected, in these few pages, the comments of Dr Yūsuf Muḥammad Mūsā on the views of the audacious Orientalist, Goldziher. This Orientalist further expanded his lies against Islam and followed a path that leaves one astonished by his attacks on our religion. His work is characterized by a methodology that is based upon lies and deeply rooted in evil and aggression. As a result, we have written a book especially for the purpose of refuting his work and the works of others like him. The book is entitled *Difāʿ ʿan al-ʿAqīdah wa ash-Sharīʿah ḍid Maṭāʿin al-Mustashriqīn* (Defending the ʿAqīdah and the Sharīʿah against the Slander of the Orientalists). There are syndicates that exploit academic research and we are obligated to deal with them harshly so as to put an end to their evil and to expose the colonialist powers that hide behind them.

Ijmāʿ[53] (consensus)

"Differences in understanding" regarding particular rulings is something that is bound to occur. However, if a ruling is agreed upon (when based upon established sources), and objectionable issues have been resolved by people of learning, it can only mean that the ruling is correct and that the community has reached consensus on it. Therefore all Muslims have to comply, without exception. This is an example of obedience to those in authority, something that the Qur'an alludes to, and whose sphere encompasses other matters that are linked to consensus as well.

After thinking about the matter for a long time, Shaykh Muḥammad 'Abduh concluded:

> *Those in authority* denotes a group of Muslims consisting of leaders and influential people such as governors, judges, scholars, generals and all other leaders that people approach when in need or to resolve issues pertaining to general welfare. Therefore, when these people agree upon a matter or a ruling, then obedience is obligatory, with the following stipulations:
>
> - That [such people] be from amongst us;
> - That they do not disobey any command of Allah or any Sunnah of the Prophet (ṣ) that has been unanimously declared as authentic, confirmed by a plurality of narrators (*al-mutawātir*);
> - That they be elected to address the matter and agree to do so; and
> - That the matter upon which they agree is for the general welfare, i.e., matters that those in authority have influence over and are familiar with.
>
> Leaders and influential people have no say as far as acts of worship and doctrine are concerned. These matters are taken from Allah and His Messenger (ṣ) alone and no one has the right to assert their personal opinions. Where consensus has been reached, the general follows the specific and the individual follows the group in all laws that have been agreed upon, taking into consideration the welfare of the community.

Scholars have defined *ijmā'* as: "The agreement of scholars from the community of Muḥammad (ṣ) (i.e., the Muslim community) upon a legislative ruling, in a particular era." Shaykh

Muḥammad ʿAbduh's comments add a further dimension to this meaning, which we should consider as well, even if other scholars have not considered them in their definition of *ijmāʿ*, because the obligation of showing obedience to one's leaders and uniformity in the conduct of the general masses are important principles of Islam. Allah, the Most Honoured and High, has ordered this in the following verses: "And whoever contradicts and opposes the Messenger (Muḥammad) after the right path has been shown clearly to him, and follows other than the believers' way, We shall keep him in the path he has chosen, and burn him in Hell—what an evil destination" (4:115).

"And hold fast, all of you together, to the Rope of Allah and be not divided among yourselves." (3:103).

The Islamic community occupies an important position in the sight of Allah and His support for it distances it from any misguided understandings or blunders in judgement. The community's agreement upon matters other than the obligatory almost prevents this from happening due to the presence of accomplished scholars. How could this happen when Allah Himself says: "You are the best of peoples ever raised up for mankind" (3:110)?

And in another verse: "Thus We have made you a just nation, that you be witnesses over mankind and the Messenger (Muḥammad) be a witness over you" (2:143).

In other words, Allah has granted Muslims authority over humankind in judging their declarations, just as He has granted the Prophet (ṣ) authority over Muslims in judging their adherence to His declarations. It is obvious that "Muslims" does not mean those that are good in actions and words, but rather indicates people of learning who are heedful, experienced and qualified to understand the Qur'an and the Sunnah. Only the directives of such people are to be followed and only their consensus is to be adhered to. In our opinion, to oppose their guidance is to slip away from Islam itself.

The Prophetic Tradition contains recommendations regarding the consensus of the community as a binding truth. These reports serve to deal with individual disputes and also to address what is odd regarding thought and behaviour, thereby making the community a single unit in the service of its sources, be it the Prophetic Tradition, or the Qur'an. The Prophetic Traditions reported in this regard demonstrate how this community is protected from falling into error and have been reported in different ways by trustworthy narrators. Consider, for example, the following statements:

"My followers will not agree upon an error."[54]

"My followers will not agree upon what misguides."[55]

"I asked my Lord to ensure that my followers do not agree upon what misguides and He acceded."[56] This narration is also reported with the phrase "upon an error."[57]

Also reported are: "Allah's hand is with the group."[58]

"Follow the greatest majority."[59]

"He who leaves the group by the distance of a hand-space has removed the noose of Islam from his neck."[60]

"There will still remain a group of my followers upon the truth until Allah's command is sent forth."[61]

"My followers will be divided into such and such sects, all of them in the fire except one." It was asked: And which sect is that? He said: "The (united) group."[62]

A sector of the Muslim community, amongst them the Mu'tizilite scholar an-Naẓẓām, does not accept *ijmā'* as a legislative source. He looked at the validity of a ruling from the perspective of its source, whether rational or textual, without considering its background. He therefore define *ijmā'* as, "Any statement whose authority has been implemented, even the statement of a single person." As far as I am concerned, this opinion does not stand firm as a source of consensus because there can be no consensus upon a matter based on weak authority. Such rulings are expected to merge and join together with other rulings that are generally accepted. They may thus contradict them if based upon weak authority.

The truth of the matter is that *ijmā'* is a valid authoritative source that the majority of scholars have relied upon. Shaykh 'Alī 'Abd ar-Razzāq said: "In reality, they speak about *ijmā'* as a genuine matter of fact, recalling examples from different situations and contexts."

Some of the examples that they put forward for established consensus are similar to those that al-Āmidī relates concerning the agreement of all Muslims—not just leaders and influential people—on the obligation of the five prayers, fasting in the month of Ramaḍān, *zakāh* (the alms tax), the pilgrimage, and other laws that are generally not required to be known by everyone out of necessity (unlike the ones mentioned above).

Another example is related by the author of *Musallim ath-Thubūt* concerning the preference of that which is conclusive over that which is doubtful: "They have witnessed that all the scholars from amongst the Companions and their followers, in all eras, would put forward what is conclusive and it is known through experience that none of them had retracted. It was thus undoubtedly established that agreement had taken place amongst them. The case is similar with regards to the Caliphate: it was witnessed that all the companions in Madīnah made the pledge of allegiance and that none of them retracted their pledges. Even those from outside of Madīnah came to pledge allegiance to the authority of Abū Bakr. This was then followed by everyone from all over and in this way it became known that consensus had been reached. Other examples of rulings entered into through *ijmā'* are the consensus reached allowing the hiring of bathrooms, the charging of fees by the barber, the collection of land-tax, the invalidity of the marriage of a Muslim woman to a non-Muslim man, the inheritance of grandparents being one-sixth, the prohibition of grandchildren receiving inheritance while their parents are still alive and many other examples."

The author of *at-Taḥrīr* quotes Abū Isḥāq al-Isfarāyīnī, who said: "We are aware that the issues pertaining to *ijmā'* are in excess of 20,000. With this we can refute those atheists who state that this religion is burdened with differences in opinion. If this were the truth, such consensus could not have been reached. We thus prove them wrong by stating that there is consensus on over 20,000 issues. Concerning subsidiary issues, the consensus reached in this regard exceeds 100,000 issues. This leaves only about 1,000 issues around which the expression of difference in opinion exists."

In reality, the implementation of *ijmā'* in matters upon which agreement has been reached should be the primary goal of all intelligent people because it leads to the unity of the Islamic community. It also serves to direct their intellectual activities towards fields that rightfully deserve independent research, fields in which their intelligence may be fully utilized. In this light, we may ask:

- What is the value of conflict in matters of the unseen?
- What is the benefit of stirring up discord in matters of worship?
- What is the significance of an irregular understanding of a text upon whose meaning scholars have already reached agreement?

All these issues—in addition to being wrong—only serve to weaken our strength and confuse our minds. However, no harm is caused if an intelligent person promotes investigation in general and universal matters, thereby giving guidance in fields not pursued by earlier scholars. This is in fact one of the shortcomings of Muslims. If only all of them could emulate the advice of the poet who said:

> And even if I may be the last
> of my generation
> I would bring forth that
> which my predecessors could not.[63]

I read a book written by an engineer in which he interprets the reality of prayer in a way that is unknown to Muslims in all of their fourteen centuries of existence. I was astonished by his foolishness and his violation of *ijmāʿ* (i.e., the consensus regarding the prayer). I asked myself: couldn't this innovator find an opportunity to express his intelligence in the field of engineering instead of busying himself, and us, with all this triviality.

No difference of opinion concerning the sources of Islam

We have thus far discussed the references of Islam, its legislative sources, the points of reference of its scholars and the boundaries of its authority. The Islamic community knows no other sources across its development and historical lifespan and, as such, only recognizes these. Differences do arise around terminology—not subject matter—concerning, for example, the binding nature of *qiyās* or *ijmāʿ*. These are minor differences that evoke inconvenience, but are not regarded as irreconcilable because any rule established by *qiyās*, for example (by those in favour of it), may just as well be established by another theory based on source-matter from the Qur'an and Sunnah by those who reject *qiyās*. That is why we say that differences lie in terminology and not in reality, thereby making reconciliation easy.

Those who reject *ijmāʿ* do not assume that general opinion is able to issue forth a ruling from itself without any link to the textual sources of Islam. One cannot issue a ruling and give it authority by general agreement; this is wrong. *Ijmāʿ* does not possess the ability to do that. People, as many as they may be, do not serve as sources for deriving religious rulings. It has been clearly established that *ijmāʿ* is completely reliant upon the Qur'an and the Sunnah. Its effect is to resolve arguments concerning issues addressed and resolved by the agreement of scholars in the position to make rulings and prohibitions.

We still have to resolve a false impression that may bother some short-sighted individuals, who suggest that the Shīʿah have other sources by which they understand the religion, thereby departing from the majority of Muslims. This is clearly taking the matter too far.[64] The Shī‘ah do not deviate from the majority in relying upon the sources that we have just explained. After the dispute around the Caliphate and the split concerning the appointment of the Caliph had settled, it becomes futile for this division to remain. Shī‘ah views, as such, have become no different than that of any other Islamic school of thought with regards to understanding the sources and their sub-divisions. This is made clear in the following extract, which we have quoted from the book *With the Imāmiyyah Shī‘ah* by Professor Maḥmūd Jawād Mughniyyah. In it he puts forward his views concerning the Qur’an, Sunnah, *ijmā‘*, and *qiyās*:

Adherence to the Qur’an

The Imāmiyyah are extremely attached to the Qur’an, guarding over it and showing it great respect. They derive their beliefs and rulings from it and use it to refute any obscurity. They regard the Qur’an as the greatest miracle and the only correct standard by which the truth and guidance is measured. They also report that their scholars order them to judge their views in the light of the Qur’an and if they contradict the Qur’an they are regarded as lies and inventions that must be completely rejected.

No fabrication in the Qur’an

It is impossible for the Qur’an to be touched by fabrication, either through addition or by deficiency, as is made clear in the ninth verse of Sūrah al-Ḥijr: "Verily We it is who have sent down the Reminder (i.e., the Qur’an) and surely We will guard it" (15:9).

Then again in Sūrah Fuṣṣilat: "Falsehood cannot come to it from before it or behind it, (it is) sent down by the All-Wise, worthy of all praise" (41:42).

The Imāmiyyah are accused of regarding the Qur’an as being deficient of certain verses in spite of the fact that their earlier and present-day scholars—in their capacity as religious authorities—clearly state that the Qur’an is no different from what is in the possession of people today.

Divisions of *ḥadīth*

The Shī'ah divide *ḥadīth* into two categories: *mutawātir* and *āḥād*. Mutawātir is a *ḥadīth* that is transmitted by a group of such a large number of transmitters that it would be impossible for them to agree or collude upon a fabrication. This type of *ḥadīth* is regarded as valid proof and it is obligatory to act upon it. *Āḥād* is a *ḥadīth* whose transmitters do not reach the level of *at-tawātur* (impeccable plurality—as above), but may have one or more transmitter. *Aḥādīth al-āḥād* are further divided into four categories:

1. *Ṣaḥīḥ* (Authentic): This is if the transmitter is from the Imāmiyyah and has been found to be just, by the required methodology.
2. *Ḥasan* (Good): If the transmitter is from the Imāmiyyah and is praiseworthy, not having any record of being unjust, or even just for that matter.
3. *Muwaththaq* (Attested): If the transmitter is a Muslim, but not a Shī'ah and is trustworthy and honest in narration.
4. *Ḍa'īf* (Weak): Anything not falling into the descriptions just mentioned; for example a non-Muslim transmitter, or one who is a deviant Muslim, or one whose character is unknown, or a chain of narration in which all the transmitters are not recorded would be regarded as weak.

Acting upon the *ḥadīth*

The Imāmiyyah regard it is as obligatory to act upon *aḥādīth* that are

Ṣaḥīḥ, *ḥasan* and *muwaththaq*, because of the strength of the chain of narrators. They reject *aḥādīth* that are *ḍa'īf* because of the weakness in the chain. They further state that *ḍa'īf aḥādīth* may come to be regarded as strong if their implementation was found to be widespread amongst the earlier jurists. Their regard for *ḍa'īf* (keeping in mind their awe and dedication to the religion, and their closeness to the first generation) exposes the existence of a link with a reality that these jurists had experienced but that we may be unaware of. Due to the existence of this link, the *ḥadīth* may be regarded as authentic and we may overlook the discrepancies of the transmitter.

Similarly, a strong *ḥadīth* may be regarded as weak if it is found to have been neglected by the classical jurists. Their lack of knowledge concerning it, even though it should have been within their sights, exposes a link that calls for the rejection of this specific *ḥadīth*, even if its transmitter is found to be reliable.

The following are some of the criteria stipulated by the Shī'ah for identifying a fabricated *ḥadīth*:

- That it is found to contradict a text of the Qur'an;
- It is contradictory to an established Prophetic Sunnah, or to reason;
- It is found to be poorly expressed, i.e., not eloquent by the standards of the Arabic language;
- The *ḥadīth* informs us of an important event that should have been transmitted widely, but is found to be transmitted by one narrator only;
- The transmitter is found to be in the service of a despotic ruler.

Ijmā' (consensus)

Ijmā' developed in Madīnah after the demise of the Prophet (ṣ), specifically amongst his companions. It is well known that in the Prophet's era there was no other authority on religious matters except him. In the era of the companions, all of the jurists—and jurisprudence for that matter—was located in Madīnah. It was thus easy to know the opinions of everyone that expressed views on a matter because they were few in number. Their status and positions in society were also well known to all. After the spread of Islam, study circles were established in every city, led by teachers of religious knowledge. It became difficult to gain the consensus of all the scholars, more so because, at that time, codification and writing were not well established practices. The Shī'ah divide *ijmā'* into various divisions which are further divided into subdivisions.

Ijmā', with regards to timeframes, is divided into three periods:

1. *Ijmā'* of the *ṣaḥābah* (Companions):
This comes into being when all the companions have agreed upon a legislative ruling. Both the Shī'ah and *ahl as-sunnah* regard it as mandatory to consider this consensus as a principle

of the *sharī'ah* (Law). They differ, however, on the reason that points to it being regarded as mandatory. The Shī'ah regard it as authoritative because of the presence of the Imam ('Alī) amongst the companions. The *ahl as-sunnah* say that it is authoritative because of the *ḥadīth* that states: "My Community will never agree upon misguidance."[65] In any case, the result is exactly the same: an obligation to act upon the consensus of the companions in all of the schools of thought.

With regards to the *ijtihād* (opinion) of one of the companions, the four schools of thought all confer that it is necessary to act upon a statement of a companion if no opinion to the contrary is found in the Qur'an or the Prophetic Sunnah. This is because he is the most knowledgeable as to what the intention of the Prophet (ṣ) may have been, through the honour of accompanying him and also because he had lived in the era of revelation. Therefore his *ijtihād* (opinion) is given preference to the *ijtihād* of anyone that came after him. Al-Ghazālī, al-Āmidī, and ash-Shawkānī are of the opinion that a statement of a companion is not authoritative or binding because the companions themselves had agreed that it was allowable for them to differ amongst themselves in matters of *ijtihād*. If a statement of a companion is not binding amongst the companions themselves, how can it be regarded—by analogy—as binding on others. This opinion is also favoured by the Shī'ah.

2. *Ijmā'* of Scholars in eras other than the Era of the Companions:

The agreement of scholars in all the Islamic precincts and cities in an era other than that of the companions and the Righteous Caliphs is given due regard by the Shī'ah and is binding for the community. Regional *ijmā'*, i.e., A specific agreement like the *ijmā'* of the people of Iraq, or the people of al-Ḥijāz, etc, cannot be regarded as a subject for research because, in reality, it is not regarded as *ijmā'*.

3. *Ijmā'* of Scholars in all Eras and Places:

If all the scholars of the different Islamic schools of thought, in all eras and places, from the era of the Prophet (ṣ) to the present time, agreed upon a matter, then under no conditions can this agreement be transgressed upon or disregarded. This ruling undoubtedly becomes a religious necessity, and whoever disobeys it is regarded as having rejected one of the principles of Islam. If the scholars of a specific school of thought agree upon a matter, then it is regarded as a ruling that would only be specific to that school and whoever rejects it has rejected a principle of that school and not necessarily a principle of Islam.

Reason as a source (*dalīl al-ʿaql*)

The scholar is required to search for his rulings—before anything else—in one of three sources: The Qur'an, the Sunnah, and *ijmāʿ*. If the ruling is found in one of these three sources then there is no room left for taking recourse to reason (as a source). If the scholar is unsuccessful in employing these three sources, he is then allowed to resort to the fourth source.

In the early stages this source was "the idea of public welfare", which differs according to differences in opinions and theories. The companions were not aware of terminology such as *qiyās* (analogy), *al-barā'ah* (freedom from liability), *al-istiṣḥāb* (presumption of continuity), and whatever other principles that were defined after the era of the companions. If a companion was questioned on an issue he would exert his reason to formulate an opinion based upon the general-welfare of the community, and the spirit of Islam, not conforming to any specific rule or principle. There are many examples to this effect, such as the following ruling by the second Caliph, ʿUmar ibn al-Khaṭṭāb: Mālik narrates that aḍ-Ḍaḥḥāk ibn Qays dug a water inlet for himself and wanted to pass it over the land of Muḥammad ibn Musallamah, but the latter refused. Aḍ-Ḍaḥḥāk said: "You refuse me but it is beneficial for you, as you can draw water from it, and it does not harm you," but Muḥammad still refused. Aḍ-Ḍaḥḥāk then spoke to ʿUmar ibn al-Khaṭṭāb about this. ʿUmar then ordered Muḥammad to grant the permission, but Muḥammad still refused. ʿUmar then said: "Do not prohibit your brother from that which benefits you and does not harm you," but Muḥammad still refused. ʿUmar then said: "By Allah, he (will be allowed) to pass through, even if he crosses over your stomach!"[66]

After the era of the companions, *ijtihād* only focused upon specific principles and rules. The various schools of thought, however, differ in the appointment of this fourth source.

The schools of thought of the *ahl as-sunnah* and the fourth source

The Ḥanafī and Mālikī Schools say that the fourth source is *qiyās* (Analogy), *istiḥsān* (Juristic Preference), and *istiṣlāḥ* (Welfare or Well-Being). The Shāfiʿī School says that it is *qiyās* and they do not rely upon *istiḥsān* and *istiṣlāḥ*. The Ḥanbalī School says that the fourth source of legislation is *qiyās* and *istiṣlāḥ*.

Qiyās is the joining of a matter that has no textual basis to one that has a textual basis, i.e., they are joined in a legal ruling because they share the same principle cause. For example, there is a legal text stating that the grandmother of a mother inherits, but there is no text stating the same for the grandmother of a father. As such, the grandmother of a father will also inherit from his estate because an analogy is drawn from the first instance, as they are both grandmothers. This is the closest example of *qiyās* by equality.

The Shīʿah reject *qiyās*, and so do the Ẓāhirī jurists of the *ahl as-sunnah*. Ibn Ḥazm has mounted a scathing attack upon *qiyās* and those who accept it. The rejection or acceptance of *qiyās* is based on academic considerations and does not concern doctrine (*al-iʿtiqād*). As we have said before, the disagreement in this matter concerns terminology and not subject-matter.

There is no harm in briefly presenting the views of a Shīʿah Scholar from Iran, who discusses the sources of legislation amongst the Imāmiyyah.

Sources of legislation according to the al-Imāmiyyah

Shaykh Muḥammad Taqī al-Qummī says:

> There are four sources of legislation according to the Imāmiyyah:
> The Qurʾan, the Sunnah, *ijmāʿ* and reason or intellectual proofs.

The Qur'an

One of the greatest blessings bestowed upon Muslims is that they do not disagree over their Book. A Muslim in the furthest point West has exactly the same Qur'an as a Muslim in the furthest point East. Manuscripts of the Qur'an in the Arab World are exactly the same as those in other countries. There is not a single difference in any verse, writing style, or letter. If the word "raḥmah" is found written with an open *tā'* (from the Arabic alphabet), this would be the case in every manuscript in every Muslim country, with no difference between Arab and foreigner, or Sunnī and Shī'ah. Over and above this complete agreement with regards to Allah's Book, Muslims also regard their Qur'an as the force by which Allah binds them together, something of momentous significance and also the primary source of the *sharī'ah*.

The Sunnah

The Shī'ah and Sunnī schools do not differ with regards to the Sunnah of Allah's Messenger (ṣ). All Muslims unanimously agree that it is the second source of the *sharī'ah*. There is also no disagreement amongst Muslims in regarding any saying, action, or tacit approval of the Prophet (ṣ) as a Sunnah that must be recognized. The difference, however, lies between one who heard something from the Prophet (ṣ) in his era and one who received a *ḥadīth* by some other means. The issue of authenticity and acceptability of transmitters thus arises, thereby leading to differences of opinion. In other words, differences centre on the means of transmission and not on the Sunnah itself. This generates disputes between the Sunnīs and the Shī'ah from time to time. The dispute is a *minor* one, not a *major* one.[67] There is no disagreement with regards to accepting what is transmitted from the Prophet (ṣ). What is disputed is that if the *ḥadīth* is transmitted by only one narrator, did it in fact originate from the Prophet (ṣ) or not.

At times, two, or even several, reports are transmitted on the same issue from the Imams of the different schools of thought as these Imams are from an era relatively closer to ours. Even Imam 'Alī—who is regarded as the stipulated Imam by the Shī'ah and is also followed by the Sunnīs'—has had two different reports transmitted from him on conflicting issues; one followed by the *ahl as-sunnah* and the other by the Shī'ah. If we seek authentication on reports transmitted from the various Imams, it is only natural that with regards to the Prophetic Sunnah the matter requires a greater degree of precision and authentication. The Prophet's statements are legislation and he is the only legislator for Muslims; what he regards as permissible will remain so until the Day of Reckoning, and, so too, what he regards as prohibited.

To reach the significance of the Prophet's statement—so that one knows whether the *ḥadīth* is conditional or unconditional, general or specific, one is required to have knowledge of the transmitter so that some link or characteristic which has an effect upon judging the *ḥadīth* is not left out. There is no disagreement about regarding the Sunnah as the second source of legislation; disagreement does, however, surround the acceptance or rejection of the transmitter. This is not something specific to the *ahl as-sunnah* and Shī'ah only, but rather a common difference amongst the various schools of thought of the *ahl as-sunnah* itself. For example, there are many transmitters that are acceptable to ash-Shāfi'ī but not to others. However, the majority of schools still accept the reports of any of the companions.

The Shī'ah stipulate that the report should be transmitted along the path of the Imams from the Prophet's household. This stipulation is because of several reasons, one of which is their belief that [the Imams] are the most knowledgeable people with regards to the Sunnah. The result in most cases does not vary. The prayer, for example, is not described in detail in the Qur'an. The details are derived from the Sunnah, from reports on how the Prophet (ṣ) performed his prayer. In spite of this, we see that the difference between the two groups is very slight, even though the pillars and smaller details regarding the prayer are many. The case is the same with regards to hajj (the pilgrimage) and other things.

Ijmā' (consensus)

Ijmā' is regarded as one of the sources of legislation by the Imāmiyyah, as it is by others, and is placed as the third

source, after the Qur'an and the Sunnah. The consensus of
the Imams upon a ruling exposes an authority lying within it,
i.e., it is safeguarded from falling into error. If it were not for
this authority, scholars—bearing in mind their devoutness
in making legal judgements—would not agree on the same
opinion. There is, therefore, an inherent authority, which the
binding nature of *ijmā'* relies upon and exposes.

His Eminence, Shaykh al-Qummī, then goes on to discuss
their fourth source, which is reason. This is, however, not the place
to explain it in detail.

After this exposition, it is my opinion that the extent of
disagreement between the two groups is not very significant.
These disagreements can easily be overcome through dedication to
authentic Islam and the unity of the community. The maintenance
of estrangement between the *ahl as-sunnah* and the Shī'ah is
therefore something that is not sanctioned by religion nor by
reason.

Notes

1. *Ṣaḥīḥ Muslim*, Book of Virtue and Ties, ḥadīth no. 4650.
2. From the article *Towards a Muslim Generation*.
3. Jean-Jacques Rousseau (2008), *Emile* (Bibliobazaar), p. 251.
4. *Ṣaḥīḥ Muslim*, Book of Leadership, ḥadīth no. 3422.
5. Buell Gordon Gallagher (1946), *Color and Conscience: The
   Irrepressible Conflict* (Harper and Brothers), p. 62. The Arabic text
   makes reference to the secondary source that quotes Gallagher, but I
   have quoted and referenced the primary source [Translator].
6. At this point in the Arabic text, Shaykh al-Ghazālī discusses
   racist legislation prevalent in the United States in the 1950s. This
   discussion has been omitted because those laws have since been
   repealed. However, the point he makes is still valid. Statutory
   racism was only abolished in South Africa in 1994 with the collapse
   of Apartheid, but has still not been completely purged in other
   countries; Israeli legislation still upholds the racist "Law of Return"
   which allows automatic citizenship to Jews from any country in
   the world but prohibits Palestinians displaced from their land and

violently dispossessed in the *nakbah* (Catastrophe) of 1948 from returning to their homes [Translator].

7. *Ṣaḥīḥ al-Bukhārī*, Book of Upliftment, ḥadīth no. 5947.
8. *Ṣaḥīḥ al-Bukhārī*, Book of Upliftment, ḥadīth no. 5947.
9. *Musnad Aḥmad*, ḥadīth no.13306.
10. *Musnad Aḥmad*, ḥadīth no. 11349.
11. *Al-Ibānah al-Kubrā*, Ibn Baṭṭah, Chapter on what was Conveyed on the Sunnah from the Prophet (ṣ), no. 203.
12. *Sunan at-Tirmidhī*, Book of Recitations, ḥadīth no. 2872.
13. *Sunan at-Tirmidhī*, Book of Virtues and Ties, ḥadīth no. 1820.
14. *Ṣaḥīḥ al-Bukhārī*, Book of Faith, ḥadīth no. 25.
15. *Sunan at-Tirmidhī*, Book of Faith, ḥadīth no. 2552.
16. *Ṣaḥīḥ al-Bukhārī*, Book of Seeking Permission, ḥadīth no. 5767.
17. Two such works are: *al-Bayān wa at-Taʿrīf fī Asbāb Wurūd al-Ḥadīth ash-Sharīf* by as-Sayyīd Ibrāhim ibn Muḥammad, better known as Ibn Ḥamzah ad-Dīmashqī (d. 1110 AH), and *al-Lumaʿ fī Asbāb al-Ḥadīth*, edited by Dr Yaḥyā Ismāʿīl.
18. *Sunan an-Nisāʾī*, Book of Awakening, ḥadīth no. 1324.
19. *Sunan ad-Dārimī*, Book of Drinks, ḥadīth no. 2037.
20. *Ṣaḥīḥ Muslim*, Book of Mosques and Places of Prayer, ḥadīth no. 827.
21. *Sunan Ibn Mājah*, Book of Foodstuff, ḥadīth no. 3305.
22. *Sunan Abū Dāwūd*, Book of Punishments, ḥadīth no. 3811. See also: *ʿAwn al-Maʿbūd Sharḥ Sunan Abī Dāwūd* for a detailed commentary on this ḥadīth.
23. *Ṣaḥīḥ Muslim*, Book of Purification, ḥadīth no. 414.
24. *Sunan at-Tirmidhī*, Book of Faith, ḥadīth no. 2562.
25. *Muṣannaf Ibn Abī Shaybah*, The Ideal of the Believer, vol. no.7, no. 69.
26. *Musnad Aḥmad*, ḥadīth no. 23968.
27. *Sunan at-Tirmidhī*, Book of Faith, ḥadīth no. 2534.
28. *Sunan an-Nisāʾī*, Book of Alms, ḥadīth no. 2395.
29. *Muṣannaf Ibn Abī Shaybah*, On what is Related Concerning Faith and Islam, vol. no.7, no. 5.
30. *Ṣaḥīḥ al-Bukhārī*, Book of Medicine, ḥadīth no. 5256.
31. *Musnad Aḥmad*, ḥadīth no.21106.
32. *Sunan at-Tirmidhī*, Book of the Virtues of the Qur'an, ḥadīth no. 2831.
33. *Majmaʿ az-Zawāid*, al-Haythamī, 5/22.
34. *Ṣaḥīḥ al-Bukhārī*, Book of Discord, ḥadīth no. 6532.
35. *Sunan Ibn Mājah*, Book of Discord, ḥadīth no. 3948.
36. *Al-Maqāṣid al-Ḥasanah*, al-Imam Mālik, 30.
37. *Ṣaḥīḥ al-Bukhārī*, Book of Discord, ḥadīth no. 6551.

38. *Ṣaḥīḥ Muslim*, Book of Faith, ḥadīth no. 70.
39. *Ṣaḥīḥ al-Bukhārī*, Book of Laws, ḥadīth no. 6611.
40. *Ṣaḥīḥ al-Bukhārī*, Book of Injustices and Usurpation, ḥadīth no. 2300.
41. *Musnad Aḥmad*, ḥadīth no. 22212.
42. *Ṣaḥīḥ Muslim*, Book of Faith, ḥadīth no. 201.
43. *Musnad Aḥmad*, ḥadīth no. 5388.
44. *Ṣaḥīḥ al-Bukhārī*, Book of Alms, ḥadīth no. 1362.
45. *Ṣaḥīḥ Muslim*, Book of Marriage, ḥadīth no. 2531.
46. Shaykh al-Ghazālī does not provide the reference details, but, he is quoting from Professor 'Abd al-Wahhāb Khallāf's famous introductory text on Source Methodology in Islamic Jurisprudence entitled *'Ilm Uṣūl al-Fiqh*. There are several editions of this work still in print today [Translator].
47. *Sunan Abū Dāwūd*, Book of Judgements, ḥadīth no. 3119.
48. *Sunan Ibn Mājah*, Book of Rituals, ḥadīth no. 2900.
49. *Sunan Abū Dāwūd*, Book of Fasting, ḥadīth no.2037.
50. *Musnad Aḥmad*, ḥadīth no. 6892.
51. *Ṣaḥīḥ Muslim*, Book of Virtues, ḥadīth no. 4358.
52. See (53:3) [Translator].
53. The majority of scholars are of the opinion that *Ijmā'* follows the Qur'an and the Sunnah and comes before *qiyās* in the deduction of Laws.
54. I have not encountered this statement with the word *khaṭa'* (error) [Translator].
55. *Sunan Ibn Mājah*, Book of Discord, ḥadīth no. 3940.
56. *Musnad Aḥmad*, ḥadīth no. 25966.
57. See note 52, above.
58. *Sunan an-Nisā'ī*, Book of the Sanctity of Blood, ḥadīth no. 3954.
59. *Sunan Ibn Mājah*, Book of Discord, ḥadīth no. 3940.
60. *Musnad Aḥmad*, ḥadīth no. 20581.
61. *Sunan at-Tirmidhī*, Book of Discord, ḥadīth no. 2155.
62. *Sunan Ibn Mājah*, Book of Discord, ḥadīth no. 3983.
63. These verses were composed by the renowned 11th century blind Arab poet, Abū al-'Alā' al-Ma'arrī, from his collection entitled *Saqṭ az-Zand* (The Tinder Spark) [Translator].
64. I am not a Shī'ah but I believe that the relationships between the different Islamic sects can follow a path that is more advantageous to Islam and closer to impartiality than the one it is upon now—only if we get to know each other better.
65. *Sunan Ibn Mājah*, Book of Discord, ḥadīth no. 3940.
66. *Al-Muwatta*, al-Imām Mālik, Passing Judgement on a Matter of Utility, ḥadīth no. 1236.

67. This is an expression common to scholars of logic. Its basis is that the first premise regarding proof is called *minor*, and the Second is called *major*. When someone says: This *ḥadīth* is a statement of the Prophet (ṣ) and all of his statements have to be followed and regarded as obligatory; therefore this *ḥadīth* is obligatory, the critique of this would be that: There is no disagreement concerning the major premise, but inquiries may surround the minor premise, i.e., is this *ḥadīth* really a statement of the Prophet (ṣ)?

2

Islamic Thought

*A*t this point, it is important to place before the reader a sketch of Islamic thought, with the stages of its development through the passage of time. We will take into consideration the factors that maintained it on its course, as well as those that distorted it, reflected its brilliance, or made it appear dull. The *Muqaddimah*[1] (Prolegomena) of ʿAbd ar-Raḥmān ibn Khaldūn, the renowned Arab Historian, contains a sober and well-composed elaboration on this subject spread across its various chapters. This book has no equal in terms of depth and methodology. Dr Muḥammad al-Bahī has presented a good summary of Ibn Khaldūn's discussion, with an explanation and an accurate commentary that brings together the various aspects of the work. We will capture the essence of his study here.[2]

The difference between Islam and Islamic thought

From the outset, we need to clarify what is meant by Islamic thought. Islamic thought is not Islam; it is the intellectual product of Muslims that aims to serve Islam by deliberating on its principles. Islam is the divine revelation inspired to the Prophet of Allah, Muḥammad ibn ʿAbdullah (ṣ). The book of this prophetic mission is the Noble Qurʾan. Its authority is consolidated by the confirmed practices of the Prophet (ṣ), which also clarify whatever needs clarification.

Islamic thought is created; it submits to the laws of growth and development and is subject to corruption. Islam, on the other hand, has a book that is incorruptible: "Falsehood cannot come to it from before it or behind it; (it is) sent down by the All-Wise, (who is) worthy of all praise" (41:42). Islamic thought is not protected from error and weakness. Islam, however, is protected. The Book of Islam—because it is protected from deviation and frailty—is of divine status and commands the absolute compliance of all believers. Islamic thought cannot demand compliance, except to the point that it is representative of Allah's Book and the Divine Message. This is because—by its very origin—it submits to criticism and difference in opinion.

The difference between Islam and Islamic thought is like the difference between that which is due to Allah and that which belongs to humanity. The relationship between the two concepts is like the bond between two objects: the one rests upon the other and depends upon it for its support and existence. However, one does not represent the other perfectly, nor is it an identical expression of it.

There is Islam, descended by divine revelation, and then there are Muslims that believe in Islam. They translate its teachings into action and are devoted to perpetuating these teachings amongst their generation as well as to the generations that follow, so that they remain devoted. They also teach their peers how to be devoted followers and how to express their faith in an acceptable way, as well as teaching them devotion to the perpetuation of Islam and to their own perpetuation as a nation of believers. Preparing the manner of these teachings, as well as defining their characteristics and then expressing them in a manner that is passed on from generation to generation via the circulation of books, etc., is what is called Islamic thought. These methods—whether planning, defining important characteristics, or expression—vary, depending upon the person, the era, and the surrounding context. Differences around this variation may be to a greater or lesser degree.

Ibn Khaldūn relates the following in his *al-Muqaddimah* concerning the science of jurisprudence (*fiqh*):

> *Fiqh* is knowledge of the rulings of Allah, the Sublime, pertaining to the actions of subjects in relation to obligation (*al-wujūb*), jeopardy (*al-khaṭr*), recommendation (*an-nadb*), detestation (*al-kirāhiyyah*), and permissibility (*al-ibāḥah*). It is derived from the Qur'an and the Sunnah, and proof-methods set up by the Legislator for this purpose. When rulings are derived from the above mentioned sources, they are described as *fiqh*.
>
> Our righteous predecessors derived rulings by this method even if it resulted in differences amongst them. Difference in opinion had to occur because most of the evidential material is textual and in the Arabic language. It is well-known that there exist differences of opinion on many of the linguistic terms of expression. The Sunnah, as well, has various chains of narration and means of verification. In many instances, its rulings conflict with one another. Giving preference to one ruling over another is therefore required and there even exists differences of opinion on how this should be done.
>
> There also exists difference in opinion regarding proofs derived from non-textual sources, as well as new developments that are not treated exhaustively by the texts. The unclear text is verified by the clear text when there is some similarity between them. All of the above are but indications of differences in opinion that occur as a necessity. From here on, differences occurred between the predecessors and the scholars that came after them.[3]

In this way, Ibn Khaldūn related what he called "indications of differences in opinion" on one of the many aspects of Islamic thought. This aspect, i.e., *fiqh*, is the least prone to differences in opinion because it is so strongly bound to the Qur'an and Sunnah. However, this does not exclude it from being regarded as human thought within the sphere of Islam. The sphere of Islam, or of any other religion, does not transform on its own, without divergence in human thought. As long as there is human thought and human intellectual output, there will always be divergence—sometimes extreme—attached to it or very close to it. Because of this divergence in Islamic thought, no opinion (of a single scholar or a handful of scholars) is expressive of Islam in a perfect manner. Islam will always remain a blessing from heaven and Islamic thought will always remain the product of people in the Muslim world; whosoever takes Islamic thought for Islam takes various different Islams for Allah's single religion.

The genesis of Islamic thought after the emergence of Islam and the elements that led to its development

Being the intellectual product of the Muslim individual, Islamic thought was generated after the revelation of the Qur'an and its explication by the Sunnah. The elements that prompted the development of Islamic thought cannot be restricted, for example, to the nature of the Qur'anic text or the authentication of *ḥadīth* from the perspective of the chain of narrators. It goes beyond these questions, and even goes beyond the issue of the rise of the Islamic State and the spread of Muslims to countries of different culture and material civilization. Therefore, it is only natural that there would be some interaction between the new religion and ancient cultures, whether through accepting certain elements or rejecting others, or through elements that stimulate deep introspection leading to the legitimation of certain issues or the rejection of others, or, more generally, through anything that stimulates intellectual engagement and challenge.

Islamic thought thus came into being as soon as the Arab Muslims—who were its original bearers—began to produce scholars and artisans. Among Arabs, it stimulated a sense of discernment and contemplation as soon as it was initiated, whereas they had previously been content to restrict themselves to approaching only the Qur'an and the Prophetic tradition.

Ibn Khaldūn explains this early development of Islamic thought is his *al-Muqaddimah* thus: The Muslim community initially lacked academic or vocational qualities due to their simplicity and nomadic nature. The Islamic legal rulings—which are the commands and prohibitions of Allah—were carried by men through memorization and were spread in a similar manner. The outlook of the people was shaped by the Qur'an and the Sunnah, as received from the Prophet and his companions.

The Arabs of that time were not very familiar with formal education, writing or codification. They were neither inclined towards these pursuits nor felt the need to acquire them out of necessity. Things remained this way through the era of the companions (*aṣ-ṣaḥābah*) and the era of the followers of the companions (*at-tābi'īn*). Those that did acquire and propagate such skills were referred to as The Readers (*al-qurrā'*), i.e., those that read the Qur'an and were not illiterate. In those days illiteracy was a general characteristic amongst the companions, who were mostly Arabs. The compilers of the Qur'an were referred to as *al-qurrā'* to indicate their skills. The title was used to refer to readers of the Qur'an and the transmitted prophetic traditions because they developed knowledge of the legislative rulings of Islam from these two sources only. These rulings were, at most, an explanation or commentary on these sources.

The Prophet (ṣ) said: "I have left you with two things which, if you hold on to them firmly, you will not go astray. [They are] the Book of Allah (the Qur'an) and my Sunnah (i.e., the exemplary practice of the Prophet)."4 After the passing of the rule of the Righteous Caliphs (i.e., the first four caliphs of Islam) the community became distanced from the transmitted traditions. There was, therefore, a need to produce commentaries on the Qur'an and to gather the *ḥadīth*, out of fear that the latter may be lost. As a result, there was also a need to have knowledge of the chain of transmitters of the *ḥadīth* as well as to be able to appraise the narrators and critique them, so as to be able to differentiate between authentic and suspicious narrations. Thereafter, there was a noticeable increase in the derivation of legal rulings from the Qur'an and the Sunnah.

All the legal sciences fell under the domain of derivation, extraction, theorisation and analogy. There was also a need for other sciences that served the legal sciences, for example, having knowledge of the rules of the Arabic language and the rules pertaining to proof-extraction and analogy. Due to the proliferation of religious innovations and disbelief, the doctrines of faith also needed to be defended using such proofs. All of these sciences thus became necessary tools that needed to be learnt, and therefore became professional vocations.

As far as the rational sciences (such as philosophy) are concerned, their manifestation in the community is only noticed after the appearance of scholars and writers and once the pursuit of knowledge had been established as a vocational practice.[5]

Some may argue that this manner of development in the Islamic community was not Islamic thought but was, rather, transmission and emulation of the Qur'an and the Sunnah. The sciences that represent this tradition are, they would argue, transmitted sciences and not knowledge that is founded upon intellectual production. However, this is not the case. We do not derive from Islamic thought an exclusively human element. That is why we prefix the description "Islamic" to it. It therefore includes transmitted Islamic elements out of necessity, in addition to the purely human intellectual elements that accompany it. That which is referred to as the "transmitted sciences" is not intended to exclude human intellectual activity or human thought processes; it simply means that it is not exclusively a product of human intellectual striving alone.

Ibn Khaldūn clarifies this in his *Muqaddimah*:

Take note that the sciences taken up and propagated by people in all regions, whether through acquisition or study, are of two types:

The type that comes naturally to humans and to which one is guided by reflection or thinking; and

The type that is transmitted, taken from whoever imparts it.

The First Type: These are the rational or philosophical sciences, which people acquire through the natural dispensation of their minds and are guided to its subject-matter and specific issues through human perception and awareness. Through investigating proofs and exploring various facets of study, a person's research and insight lead him to that which is correct and he is, from this perspective, a rational being.

The Second Type: These are the transmitted or established sciences. They are all based upon the enunciations of the legitimate transmitter (God or the Prophet). There is no room in this category for rational speculation except by way of linking peripheral issues with universal principles because these particular issues do not fall under the transmitted universals when plainly expressed (by the Legislator), and therefore need to be linked to it by means of analogy. However, this analogy is derived from the account where the ruling is established in the origin, which is already established by transmission.[6]

Therefore, the transmitted sciences incorporate rational exertion and human thought processes, but are based upon and linked to that which is transmitted and is not completely independent.

Regarding the transmitted sciences prevalent in the Islamic community, Ibn Khaldūn states:

The foundation of all of these transmitted sciences is that which is legislated in the Qur'an and the Sunnah, i.e., which is legitimated for us by Allah and His Prophet, as well as the sciences associated therewith, which act to facilitate deriving of benefit from them. The categories of these transmitted sciences are many because the believer is obligated to know the laws that Allah has made compulsory upon him and his community; these are derived from the Qur'an and Sunnah, either literally, by consensus (*ijmā'*), or through association.

1. Firstly, it is necessary to ponder over the Qur'an so as to clearly understand its expression. This leads to the *Science of Tafsīr* (interpretation or explanation).

2. One must then examine the chain of narrators leading back to the Prophet (ṣ), who has brought it to us from Allah, in addition to examining the narrations pertaining to the

various reciters and recitations. This leads to the *Science of Qirā'ah* (recitation).

3. Thereafter, one must examine narrations pertaining to prophetic utterances and their link to the Prophet himself. One must also discuss the narrators and their backgrounds to establish their impartiality and to have an informed opinion on their reliability, so as to be able to enact what they transmit. This leads to the *Sciences of Ḥadīth* (Prophetic traditions).

4. Then, one must be able to derive legal rulings (the rulings made obligatory by Allah) from their sources in a legitimate manner that reflects knowledge of proof derivation. This leads to the *Science of Uṣūl al-Fiqh* (legal source methodology).

5. Thereafter, one attains the fruits of knowing the laws of Allah pertaining to the actions of those who submit in faith. This leads to the *Science of Fiqh* (jurisprudence).

6. Religious obligation, then, is both physical and spiritual. The latter is concerned with faith and what is obligatory belief. This is the *Science of al-'Aqā'id al-Īmāniyyah* (the doctrines of faith), concerning the essence and characteristics of Allah, resurrection, reward, punishment, and predestination. Argumentation concerning these rational proofs leads to the *Science of 'Ilm al-Kalām* (dialectic theology).[7]

These are the subjects of authentic Islamic thought dealt with by Muslims and which formed the platform for their intellectual activities in terms of the extraction and provision of proof. The subject matter is transmitted (*naqlī*), but expounded upon by the rational or intellectual activity of the Muslim scholar. Authentic Islamic thought thus emerged and developed, reaching a particular juncture that we will now discuss.

Muslims were compelled to create the science of *tafsīr* (exegesis) and, as such, they "explained the Qur'an, firstly, by the use of narrations that were derived from the transmitted corpus of the earlier scholars. These narrations dealt with scholarship on the abrogated and abrogating verses (*an-nāsikh wa al-mansūkh*), the occasions of revelation (*asbāb an-nuzūl*), and the aims and objectives of revelation (*maqāṣid al-āyāt*)."[8] Exegesis by way of narrated reports—as stated by Ibn Khaldūn—included "what was inferior and what was enriching as well as what was acceptable and what was contemptible."[9]

A second type of exegesis was influenced by a specific form of sectarianism, in exegetical works like *al-Kashshāf* (The Exposition) by az-Zamakhsharī and *al-Kibrīt al-Aḥmar* (The Red Sulphur), by Muḥyī ad-Dīn ibn 'Arabī. The opinions expressed in *al-Kashshāf* represent the Mu'tazilī School. The opinions in *al-Kibrīt al-Aḥmar* represent the views of the later sufis (mystics) specifically pertaining to the issues of Transfiguration (*at-tajallī*), immanence (*al-ḥulūl*), and unity of being (*waḥdah al-wujūd*).

Muslims were compelled to create the science of *fiqh* (jurisprudence) due to the requirements of political and social life, the expansion of the Islamic State and the embracing of Islam by people from different religions and cultures. *Fiqh* is defined as the study of the laws of Allah pertaining to the actions of the believers. The most famous schools of *fiqh*, which represent the majority of Muslims, are as follows:

1. The School of opinion and analogy (*madhhab ahl ar-ra'y wa al-qiyās*). This school originated amongst the people of Iraq, who followed and mastered analogy because of the scarcity of transmitted prophetic traditions in this region. This is why they are referred to as 'People of opinion'. Foremost within this group was Abū Ḥanīfah and his companions.

2. The School of tradition (*ahl al-ḥadīth*). This school originated amongst the people of Ḥijāz (the region of Makkah and Madīnah). Foremost amongst them was Mālik ibn Anas al-Aṣbaḥī, the Imam of Madīnah (the city is also known as *dār al-hijrah* because it was the place to which the Prophet (ṣ) and his early Muslim community migrated to after being persecuted in Makkah). After him came Muḥammad ibn Idrīs ash-Shāfi'ī who conflated the jurisprudence of the people of

Madīnah with that of the people of Iraq, after having travelled to the latter region.

3. The Literalist School (*madhhab aẓ-ẓāhiriyyīn*). The foremost scholars of this school were Dāwūd ibn 'Alī and his son. Their school is founded upon the denial of analogy and the refutation of its usage. "They restrict everything that can be perceived to the texts (of the Qur'an and Sunnah) and to consensus (*ijmā'*). They link any apparent analogy (*al-qiyās al-jalī*) and its underlying textual motive (*al-'illah al-manṣūṣah*) to the text, because a text with a clear motive (*al-'illah*), they argue, is a text that indicates a ruling in all possible fields of application."[10]

4. Together with these schools of jurisprudence, which are associated with the majority of Muslims, one finds another unique school associated with the *ahl al-bayt*—i.e., the Shī'ah. This school is founded upon belief in the Infallible Imam.

5. There is also a school of *fiqh* associated with the Khawārij sect. When deriving rulings from the primary texts, they take into consideration their unique position on leadership and the duties of the leader towards his followers, in addition to the obligations of the followers towards the leader.

Muslims were also compelled to create the science of *uṣūl al-fiqh* (legal source methodology) alongside *fiqh*. *Uṣūl al-fiqh* entails inquiring into juridical proofs, since they serve as the basis for deriving laws and obligatory actions.

As Ibn Khaldūn explains, the creation of this discipline was essential:

> Know that this is one of the disciplines that was invented and specially created by the Muslim community. The predecessors were in no need of it because the meanings of various expressions were within their grasp, due to their highly developed linguistic capabilities. They were also not in need of the rules or principles required to derive laws specifically, because most of these laws have come down to us from them. They were also not in need of the chain of narrators in order

to assess the validity of transmitted accounts, or accounts of the narrators themselves pertaining to their knowledge, because these accounts were narrated in their era. Once the early predecessors had died out and the first generation vanished and the sciences had become vocational pursuits—as has been explained earlier—scholars and jurists came to be in need of such rules and principles to derive laws from existing sources. They, therefore, recorded these principles, thereby establishing an independent science, which they named *uṣūl al-fiqh*.[11]

Muslims were also compelled to defend the Islamic faith—when it was overwhelmed and attacked by other faiths and beliefs—and they therefore created the science of *kalām* (dialectic theology): "The subject matter of the science of *kalām*—according to its proponents—deals with the doctrines of faith after they have been made obligatory in a correct manner by the Law, in that rational proofs are also sought to defend these doctrines. In this way, the doctrines of faith are disassociated from any innovations and doubt or uncertainty that may surround them."[12]

Therefore, *tafsīr*, *fiqh*, *uṣūl al-fiqh* and *'ilm al-kalām* capture the various facets of authentic Islamic thought. They were created out of necessity, and as a consequence of the pressures under which Muslims lived at that time, in different regions and generations, and to bridge a chasm in the life of the Islamic community or to defend against accusations or speculation cast at the face of Islam. These sciences represent authentic Islamic thought because they spring forth from Islam itself and branch out from where Muslims applied their minds. No matter how different the ideas of Muslims may be when branching out from Islam, their differences have not forced the majority of them to sever their link with Islam or to show intolerance to those who think differently.

The Principle of "movement" in Islamic thought and its effects

"Movement" results from the fact that the thought of all Muslim scholars emanates from a single principle: whosoever applies his mind and reaches a correct judgement is rewarded twofold, and whosoever applies his mind and errs is rewarded a single reward only.[13] Everyone is rewarded because they all strive towards the truth, taking every precaution in order to extract it. Every one of these scholars also tries to be a Muslim in faith as well as in action. *Ijtihād* (mental exertion) is not only an expression of a Muslim's vitality towards Islam and life, or an expression of the ability that a Muslim possesses to continuously reconcile the life he lives here and now—or in the future—with the Islam that he believes in; it is also an expression of the spirit of ease and freedom of thought, even if this is a limited freedom.

The principle of *ijtihād*, upon which authentic Islamic thought is founded, is a principle of construction, of movement, of freedom, and, as a result, of facilitation and ease. At the same time, it is also a principle of purity and tolerance because the personal antagonism that results from intense intellectual antagonism has no place amongst the practitioners of *ijtihād* in Islam. It does, however, happen that when compulsion and strict compliance are enforced by some of the legal schools, they are judged to be backward and not completely judicious. Therefore, when authentic Islamic thought is initiated on the basis of unadulterated and free *ijtihād*, we find that the character of this thought is honesty and progress. We are hardly able to detect antagonism or disputation that goes beyond the spirit of sane inquiry between adversaries engaging on a subject or issue. In terms of the various ways in which they reasoned, we find that the Muslims of that era were people of opinion, knowledge and proof.

Ibn Khaldūn states:

> Indeed, these Transmitted Religious Sciences were pursued vigorously in the Muslim community, reaching a point where no more could be added, the intellectual capacities of the scholars having reached the extreme limit, beyond which nothing new could be found. All terminology was perfected and the various disciplines had been classified. They were only improved beyond this point in terms of excellent exposition and literary

embellishment. Every discipline thus had an authoritative spokesperson that was invoked and conditions under which knowledge production had benefited from.[14]

The growth of Islamic thought

However, the growth of authentic Islamic thought did not continue in the direction it had initially followed, and was, within a short space of time, no longer accompanied along its path by the principle of "movement", i.e., *ijtihād*. In fact, it took another turn, towards foreign ideas that penetrated the Islamic community in the era of the Abbasid Caliph al-Ma'mūn. From then onwards, this foreign element imposed itself upon Islamic intellectual life. Thus, less attention was paid to *ijtihād*, and its influence within Islamic thought was diminished. With these two factors together, Islam was no longer the only source of Islamic thought, as it was now also influenced—lamentably—by this foreign element. In addition, its progress slowed down to the point where growth could hardly be discerned.

With the introduction of foreign thought elements into Islamic thought, the intellectual orientations and various philosophies within the Islamic community were injected with different incentives and objectives. New tendencies were added to the gruelling intellectual tendencies of the past, which very rarely concurred with and were, in most cases, in opposition or even contradictory to the established tendencies. The sciences of logic, metaphysics, biology and illuminative asceticism were introduced to the Islamic community after the translation of the pagan philosophical thought of the Greeks and the illuminative religious tradition of the East.

In this period, the disciplines of mysticism (*taṣawwuf*), magic (*siḥr*), talismanry (*al-ṭalmisāt*) and numerology (*asrār al-ḥurūf*) were innovated as well. These disciplines, which were transmitted or innovated in the Islamic community, did not remain isolated, and managed to infiltrate the religious sciences of authentic Islamic thought as well.

Ibn Khaldūn gives a summary description of these disciplines and their effects:

Islamic scholars dedicated themselves to the pursuit of these sciences and mastered their disciplines, excelling in them and even rejecting many of the opinions of "The First Teacher," Aristotle. They paid special attention to either affirming or rejecting his views because of his fame, and, as a result, much was written in this regard. They even surpassed their predecessors in these sciences. Abū Nāṣr al-Fārābī was one of the most accomplished of such scholars amongst the Muslims of the fourth century (AH), during the reign of Sayf ad-Dawlah. Abū 'Alī ibn Sīnā gained fame in the East in the fifth century (AH), in the reign of Niẓām al-Mulk of the Bani Buwayyhi from Isfahān. Also worthy of mention, due to their fame, are the judge Abū al-Walīd ibn Rushd and the minister Abū Bakr ibn aṣ-Ṣā'igh of al-Andalus (Spain), in addition to many others who also excelled. Many restricted themselves to taking up alchemy and its related disciplines like astrology, magic and talismanry. In these professions, Maslamah ibn Aḥmad al-Majrīṭī of al-Andalus (Spain) and his students were the most famous.

Foreign elements entered the Muslim community through these sciences and their practitioners. Many people were seduced by inclining towards them and through blindly following their opinions. Blame only falls upon the indulgent, and if Allah had so wished, they would not have indulged in these practices.[15]

The corpus of authentic Islamic thought, represented by *tafsīr*, *fiqh*, *uṣūl al-fiqh* and *'ilm al-kalām*, did not escape the influence of these translated and innovated sciences after they became available in Arabic. The exegetical work *al-Kashshāf* by az-Zamakhsharī, who was a Mu'tazilite, was influenced by Mu'tazilite methodology and thought. The Mu'tazilī School was influenced by Aristotelian and Neoplatonic thought in its development, especially on the issues of *tawḥīd* (unity—especially the unity of God) and the problem of the Divine Attributes. The exegesis of Muhyī ad-Dīn ibn 'Arabī—as has been mentioned—was influenced by Brahmin philosophy on the issue of unity of being and by Christian philosophy on the issue of the incarnation of the divine in the human. This was in addition to the views of Ibn Sīnā, the Ikhwān aṣ-Ṣafā (the Brethren of Purity), and other extremists who fell under the spell of foreign thought.

After the translation of works on asceticism and eastern mysticism, Islamic jurisprudence had to compete against Islamic mysticism. While Islamic jurisprudence remained committed to the human comprehension of the texts of the *sharī'ah* in gaining knowledge of the rulings pertaining to the actions of the believers, Islamic mysticism relied upon *adh-dhawq* (personal spiritual inclination) and *muḥāsabah an-nafs* (self-accountability) as a source of knowledge after *īmān* (belief).

Human actions thus came to be judged by two standards: occasionally by the standard of juristic rulings pertaining to rituals, customs and conduct, and, at other times, by the standard of personal spiritual inclination and self-accountability. This contestation developed into antagonism and hostility. Al-Ghazālī, who is a representative of the intermediate stage in the development of Islamic mysticism, said:

> The guides along the path are the scholars who are the heirs of the prophets, whose time has passed; all that is left are those that follow in their footsteps. Now, everyone seems to hasten his fate as if enchanted, and what is good is seen as abhorrent, and what is abhorrent is seen as good.
>
> Even the science of religion has been obliterated and the torch of guidance in the various lands has been extinguished. People thus seem to think that there is no knowledge except what is expressed in the legal directives of a government and upon which judges rely to settle disputes when dissension is sewn amongst the populace, or what arises out of disputation advanced as an argument by someone boastful in order to refute another opinion, or rhymed prose employed by preachers to entice the masses. They do not regard anything except these three as a snare for that which is prohibited and as a net for rubble.

The science of the path of the Hereafter—i.e., spiritual exercise (*ar-riyāḍah an-nafsiyyah*)—and that which was practised by the pious predecessors and has been described by Allah, the Most Sublime, in His Book as understanding, wisdom, knowledge, illumination, light, guidance and uprighteousness, has been ignored by people and has been almost forgotten.[16]

In spite of this, hostilities did not reach the point of enmity and dogmatism because the science of mysticism—until today—has not reached the zenith of its development. Most of its elements are Islamic, but it is distinguished by what is known as striving against the self and self-accountability. Ibn Khaldūn describes it in the following manner:

The active and engaging soul in the body arises out of perceptions, desires and circumstances, and this is what characterises the person. Some of these elements arise out of others, just as knowledge arises out of proof, and joy and sadness out of feeling pain or pleasure, or vitality out of striving, or laziness out of incapacity. In a similar manner, the *murīd* (Sufi initiate), in his rituals and spiritual striving, brings about a certain state as a result of his striving. The *murīd* continues to ascend from one level to the next, until he achieves union with the divine (*at-tawḥīd*) and knowledge (*al-maʿrifah*), which is the sought-after-goal to achieve happiness. It is essential that the *murīd* ascends through these stages. Its basis is complete obedience and sincerity, which is preceded and accompanied by faith. It is from these states and characteristics that results and fruits are borne.

Thereafter, other stations (*maqāmāt*) arise until the seeker reaches the station of union with the divine (*at-tawḥīd*) and gnosis (*al-ʿirfān*), spiritual knowledge and insight. If some change occurs in the expected outcome, or some blemish is manifest, we then know that it is a result of shortcomings in the effort prior to it. This applies to the state of self-consciousness and the emotions of the heart as well. For this reason, the *murīd* requires self-accountability in all of his actions and has to consider their realities. It is inevitable that results arise out of actions and that shortcomings are a result of laxity. The *murīd* is able to find personal flaws by his spiritual sense (*adh-dhawq*) and is able to make himself accountable for their manifestation. Only a few people have this ability. It is as if unawareness of this is all-encompassing.

The objective of the people of worship (*ahl al-'ibādāt*) (i.e., those that heed the teachings of *fiqh*), is to approach good deeds exclusively from the perspective of jurisprudence, in compliance with its detailed expositions. The *murīds*, in contrast, search for outcomes by means of spiritual sense and emotion so as to know that they are, in essence, free of any shortcomings. It is thus apparent that the basis of the *murīd*-method is self-accountability in terms of action and abstention. This is followed by deliberation on the spiritual senses and emotions that are acquired through striving, and which settle within the *murīd* initially and thereafter passes on to others.

In addition to this, they also have certain customary practices and terminology that is specific to them. They have, thus, specialised in this type of knowledge, since no one else from amongst the people of the *sharī'ah* is proficient in it. The science of *sharī'ah* thus became divided into two categories. The first category pertains specifically to the jurists and jurisconsults (*ahl al-futyā*), and deals with the general rulings of rituals, customs, and conduct. The second category pertains to the mystics, who are practitioners of striving and self-accountability, who deliberate on the spiritual senses and emotions encountered along the path, and on how to ascend from one experience to the next, and who explain the terminology that they employ.

When the sciences began to be recorded and codified, and jurists began writing on *fiqh*, *uṣūl al-fiqh*, *al-kalām*, *tafsīr*, etc., mystics also started writing about their paths and practices. Some of them wrote on piety and self-accountability in terms of abstention and permissibility, as was done by al-Qushāyrī in the book *ar-Risālah* and by as-Suhrawardī in the book *'Awārif al-Ma'ārif*, in addition to many others. Al-Ghazālī brought *fiqh* and mysticism together in his book *Iḥyā' 'Ulūm ad-Dīn*. In it he recorded the rules pertaining to piety and emulation and then clarified the customs of the mystics and their traditions, in addition to explaining their terminology in their words.

The science of mysticism (*at-taṣawwuf*) thus became a codified discipline, whereas, prior to this, the only way was worship (i.e., the way of jurisprudence). Its rulings were received from "the hearts of Men" (i.e., from the lived experiences transmitted by scholars), as was the case with the other sciences that were eventually codified by means of writing, such as *tafsīr*, *ḥadīth*, *fiqh* and *uṣūl al-fiqh*.[17]

Islamic dialectic theology (*'ilm al-kalām al-Islāmī*) was—in comparison to other trends in authentic Islamic thought—strongly influenced by and the most engaged with the corpus of foreign thought transmitted into Arabic. Ibn Khaldūn states:

The later scholars wrote on the sciences of the people of their times and al-Ghazālī refuted much of what was written. Thereafter, the later dialectic scholars (*al-mutakallimūn*) conflated many of the issues pertaining to dialectic theology (*'ilm al-kalām*) with issues of philosophy—as these were prevalent in their inquiries—so the subject-matter of dialectic theology resembled philosophy and their inquiries resembled each other as well. They thus appeared to be a single discipline. Dialectic theology was also conflated with the concerns of the science of aphorisms (*al-ḥikmah*) and its books were filled with aphorisms. It was as if the objective and concerns of the subject were the same, and this was confusing to people. This is lamentable because dialectic theology is concerned with the doctrines of belief derived from the *sharī'ah* as conveyed by the early generation, without having recourse to the intellect or relying upon it. Therefore, the suggestion that these doctrines are affirmed exclusively by the intellect is false.

Indeed, the intellect is separate from the revealed law (*ash-shar'*) and its purview. That which is deliberated upon by the dialectic scholars concerning the provision of proof does not concern the search for truth in the divine law. Having recourse to evidence—to prove a fact that was not known to be factual— is the concern of philosophy. The methodology of dialectic theology, on the other hand, is to search for rational proofs that support the doctrines of faith and the teachings of the early generation and which repel the obscurity of the heretics (*ahl al-bida'*). This would occur after these doctrines had been, firstly, verified as correct according to transmitted proofs, as was received and accepted by the early generation, and which were then verified again from a rational perspective.

Ibn Khaldūn also states:

The insight of the Legislator is far deeper because its frame of reference extends beyond the scrutiny of rational insight. The Legislator's insight is above rational insight and encompasses it, as it flows from the divine light and does not fall under the legislation of weak rational insight. So if the divine law (*ash-shar'*) guides us to a certain insight, we should give it precedence over our insights and show confidence in it. We should not attempt to adjust it by rational insight, even if it is seemingly contradictory.[18] In fact, we should rely upon that which we are obligated to, in terms of belief and through knowledge, and we should remain silent concerning whatever of it we do not understand, leaving the matter in the hands of the Legislator, and excusing the intellect from issuing judgement.... The remonstrations of the dialectic theologians seemed—after this conflation—to be instituting the search for a mean through the provision of rational proof, but this is not the case. Their efforts are no more than a refutation of the atheists, and what is sought is to establish the truth and make it known.[19]

In this manner, Ibn Khaldūn explained the extent of the difference between the method of the dialectic theologians and the method of the philosophers, the effect that this has had upon the worth of religious doctrines, as well as the way in which it has concealed the sources from which it is taken and given standing i.e., the Qur'an and the Sunnah. The negative effects of the foreign thought elements translated into Arabic are not only restricted to turning Qur'anic exegesis in a direction opposed to its original orientation, nor to placing mysticism in competition against jurisprudence, nor to conflating the methods of the dialectic theologians with those of the philosophers. It, in fact, transcends all of this, and has created in jurisprudence a trend that is antagonistic to Islam, in addition to creating a similar trend in mysticism. This is due to the pagan philosophic elements conveyed in the foreign thought, in addition to Brahmin and Indian elements.

In its exposition of the reality of existence, this foreign thought brought with it the trinity of neo-Platonism, which holds that The First Cause (by which they mean God) is the origin of all of existence, then comes the intellect, and then the universal soul as existing matter, which is regarded as the basis and the highest example for everything in existence except itself. It brought with it this trinity—after having thrust it upon sacrosanct Christian beliefs prior to Islam—which brought about the well-known Christian belief in the trinity of God, the Son and the Holy Spirit.

This notion, which is foreign to Islam, also brought with it the belief of complete unity of existence (*waḥdah al-wujūd ash-shāmilah*). It holds that whatever is in existence—no matter how profuse—is a manifestation of only one thing, and an extension of a singular existent, which is the cause and the origin, or the divine object of worship. This divine object of worship is the essence of existence and is manifest in all that is perceived to be, no matter how profuse and unending. It also brought with it the arrangement of existent matter as it sprung forth or emerged by means of emanation, as well as its contraction and return to the origin from which it had emanated. This idea is referred to as the "ascending disputation" and the "descending disputation" in the Alexandrian School. It resulted in the extremist trend in Shī'ah jurisprudence, amongst those who are referred to as the Ismā'īlī, Bāṭinī, Tā'līmī, or the Rāfiḍah. Some of these groups came to be known as the Qarāmiṭiyyah, and others as the Druze or the Ḥākimiyyīn (in the Levant). A third group came to be known as the Fāṭimiyyīn or the 'Ubaydiyyīn (in Egypt). A fourth group was known as the Companions of the Absolute Herald (*aṣḥāb ad-dā'ī al-muṭlaq*) (in Yemen). A fifth group was the Naẓāriyyīn (in India), with the Aga Khan as one of their leaders, and so forth.

The jurisprudence of these extremist Shī'ah groups is founded upon the belief in the trinity of Allah, Muḥammad and the

Imam, with the belief that the spirit of Allah is incarnated in the Imam, and he is therefore infallible in terms of his actions and pronouncements. The Imam's pronouncement is regarded as authoritative in terms of Islamic law and is no less authoritative than the Qur'an and sometimes of a higher status because, by his pronouncement, some Qur'anic laws may be abrogated or suspended. As such, the jurisprudence of these extremist groups is based on the pronouncements of the Imam to a greater degree than upon the text of the Qur'an. Later groups, such as the *Imāmiyyah* and Twelver Shī'ah regarded these former groups as beyond the fold of Islam, and as rejecters of the faith, as is the view of the rest of the Muslim community.

These same developments also unfolded amongst the Sufis. The *taṣawwuf* that we alluded to earlier, i.e., the *taṣawwuf* founded upon obedience, faith, exertion and self-accountability, was transformed under the influence of this alien thought, leading to a predicament similar to that of the extremist Shī'ah. These Sufis also advocate a trinity consisting of Allah, Muḥammad and the *quṭb* (the Charismatic Leader). The spirit of Allah is incarnated in the *quṭb*, who is therefore seen as infallible, and is absolved of religious obligation. His followers are consequently required to seek his intercession as he is also regarded as the centre of human salvation.

The influence of alien ideas from the extremist Shī'ah upon *taṣawwuf* was so pervasive that later Sufis adopted their belief in absolute unity (*al-wiḥdah ash-shāmilah*) and divine manifestation (*at-tajallī*), which implies that these creatures are the essence of Allah, as is expressed in the saying: "I [Allah] was a hidden treasure and wanted to be known, so I created creation so as to know me."[20]

Concerning these later Sufis, Ibn Khaldūn said: "Then came the later extremist Sufis who also addressed issues of dialectic theology, and, thereby, conflated separate disciplines and, as such, addressed issues of prophecy, divine union, incarnation, unity of existence, etc."[21] He elaborates further:

Later scholars focused their attention on unveiling the unseen and the consciousness behind it. The means of spiritual exercise in this regard differed according to the differences in their training to suppress the physical senses, and the sustenance of the intellectual spirit with *dhikr* (ritual recitation), until the soul attains an awareness from within its essence, through its proper nurturing and sustenance. If this is attained, these Sufis claim, existence is contained in the consciousness of the soul and they would unveil the essences of creation and would portray the reality of all things from the throne to the furniture. The consciousness of those who do not share their path is restricted and they are not able to understand their tastes and inclinations.

The jurisconsults are divided into those who reject these Sufis and those who affirm them. Proof and evidential statements do not benefit this path, whether to legitimate or to refute, as it is—according to their claim—a matter of emotional sentiment. Some writers try to clarify their positions pertaining to the unveiling of existence and the hierarchy of things. They only make matters even vaguer, in comparison to rational scholars who depend on evidence and use the terminology of the sciences. This vagueness is seen in the writing of al-Firghānī, the commentator on Ibn al-Fāriḍ's *ad-Dībājah* (The Preamble), in the heart of the commentary itself. Concerning the emanations of existence and their sequence, emanating from the First Cause (*al-fāʿil*), he mentions that all of existence emanates from the characteristic of emotion, which is the form of singularity. Together, both of these emanate from nothing other than the Noble Essence, which is the essence of singularity, and this emanation is referred to as divine manifestation (*at-tajallī*).

The first level of manifestation, according to these Sufis, is the manifestation of the essence upon itself. It encompasses perfection and the emanation of creation and appearance. This is in regard to the prophetic utterance that they transmit: "I [Allah] was a hidden treasure and I wanted to be known, so I created creation so as to know me".[22] This perfection of the creation descended upon existence and the details pertaining to reality—which is the true existence according to them—takes the following order:

1. The world of meaning and the perfect presence;

2. The Muḥammadan reality, which encompasses the reality of the attributes, the preserved tablet (*al-lawḥ*), the pen and the reality of all the prophets and messengers; and

3. The remainder of the followers of Muḥammad's faith.

All of this explains the Muḥammadan reality. Other realities emanate from these realities in the Glorious Presence, which are:

1. The symbolic level, then the throne, then the pedestal, then the planets;

2. Thereafter, the world of elements;

3. Thereafter comes the world of objects, and this is in the conjoined world, and if it is made manifest then it is in the separated world: "The heavens and the earth were joined together as one united piece, then we parted them" (21:30).

This school of thought is known as the school of the believers in the manifestation, the forms and the presences (*madhhab ahl at-tajallī wa al-maẓāhir wa al-ḥaḍārāt*). The followers of rational opinion cannot understand the import of these views, because of their vagueness. There is a vast gap between the followers of spiritual experience and emotion and the followers of evidential proof.

Similarly, others amongst them speak about unity and its branches. This view is closer to the first in terms of its attachments and branches. They accordingly claim that existence has a force, in its finer details, through which the realities of existent objects, their forms and substances are brought about. The elements are also a result of this innate force, as well as its matter, that has within it a force that brings about its existence. Thereafter, all objects have within them this force, encompassing the forces of their constituent components—like the force of minerals, which contains the forces of their primordial elements and the force of the mineral itself. Thereafter, the animal force encompasses the mineral force in addition to its own force. Similarly, the human force is combined with the animal force. The planets, thereafter, encompass the human force and all its additions, as well as the spiritual essences.

The all-encompassing force, without any elaboration, is the Divine Force, which circulates in everything in existence, in part or in full, and brings together and encompasses it all from every perspective, not only from the perspective of appearance, or the perspective of concealment, or from the perspective of the form or the perspective of matter. The collective is one and it is the same divine essence. It is also the reality—singular and simple, and the way it is apprehended is what explains it. This applies, for example, to humanness and animalness. Do you not see that animalness is a part of humanness and exists through it? It is sometimes expressed as the genus within the species in all that exists, as we have already mentioned. And, it is sometimes expressed with the whole and the part, as in symbolic expression.

By such explanations they flee from the composite and the plural, even though they have been obligated to accept such beliefs through speculation and imagination.

What is made manifest by Ibn Dahqān in his report of this school of thought is that the reality of what they speak of concerning unity is similar to what the philosophers say concerning colours: that their existence is dependent upon light and that if light is non-existent then colours cannot exist in any form. Similarly, according to them, the existence of all tactile objects depends upon the existence of the sense of touch and the existence of all rational or imagined objects depends upon the existence of the intellect. Therefore, preferred existence, all of it, is dependent upon the existence of the human subject.

The later Sufis, those who concerned themselves with unveiling (*al-kashf*) and metaphysics, immersed themselves in this school of thought. Many became exponents of incarnation and unity of existence, as we have pointed out, and wrote extensively on these subjects, like al-Harawī in his book *al-Maqāmāt (The Ranks)*, and many others. They were followed by Ibn ʿArabī and Ibn Sabʿīn and their students, Ibn al-ʿAfīf, Ibn al-Fāriḍ and an-Najm al-Isrāʾīlī, who wrote poems on these issues.

Their followers integrated with the later Ismāʿīlīs and Rāfiḍah, who also preached incarnation and the divinity of the Imams, which was not known to their earlier scholars. Each of the two groups drew from the other's school of thought and their discourse was integrated, with many similarities appearing in their doctrines.

The Sufi discourse started advocating the idea of the *quṭb*, which is a reference to the head of the Gnostics. They claimed that it was not possible for anyone to reach his level of knowledge until Allah had taken his soul, after which another Gnostic would inherit his position. They then advocated the idea of the existence of a hierarchy of alternatives after this *quṭb*, in a manner similar to the idea of the *nuqabā* amongst the Shī'ah.[23]

The influence of disciplines transmitted from the outside increasingly impacted upon the Sufis. They were influenced—in addition to neo-Platonic, Brahmin and Indian thought—by the ideas of the Kaldanians and the Ashurites of Babel. In turn, they were influenced by the discipline of talismanry, which is a discipline dealing with the means and preparation of talismans that enable humans to be influenced by the world of elements, through invoking the help of the heavens.

They invented a discipline that came to be called "The Secret of the Alphabets". This discipline appeared in the Islamic tradition with the appearance of the extremist Sufis and their devotion to exposing the veil of the senses, including the performance of supernatural acts by their hands and delving into the world of elements, with the writing of books and the invention of terminology and with claims of the descending of existence from the One and its consequent ordering. They claimed that the perfection of the heavens are manifest in the souls of the planets and the stars and that the nature of the alphabet and its secrets are posted in the heavens and in creation according to this order. Creation is a shade of primary innovation that is transmitted in its spheres and gives expression to its secrets. For this reason, the discipline of the secrets of the alphabets was created. Al-Būnī, Ibn 'Arabī, and others have written on this. The import of their thought is that divine souls are able to effect changes in the natural world by invoking the beautiful names of the Creator and the divine words, which arise from the alphabets by secret and which are posted in all of creation. Their thought is based upon spiritual sensibility (*adh-dhawq*) and unveiling (*al-kashf*).

Al-Būnī states in his book *al-Anmāṭ (The Patterns)*: "Do not think that the secret of alphabets is a discipline that can be attained by analogical reasoning; it is reached by attaining witness (*al-mushāhadah*) and by Divine Grace. The actions of the companions of the heavens (upon nature) are as a result of what they have attained through earnest striving and through the unveiling from the divine light and through the divine extension. They are thereby able to manipulate nature voluntarily, without difficulty, and they do not require the intervention of planetary forces or anything else."[24]

Writings on magic were transmitted to the Arabic language by way of the ancient Babylonian culture and certain Muslim scholars—who were not from within the Sufi tradition—inclined towards it and wrote about it. Ibn Khaldūn states:

> The books of the Babylonians (the Assyrians and Kaldanians) were not translated for us. The Coptic people of Egypt accumulated some knowledge of the disciplines of magic and talismanry, such as accounts of the Nabataean farmers of Babel. People acquired this discipline from the Copts and further inquired into it. Thereafter, Jābir ibn Ḥayyān, the greatest Sorcerer of the Islamic tradition, appeared in the East. He studied the Babelian texts and distilled from them the discipline of chemistry. He wrote on this subject, and on many others, and discussed alchemy in detail because it was closely related to chemistry. Since the transformation of objects from one form to another is achieved through an inherent force in alchemy and not through practical industry, it is regarded as magic. Maslamah ibn Aḥmad al-Majrīṭī appeared after him. He was the leading Andalusian scholar of mathematics and the sciences of magic. He summarised and refined all the extant works on the subject and integrated the different schools into his book, which he called *The Objective of the Wise (Ghāyah al-Ḥakīm)*; none have written on the subject after him.[25]

The suspension of the principle of "movement" in authentic Islamic thought

Thus the influence of the transmitted philosophical sciences drove various trends within authentic Islamic thought. Alongside this fate—manifested in the above trends—we notice that this thought became afflicted by the inability to continue with constructive movement, as was the case at the beginning of its inception, reaching its height at the end of the third century after the Hijrah.

Authentic Islamic thought was afflicted by stagnation. With regard to deriving legal rulings and the understanding of texts, free thought was prohibited. By public opinion, Islamic jurisprudence culminated in the blind adherence to specific schools, except in the case of the *ahl al-bayt* and the Khawārij. Jurisprudence became a secondary practice within the framework of the imitated school, and imitation was restricted to a specific school with no extension into other schools.

Ibn Khaldūn explains:

> When the splitting of terminology became widespread in the sciences, and short-sightedness impeded the process of free thought (*ijtihād*), and when it was feared that learning would be attributed to the unqualified whose opinion and religious commitment could not be vouchsafed, inability was proclaimed and people were advised to imitate the four Imams in order to understand the Sunnah. People were warned against constantly changing their allegiance from one to another school of thought as this would lead to manipulation. Therefore, no Muslim was allowed to follow more than one school of thought. All that they were allowed to do was to transmit their schools of thought, and each adherent (*muqallid*) stuck to his specific school after its principles had been corrected and its chain of narration had been linked to the narrative account (*riwāyah*). There was no other output of jurisprudence and those who claimed freedom of thought in this era (the seventh century AH) were rejected and their opinions were not followed.[26]

By prohibiting exchange between the various schools, the divisions between them became more pronounced and the chasm between their adherents was consequently widened. According to Ibn Khaldūn, "When the school of every Imam became a specific discipline for its followers with no recourse to free thought and analogical reasoning, they needed to theorise on issues by way of comparison and to differentiate between them when in doubt by taking recourse to predetermined principles developed in the school of their imam. To be able to theorise and differentiate in this manner so as to comply with the school of their imam required a firmly established aptitude. This aptitude became the science of jurisprudence of this era."[27]

If free thought had transformed into blind imitation and the aptitude to derive and extract rulings had transformed into emulation and conformity to the teachings of the imam of a school, and if a barrier was created between a school's adherents and the capacity to test their school, it would be only a matter of time before the various schools of jurisprudence would become similar to separate religious traditions in terms of bigoted attachment and disputation amongst their adherents. This was, in fact, what transpired, leading to the creation of what became know as the Science of Disputation (*'ilm al-khilāfiyyāt*) in the Islamic community. This science is founded on debate amongst the various schools of thought that argue the merits of a certain school and the importance of adhering steadfastly to it.

Ibn Khaldūn explains:

Know that there was much disputation amongst scholars over jurisprudence, which was derived from textual evidential material, and, due to differences in opinion and apprehension, disagreement was inevitable. This took on tremendous proportions in the faith community and there developed many schools of thought. Finally, the schools of thought of the four Imams gained ascendancy due to their high regard and people constrained themselves to following one of these four schools and prohibited adherence to any other schools due to the decline of free thought (*ijtihād*) and the difficulties associated therewith.

The disciplines within the four schools of thought multiplied with the passing of time and, due to the neglect of other schools, the principles of the faith community were established within these four schools. Differences also arose amongst adherents of the four schools due to diverse understandings of religious texts and differences concerning juristic principles. Debates were held in defence of the schools of the various Imams and were based upon set principles and rules in which the adherent to a specific school would provide evidence in defence of the school he was devoted to and which he defended. This discipline came to be known as disputation (*'ilm al-khilāfiyyāt*). Ibn as-Sā'ātī has compiled everything related to the science of disputation in his compendium on the principles of jurisprudence, pointing out all the differences of opinion pertaining to each problem.[28]

Islamic thought began with clearly defined features after the beginning of Islam, the establishment of the Muslim community, the founding of its state and the emergence of its civilisation. This thought set out along an authentic trajectory, guided by the Qur'an and the Prophetic tradition, after the requirements of everyday existence compelled it to seek such guidance and inspiration. It began establishing itself, guided simultaneously by the Islamic texts and human reason.

Islamic thought was required to respond to the changes brought about by the spread of Islam and the increasing demands placed upon it through increased contact between Muslims and other civilisations. The thinking of our early ancestors was informed by Islam and rational engagement. By this means, they were able to create a paradigm of Islamic thought which was unique to them, and, by expanding upon it, they reached great heights.

They were not motivated only by the requirements of everyday life in their efforts to create this paradigm, but also by their desires and aspirations. In addition to the requirements of everyday necessities, the sphere of Islamic thought also gave expression to political trends, as well as to questions of leadership.

The tensions in the systems of governance in the Islamic lands lamentably contributed to cultural chaos. Foreign thought found its way into the Arabic language, and Muslims began advocating it. This was due to Muslims seeking assistance from foreign ideas and their persistent exposure to these. Foreign thought had a visible influence upon authentic Islamic thought, as can be seen from:

1. Confusion in portraying the objectives and interpretive methods of the noble Qur'an;
2. Confusion in understanding the Prophetic tradition and its status, as well as attributing false statements to the Prophet (ṣ);
3. Going beyond the set objectives of Islamic dialectic theology;
4. The withdrawal of certain jurisprudential and doctrinal schools from the sphere of Islam and its beliefs, like the extremist Shīʿah and Sufi groups;
5. The creation of the Sufism of the extremists, which became a competitor to jurisprudence, and which ultimately became hostile to it and to Islam in totality;
6. The creation of alternative disciplines of learning in the Muslim community, like the disciplines of magic, talismanry and the secret of the alphabets, which resulted in people turning away from the truth and its teachings, causing them to believe in baseless superstitions. Matters were made worse by the constant degeneration of authentic Islamic thought to the point where it lost its authenticity, and where intellectual stagnation weakened the foundation upon which it was constructed.

Having recourse to the religious texts became less common, and the invoking of the opinions of the Imams of the various schools of thought became the norm. The principle of movement in Islamic thought (*ijtihād*) was suspended and was replaced by blind imitation (*taqlīd*). Islamic thought was, as such, incapacitated and frozen, and the Qur'an and Prophetic Tradition were forgotten.

Evaluation and appraisal were referred to the schools of thought; to the book of man and no longer to the book of God. Man thus enjoyed the infallible status of God in his pronouncements. The Islamic environment was polluted by countless superstitions and delusional claims, which quickly brought about its collapse. Islam was no longer the religion of principles that defined people; rather, piety became associated with people who pronounced their own principles. The religion of pure monotheism was no more and had become the religion of *unity of being*, of *intercession* and *intermediation*. The religion of the single community was no more and the *ummah* had become sectarian, divided into a multitude of doctrinal schools.

Thereafter, the state was weakened, and collapsed, and central authority was passed on to the provinces, which further divided into independent principalities. Muslims divided into sects and every tribe proclaimed its own prince of the believers, with his own pulpit. When the Islamic community weakened intellectually and spiritually, and when the bonds that held it together weakened, thereby weakening its unity, foreign forces were spurred on, the spirit of resistance was broken and the Muslim empire was stormed by the Tartars from the East and the Crusaders from the West. This was its position just before the seventh century AH.[29]

However, the earth was not emptied of those who stood as witnesses for Allah. Certainly not! Every era produced someone who put fear in the heart of the oppressor so as to set him on the straight path. There was always someone in our *ummah* who stood against deviance if it appeared, who resisted it if it took root and who violently opposed it so that the flag of truth was raised and could take its place. The story of this gruelling intellectual struggle is a long one. To gain some insight into it, we recommend Abul Hasan Ali Nadwi's book, *Men of Intellect and Propagation in Islam*.[30]

Notes

1. There have been a number of translations of *al-Muqaddimah* into English. The most famous of these is probably Franz Rosenthal's (1958) three volume version: *The Muqaddimah: An Introduction to History. Pantheon/Bollingen.* Rosenthal's translation is available online at http://www.muslimphilosophy.com/ik/Muqaddimah/ [Translator].

2. He presented this study at Egypt's Ministry of Endowments in a lecture delivered at the invitation of the Culture Ministry. A few additions and slight changes in the presentation style have been made to suit the needs of the current book. In addition, care has been taken to be as faithful as possible to Ibn Khaldūn's work when quoting from it.

3. *Al-Muqaddimah*, p. 372 (All page numbers make reference to the edition printed by *al-Maṭbaʿah al-Amīriyyah*).

4. *Mishkāh al-Maṣābīḥ*, critically appraised by al-Albānī, ḥadīth no. 184.

5. *Al-Muqaddimah*, pp. 477-479.

6. *Al-Muqaddimah*, p 364.

7. *Al-Muqaddimah*, p. 364.

8. ibid.

9. ibid.

10. *Al-Muqaddimah*, p. 372.

11. *Al-Muqaddimah*, p. 379

12. ibid., p. 389.

13. *Ṣaḥīḥ al-Bukhārī*, Book of Holding Fast to the Book of Allah and the Prophetic Practice, ḥadīth no. 6805.

14. *Al-Muqaddimah*, p. 364.

15. *Al-Muqaddimah*, p. 401.

16. Al-Ghazālī, *Iḥyāʾ ʿUlūm ad-Dīn*, vol. 1, page 2.

17. *Al-Muqaddimah*, p 391-392.

18. There is nothing in the Divine Legislation that contradicts Reason. What is intended here is anything whose underlying wisdom remains hidden to the mind, like some of the rituals of hajj, for example.

19. *Al-Muqaddimah*, p. 413-414.

20. See note 22, below.

21. *Al-Muqaddimah*, p. 441.

22. *As-Silsilāh aḍ-Ḍaʿīfah*, al-Albānī, ḥadīth no. 6023. This is a very commonly invoked tradition by the Sufis but has no basis; this entire subject is unfamiliar to Islam and is not in anyway related to its obligatory or voluntary practices.

23. *Al-Muqaddimah*, pp. 392-395. The Sufi discourse on these subjects vacillates between falsehoods and lies and has no relation to

academic inquiry. It is extremely lamentable that this subject matter should occupy a place in our traditional heritage.

24. *Al-Muqaddimah*, p. 423. This talk is all superstition that has been contrived by overindulging in delusion. Islam is absolved from it and those that busy themselves with it are impostors.

25. *Al-Muqaddimah*, pp. 414-415. Chemistry is today a science that enjoys an established status as it is based on experimentation and observation. In ancient times it was a fake discipline concerned with transforming base elements into gold.

26. *Al-Muqaddimah*, p. 374.

27. *Al-Muqaddimah*, p. 375.

28. *Al-Muqaddimah*, p. 381.

29. 13th Century CE [Translator].

30. Shaykh al-Ghazālī makes reference to the Arabic translation of Nadwi's book, published as *Rijāl al-Fikr wa ad-Da'wah fī al-Islām*. The original work was written in Urdu, entitled *Tarikhi Dawat-o-Azimat*. The book has also been translated into English, in four volumes, by Mohiuddin Ahmad, under the title *Saviours of Islamic Spirit* [Translator].

3

Innovation in Religion

The perceptive scholar, familiar with the sources of Islam and its subdivisions, does not fail to notice the innovations that have been added to this religion. These innovations are not a part of Islam but totally blemish its purity, and damage its authenticity and image. Such innovations have been introduced by people who, thereby, make additions to that which Allah has legislated. We need to carefully consider this development from various perspectives. Why do people come forward with new things of their own doing, mixing them with Islam and thereby attempting to draw the sanctity of Islam onto these innovations? Do they see a deficiency in the teachings that Allah has revealed? If this is the motivation for their innovations then it is indeed great foolishness, because Allah, the Most High, says in His Book: "This day, I have perfected your religion for you, completed My favour upon you, and have chosen for you Islam as your religion" (5:3).

Whoever thinks that there are shortcomings or deficiencies in the teachings of Islam, thereby warranting additions to discipline the self or bless the masses, is a disbelieving idiot. The majority of innovators most probably concoct inventions because of religious extremism and not because they find the religion deficient. Extremism—in any matter—leads to deviation from set objectives. In most instances, it causes one to lose track of reality and contributes to establishing falsehood. The extremism of the Christians resulted in them associating partners with Allah; others went to extremes by prohibiting that which was permissible. With regards to those before us, Allah, the Most High, says: "O people of the scripture (Jews and Christians)! Do not exceed the limits in your religion nor say of Allah aught but the truth." (4:171). With regards to the believers, Allah states: "O you who believe! Make not unlawful the good things which Allah has made lawful to you, and transgress not." (5:87). Allah then orders His righteous servants to strictly adhere to one path, without deviation. If they were to deviate, they would be misled: "And this is the path of your Lord leading straight. We have detailed Our revelations for a people who take heed" (6:126).

The Prophet (ṣ) has advocated the adherence to his Sunnah and the following of his example in many aḥādīth. Muslim narrates from Jābir ibn 'Abdullah: "Allah's Messenger (ṣ) would say in his sermon: "The best of statements is (from) the Book of Allah and the best of guidance is the guidance of Muḥammad. The worst of matters are innovations and all innovations are bid'ah (heresy) and all bid'ah leads to misguidance."[1]

'Abdullah ibn Mas'ūd narrates on the authority of the Prophet (ṣ): "Indeed they are two: speech and guidance. The best of speech is the speech of Allah and the best of guidance is the guidance of Muḥammad. In spite of this, you will introduce innovations and innovations will be introduced for you; all innovations lead to misguidance and misguidance leads to the fire."[2]

The forms of these despised innovations vary in degree and extent, and the harm and deviation resulting there-from vary as well. Scholars have rejected the most insignificant innovation, showing no laxity, because accepting even seemingly-insignificant innovations leads to widespread innovation in the fields of belief (al-'aqā'id), legislation (al-aḥkām), worship (al-'ibādāt), and behaviour (al-akhlāq). As the saying goes: "The majority of the inhabitants of the fire have entered due to small evils."

It is reported that a man sneezed next to 'Abdullah ibn 'Umar and said: "Praise be to Allah and blessings upon the Messenger of Allah!" 'Abdullah ibn 'Umar said to him: "That is not what the Messenger of Allah had taught us to say when we sneezed; he taught us to say only: 'Praise be to Allah.'"[3] Ibn 'Umar refused to keep silent regarding an addition that some see as being of no harm and took it upon himself to guide the man to comply with the boundaries set by the transmitted Sunnah, without adding or subtracting from it in the least. If the door to this addition was left open, extravagant individuals would have invented lengthy sayings to be recited by the one who sneezes, and even lengthier responses. Innovations surrounding these minor matters would then lead to innovations in matters of greater significance.

The one who innovates in matters of religion grants himself a position he is not entitled to. Allah, the Most Honoured and High, is the only Legislator. How can someone—no matter what his intention or his position—add to Allah's rulings things that he puts forward by his own initiative, saying that this is good and should be carried out or that this is detestable and should be ignored? Allah has not granted anyone such authority in His revelation, nor is it given any credence by the Sunnah of the Prophet (ṣ): "Or have they partners with Allah, who have instituted for them a religion which Allah has not allowed? And had it not been for a decisive word (gone forth already), the matter would have been judged between them. And verily, for the wrongdoers there is a painful torment" (42:21). By encroaching upon this divine right, humankind transgresses upon its own restricted capacity and exceeds its own limits. For this reason, going along with this trend is regarded as associating other lords with Allah, thereby permitting what is prohibited, and prohibiting what is permissible.

Ath-Thaʿlabī narrates the following from 'Adiy ibn Ḥātim: "I came to Allah's Messenger (ṣ) wearing a cross made of gold around my neck. He said: 'O 'Adiy, expel the idol that is on you.' I heard him then reciting: 'They (the Jews and Christians) took their rabbis and their monks to be their lords besides Allah' (9:31). I said: 'O Messenger of Allah, they do not worship them.' He said:

'Do they not prohibit that which Allah has made permissible and make permissible that which Allah has prohibited?' I said: 'Yes, they do.' He then said: 'That is their worship.'"[4]

Referring to this verse (9:31) that the Prophet (ṣ) recited, al-Alūsī said: "The verse points to many of the deviant sects that ignore Allah's Book and the Sunnah of His Prophet (ṣ) in favour of the statements of their scholars and leaders." Only the truth deserves to be followed, and when it is made apparent, all Muslims are obligated to follow. There is no doubt that adding to the religion reflects an inclination towards vanity, and abandoning the truth results in deviation from the path: "So after the truth, what else can there be, save error? How then are you turned away?" (10:32).

Those that devise these innovations carry the burden of their own misguidance as well as the burdens of those that are fooled and respond to them, as is stated in the *ḥadīth*: "Whoever established a bad practice shall be burdened with its burden as well as the burdens of those who act upon it."[5] Allah, the Most High and Honoured, also states: "They will bear their own burdens in full on the Day of Resurrection, and also of the burdens of those whom they misled without knowledge" (16:25).

Every act of worship occupies a place in the heart in which it descends and settles. These acts of worship also require an effort for them to be fulfilled. No man has two hearts and cannot exert any effort greater than that which he possesses and is characterised by. As a result, he cannot place himself between two positions; he either orientates himself with his heart and strength towards the Sunnah, or towards *bid'ah* (heretical innovation). Any activity in either of these two categories would be at the expense of the other category. Those that busy themselves with heretical innovations, regarding them lightly, inadvertently lose track of some of the realities and clear obligations of correct Islam, emphasizing these superstitions and being attracted by these innovations.

The danger of *bid'ah* is not only that it is a blemish that stains the face of authenticity; it is also a disease that causes religion to lose its health and weakens its heart and limbs. For this reason, Ibn Mas'ūd said: "Moderation with regards to the Sunnah is better than exercising an opinion that is based on innovation."[6] The Prophet (ṣ) said: "Any *bid'ah* introduced by people results in them losing an equivalent portion of the Sunnah."[7]

Abū Dāwūd relates that Mu'ādh ibn Jabal once said: "Ahead of you lies discord in which there will be an abundance of wealth and the Qur'an will be opened and taken hold of by the believer and the hypocrite, men and women, young and old, freeman and slave. A person will almost say: 'Why do people not follow me, even though I have recited the Qur'an? They will not follow me until I innovate for them something other than the Qur'an!' So beware of innovation, because it is misguidance. I also warn you of the deviation of the wise, as Satan may utter a word of misguidance by the tongue of the wise and a hypocrite may utter a word of truth."[8]

Mu'ādh's words explain to us how people of religion—especially the Sufis—construct prayers and *dhikr* (ritual invocations) for ordinary people just as an ignorant doctor dispenses bad medicine. This is then accepted by those who are fooled and they waste their time performing acts that have not been ordained by Allah, neither as an obligation nor as a voluntary practice. They forget the requirements of Islam (that serve to uplift their spirits and set aright their minds) to the extent that they occupy themselves with these innovated *adhkār* (pl. of *dhikr*).

Abū Dāwūd narrated that a man wrote to 'Umar ibn 'Abd al-'Azīz, asking him about predestination. 'Umar replied: "I advise you to be heedful to Allah and to maintain frugality in carrying out His orders, to follow the Sunnah of his Prophet and to leave that which has been innovated after the establishment of the Sunnah. You should heed completely to the Sunnah because—with Allah's permission—it is infallible. Know that people have not innovated any *bid'ah* whose falsity cannot be proven. The Sunnah was established by one who knew of the errors that lie in rejecting it either deliberately or through ignorance and carelessness. So satisfy yourself with what people before you were content with as they possessed knowledge and insight; they were far more capable at resolving matters and were people of honour."[9] The people of honour that are referred to by 'Umar ibn 'Abd al-'Azīz were the Companions of the Prophet (ṣ), who adhered to his word without the slightest deviation.

Some people are gifted with the ability to invent and originate. This is approved of and welcomed by Islam because the ability to innovate can be well utilized. It is welcome in worldly matters as it broadens the horizons of life. Westerners have exercised their ability in this field with great benefit and success. Instead of showing compliance in matters of religion and innovating in worldly matters, we have done exactly the opposite. In religious matters we have innovated meaningless things, and we have remained stagnant in worldly matters. People have flown between the heavens and earth but we still remain crawling on the ground. What would have been our state had we adhered to Allah's revelation and shown innovation in matters relating to our intellects and worldly pursuits? Would this not have been better for our religion and more beneficial to our livelihood?

It is not permitted for a person—no matter how learned and experienced—to give credence to an action by placing upon it the characteristic of religion, allowing him to circulate it amongst people under the pretence that it is from the Lord of all creation, leaving the impression that carrying out this action results in reward or that ignoring it indicates shortcoming. This is the essence of falsehood, no matter what the intention of the person or the nature of the action that is introduced.

There are certain narrations that have been misunderstood. Some regard these narrations as giving approval for certain acts, encouraging their performance and describing them as acceptable devotions. For example, the Prophet (ṣ) said: "Whoever establishes a good action will have its reward and the reward of those who perform it, without having their reward reduced in any way."[10] Another example is the following statement attributed to the Prophet (ṣ): "That which Muslims see as good is regarded by Allah as good."[11] The first *ḥadīth* is narrated by Muslim. It does not in any way suggest that innovation in religion is allowable, because there is no good action sanctioned by this religion that is not based upon the Qur'an or the prophetic practice. The first *ḥadīth* is similar to another statement of the Prophet (ṣ): "Whosoever invites to guidance will receive its reward and the reward of one who acts upon it, without detracting from their reward in any way."[12]

Another example: "One who points towards good is like one who does good."[13] The guidance invited to is good actions, actions that Allah is pleased to see his servants follow. There is no guidance that is able to point out something that Allah has overlooked or a matter that the Prophet (ṣ) may have forgotten! Yes, there may be guidelines that have a broad frame of implementation and that may be portrayed in different ways, thereby renewing methods of implementation with the passing of time. Such guidelines leave open the sphere for the innovation of methods and the viewing of concerns. This cannot be described as innovation in religion, or deviating from its established practice, even though it was not established by our predecessors; the requirements of their era did not call for this. A good action—after being settled—should be revelation from Allah or guidance from His Prophet, or an action in line with this orientation, drawing from this very same well-spring.

The narration which states "That which Muslims regard as good, is regarded as good by Allah" is not a *ḥadīth* of Allah's Messenger (ṣ) but rather a statement of 'Abdullah ibn Mas'ūd. This respected Companion enjoys a high status in jurisprudence, which warrants us to welcome whatever he says. Ibn Mas'ūd, without doubt, did not intend to give the Muslim community permission to make additions or subtractions to their Book by this statement. He was the most sensitive of the companions in rejecting the infiltration of vain practices into general behaviour. He therefore took an extremely harsh position towards *bid'ah* and would expel it even if it concerned a minor matter, wrestling with any innovation from its inception, thereby extinguishing it at its origin. It would therefore be utter foolishness to suggest that the above-mentioned statement acts as evidence to allow innovation in matters of religion. Perhaps his statement is a recommendation of some sort that was made in reference to the consensus (*ijmā'*) of the companions and those that follow them in righteousness, expressing the hope that they would not lose sight of any truth that is acceptable to Allah. It may even be referring to that which serves Islam and fulfils its major objectives, i.e., methods upon which the *sharī'ah* has not placed any strict stipulations. Or perhaps it is a reference to general matters in which—from the perspective of Islam—only a good intention is a requirement.

Allowing additions to Islam under the pretence that they are good is the same as cancelling some of its teachings under the pretence that they are not beneficial or not suited to development; both scenarios are deviant and unacceptable. No one is allowed to ignore what Allah has legislated or to legislate what Allah has chosen to remain silent about, as is explained in the following *hadīth*: "Allah has obligated the fulfilment of certain things so do not be neglectful of them; He has set certain boundaries so do not transgress them; He has prohibited certain things so do not violate (His prohibitions) and He has remained silent on certain things as a mercy to you and not out of forgetfulness, so do not inquire about them."[14]

Mālik ibn Anas said: "Whoever regards a *bid'ah* as something good has suggested that Muḥammad has betrayed his mission." Ash-Shāfi'ī said: "Even if I saw an innovator walking on air, I would not accept (his *bid'ah*)." He also said: "Whoever authenticates something, legislates it." And: "Any innovation—contrary to the Qur'an, sunnah, *ḥadīth*, or *ijmā'* is a *bid'ah* that leads to misguidance." Wakī' said: "I regard committing adultery as being of a lesser consequence than asking an innovator for an opinion."

Previous religions failed to implement their teachings not because of the disobedience of their people, but because their scriptures were taken lightly and interpreted vainly, or even fabricated, thereby leaving people to submit in ignorance or to transgress because of arrogance. Allah has protected the Noble Qur'an and it has therefore not been touched by fabrication or modification. He has also safeguarded the Sunnah by destining that it be protected by righteous critics who refuse any lies against it and who ensure that it is not manipulated by fabricators. He safeguards Islam by sending forth, in every generation, guardians who protect its authenticity against superstition and its purity from foreign influences. Ancient religions have perished because their principles were deviated by vain desire, leaving only their names untouched. With Islam, no matter how widespread *bid'ah* may be amongst its followers, there will always be dedicated scholars who will expose the evils of such heretical innovations. In this way, the truth prevails and falsehood is restrained. Even if falsehood is destined to exist, it will always be despised and scorned.

Scholars of religion carry the obligation of directing people to adhere to the plain realities of Islam as they have been conveyed by the Prophet (ṣ). Ibn Mas'ūd said: "Take hold of knowledge before it is lost, as it will be lost when one who possesses it passes on. You will come across people who claim to be inviting to Allah's book but they will have flung it behind their backs, so take hold of knowledge. Beware of innovation, exaggeration and speculation, and rather adhere to that which is well established."[15]

'Umar ibn Yaḥyā narrated:

I heard my father speaking about his father and he narrated the following: "We were sitting outside 'Abdullah ibn Mas'ūd's door before the early morning prayer so that we could accompany him to the *masjid* when he came out. Abū Mūsā al-Ashʿarī came to us and asked: 'Has Abū ʿAbd ar-Raḥmān left as yet?' We said 'no,' so he sat down with us, waiting for him. When he came out we all stood up and Abū Mūsā said to him: 'O Abū ʿAbd ar-Raḥmān (i.e., Ibn Masʿūd), I have just seen something in the *masjid* which is unknown to me and which I think—Praise be to Allah—is something good.' Ibn Masʿūd asked: 'What is it?' He said: 'Come along and you will see.' He then said: 'I saw people in the *masjid* sitting in small groups waiting for the prayer. Each group was led by a man and they all held pebbles in their hands. The leader of each group would say: "Recite *Allahu Akbar* 100 times," and they would repeat this a hundred times. He would then do the same asking them to repeat "*Alḥamdulillah*" and "*Subaḥānallah*"'. Ibn Masʿūd asked: 'What did you say to them?' He replied: 'I did not say anything to them; I wanted your opinion and command first.' Ibn Masʿūd said: 'Did you not command them to count their bad deeds, or try to reassure them that nothing could wipe out their good deeds?' Ibn Masʿūd then took off and we went with him until he reached one of those groups and stopped. He then said: 'What is it that I see you doing?' They said: 'We are counting the praises of Allah with these pebbles.' He then said: 'Count your bad deeds rather; I guarantee you that there is nothing that can cause you to lose any of your good deeds. Be warned, followers of Muḥammad, that your destruction is near! The Companions of your Prophet are amongst you in abundance, his clothing has not yet deteriorated and his utensils are still intact, and by my own life, you are either following a religion that is more instructive than the religion of Muḥammad or you have opened the door of misguidance.' They said: 'By Allah, O Abū ʿAbd ar-Raḥmān, we did not intend anything except what is good!' He said, 'There are many who seek good but do not achieve it. Indeed, Allah's Messenger (ṣ) had spoken to us about those that recite the Qur'an, but it does not go beyond their throats. It may just be that most of them are amongst you.' He then turned away from them. ʿAmmār ibn Salmah then said: 'I saw most of those people siding with the Khawārij, fighting against us, on the day of an-Nahrawān.[16]

'Abdullah ibn Mas'ūd also said: "Follow and do not innovate, this is sufficient for you."[17] Ibn Mas'ūd disliked additions that were not present in the era of the Prophet (ṣ) and looked upon these innovated images with suspicion and misgiving. He saw the seeds of extremism flourishing within these individuals, through their attitude towards *dhikr* (ritual invocation). This led to their fundamentalist outlooks towards governance and reached the point where they accused the believers of disbelief. They were killed in battle, ridding the Muslim community of this thorn, but their ideas still remained. Ibn Mas'ūd also saw within them the seeds of innovation that would turn *dhikr*-gatherings into platforms where mobs would dance, claiming they had been overcome by some divine spirit.

Harsh criticism does not ward off the spread of *bid'ah*. When the ordinary masses turn away from the plain truth and the pure religion, they are easily attracted to these deviant practices, as if they were a long-pursued objective. One is amazed to see how these blemishes develop—through ignorance and bigotry—until they are accepted as being part of Islam and whoever is opposed to them is regarded as vain. Consider the following statement of 'Umar ibn 'Abd al-'Azīz, in which he refers to the difficulty one is faced with in repelling *bid'ah*: "I have to deal with matters upon which elders have perished and with which the young have been brought up, which foreigners have learnt fluently and which has even been accepted by the Bedouins. They all regard these matters as part of Islam and do not regard anything other than this as the truth." If this was the extent of the growth of *bid'ah* in the era of 'Umar ibn 'Abd al-'Azīz, imagine what it was like thereafter.

What is *bid'ah*?

Scholars define *bid'ah* as: "An innovated procedure in religion, emulating something legitimate, having the same purpose as the legitimate procedure, or with the intention of showing extreme devotion to Allah." Innovation is the introduction of something new, something which people did not know before. Scholars in the West—who have invented the airplane, the train, the radio, etc.—are also innovators because they introduced things that were not known to their predecessors. Their innovations in these fields are praiseworthy. However, those that innovate sayings and actions and then embellish them so that people may regard them as part of Islam are innovators that introduce things that were not revealed by Allah or taught by His Prophet (ṣ).

The essence of innovation is the creation of something that has no prior equivalent or any evidence as to its existence. Allah is referred to as *al-Badīʿ* (The Originator) because He created this world without there being anything similar to it before: "The Originator of the heavens and the earth. When he decrees a matter, he only says to it: 'Be!'—and it is" (2:117).

The innovator has to make sure that his deception appears to be the truth. He therefore tries very hard to emulate the *sharīʿah* in outlook, even if he opposes it in essence. The one who circulates *bidʿah* is, therefore, similar to a counterfeiter. Counterfeit syndicates try very hard to use colours and characteristics that imitate the original currency as closely as possible, so that the naïve may easily be deceived. After the currency is counterfeited, it is mixed with some of the original so that it may appear to be all the same, making it easy to circulate.

The earlier Imams of Islam were extremely dedicated to searching for and putting an end to *bidʿah*, in a way similar to the dedication shown by current governments in tracing counterfeit money and punishing the criminals who produce and circulate it. The Imams were sustained by the teachings of the Prophet (ṣ), who said: "Whoever innovates something concerning our affairs, which has nothing to do with us, is indeed rejected."[18] Similarly, he said: "Whoever carries out an action that we have not ordered is indeed rejected."[19] Both these *aḥādīth* declare war against *bidʿah*; the first with regards to its innovation and the second with regards to its acceptance and implementation. If innovations in Allah's religion were met with one-tenth of the force with which money counterfeiting is met, the essence of Islam would have remained pure, making it all the more attractive and easier to adhere to. Unfortunately, people grant more importance to matters of their livelihood and exert greater effort to safeguard it. Matters of religion are given less importance, thereby allowing *bid'ah* to become widespread, which results in the truth slowly vanishing.

The enemies of Islam dedicate themselves to promoting these innovations, creating the impression that this is all that the religion consists of. In this way Islam loses its natural attraction and clear sense. One notices the evil intent directed towards Islam and Muslims in the following article published in *The Times* newspaper, under the title "Colonialism and Islam": "Islam is spreading quickly in West Africa, causing great concern amongst missionaries and Europeans as to what outcome this may bring about in the region. The belief in the past had been that Islam was a religion of desert communities that may proceed towards civilization; the current turn of events indicates that the circle of Islam is widening. One can hardly believe that it has been able to penetrate the equatorial regions and reach as far as the South, as is the case with Sierra-Leone, the Ivory Coast, and the Gold Coast.[20] Bureaucrats have expressed fear that the spread of Islam in this area will be followed by the establishment of links with Cairo and the Arab world. Western thinkers differ on the future of Islam in Africa. Some say that the progress of Islam will not harm the welfare of colonialism as long as it stays within the course set by the colonialists. Others deem it necessary to limit the progress of Islam by spreading innovations and superstitions so that these may act as a barrier against the increasing pressure of Islam." Do you see how *bid'ah* acts as a stumbling block in front of Islam, weakening its strength, tearing apart its state?

A specific characteristic of these innovations is that they are very similar to business fraud, in which different products are mixed with inferior components and then sent to the markets as if they are products of high quality. Someone who wants to introduce something into Islam does not do so openly, proclaiming it to be a part of the religion. He covers his innovation so that it appears to emulate the *shari'ah*, or he draws some false links with its principles and sources. Look at the idolaters who sought to justify the worshipping of their idols by claiming that they acted as intermediaries with Allah.[21] When they circumambulated the Ka'bah naked, they claimed that they did not want to do so in clothing they had worn while showing disobedience to Allah!

Innovations that occur under the category of acts of worship creep into and infiltrate the body of teachings introduced by Islam. As is well established from its texts, Islam comprises of beliefs, acts of worship, ethics, politics, personal laws, civil laws, criminal laws, and so forth. Committing excesses in trying to gain closeness to Allah is initially manifested in acts of normal obedience, through additions and unnecessary difficulty. Such excessiveness may also be directed towards other teachings of Islam, by stipulating customs and rules with the intention of incorporating them into the religion when, in fact, they are based only on pure vanity. In this way innovation encompasses acts of worship and conduct.

However, innovation in the category of conduct is not regarded as *bid'ah* if it does not aim to emulate the objectives and practices of Islam. This type of innovation is, in fact, viewed positively by the *shari'ah*, which stipulates very precise measures for the general welfare of the community. This means that innovation and modernization are approved of as long as they fall within the framework that we have just indicated. The fundamental principle regarding acts of worship is to adhere very strictly to the standards that have been preordained; innovation in this category is viewed as oppressive and misguiding.

One might ask: is there a difference between innovation in conduct and innovation in acts of worship? In this regard, it must be said that the acts of submission stipulated by the Lawgiver are based upon specific texts and take very specific forms, leaving no place for the creation of new forms. As far as general principles and worldly matters are concerned, one sees that the Lawgiver pays no attention to their forms or framework, but is rather concerned with their implications and objectives.

Introducing a new prayer to the prescribed prayers, or increasing the number of cycles (*raka'āt*) that have already been predetermined is something that is completely rejected. However, if people set out to establish sewage systems underground and to provide running water to *masjids* because Islam stipulates cleanliness, thereby introducing systems that were unknown to our predecessors, then these developments cannot be regarded as objectionable innovations. Indeed, *bid'ah*—according to the definition we have provided—has no link to worldly matters and cannot be implicated in the modernization and development introduced to uplift humankind.

Bid'ah cannot simply be regarded as a sin. A sin is something that goes contrary to a text or transgresses upon a principle with both still remaining intact and clearly defined as outlined by the *sharī'ah*. An act that is *bid'ah* undermines and neutralizes both the text and the principle; it deviates from the authenticity of the Divine Address by incorporating vain desires. This only serves to lead away from the straight path. A sinner transgresses the command of Allah but is still aware of what Allah has commanded; he may even repent in the near or distant future. The innovator does not understand the requirements of the religion so he tries to gain closeness to Allah by methods that are invalid; he performs acts that are not obligatory, which may even be prohibited. However, a sin may transform into an innovation if it comes to be regarded as part of the religion. To charge money for reciting the Qur'an, for example, is strictly prohibited as it contradicts the following statement of the Prophet (ṣ): "Do not earn your living by it (i.e., the Qur'an)."[22] If this act is adopted as a religious practice and people are hired to recite at funerals as a means of gaining closeness to Allah, they have inadvertently committed a compounded sin, i.e., disobedience and innovation.

Some scholars regard all infringements and innovations that emerged after the Prophet (ṣ) as *bid'ah*, whether a sin that is repelled by the Lawgiver or an innovation fabricated by ignorant and prejudiced individuals under the pretence that it is part of the religion when, in fact, it is not. This generalization is far from being precise. Even further are those who regard *bid'ah* as encompassing all innovations that occurred after the Prophet (ṣ), whether in conduct or worship, good or bad, praiseworthy or reprehensible.

The first definition was adopted by Imam ash-Shāṭibī. He studied all reprehensible innovations in this light in a very original and praiseworthy book, which he called *al-I'tiṣām* (The Refuge). To regard everything that is new in Allah's religion or in worldly matters as *bid'ah* would be closer to its linguistic meaning than to the meaning that is implied by the *sharī'ah*. Al-Qarāfī and 'Izz ad-Dīn ibn 'Abd as-Salām have inclined towards this meaning. Their position is not flawless, even if it leads to the rejection of all conspired additions to Islam. From this perspective, there is no disagreement amongst the scholars, even if they disagree as to the precise meaning of the word *bid'ah*.

Between *bid'ah* and *al-maṣlaḥah al-mursalah* (public welfare)

Professor 'Abd al-Wahhāb Khallāf states in his book *The Science of Uṣūl al-Fiqh*: "One who peruses the verses of the Qur'an pertaining to laws regarding worship finds that they are very detailed. This is also the case with personal matters such as inheritance, partly because most laws of this type are devotional and do not fall into the sphere of applied reason or change with the changing of the environment. Allah's rulings pertaining to laws other than worship and personal matters, like civil law, criminal law, constitutional law, economic law, etc, are, in the majority of cases,[23] basic principles that rarely go into specific details. This is because these rulings tend to change with the changing of the environment and according to the public welfare. The Qur'an limits these rulings to general normative and foundational principles so that rulers in any era are able to stipulate the specific details of the law in accordance with their own welfare, keeping them within the general boundaries set by the Qur'an and without any contradiction."

Najm ad-Dīn at-Ṭūfī said: "We only consider the public welfare in matters of conduct and not in matters of worship and the like, because these fall within the rights of the Lawgiver and are specific to Him. It is not possible to have knowledge of His rights, in relation to time, space, quantity, etc., except as He has directed and the servant is therefore compelled to comply to the stipulations set by Him. This is because a slave is only regarded as obedient if he complies with the directions of his master and does only that which he knows will please him. This is exactly the case here; when philosophers rejected the law and approached religious devotion as an application of their intellects, they incurred the wrath of Allah and were misled and led others astray. This is, however, not the case with commissioned rights, as these concern political rulings implemented for the general welfare and determined by it."

'Izz ad-Dīn ibn 'Abd as-Salām stated in relation to this: "Whoever considers the general purposes of the law, which are based on the obtaining of welfare and the repelling of perversity, realizes that it is not permissible to be lax in obtaining welfare or in overlooking perversity even if it is not stipulated by *ijmā'* (consensus) or *qiyās* (analogy) or any specific text; the understanding of the law makes this an obligation."

From these statements we learn that the position towards enactments dealing with acts of worship is not the same as enactments dealing with conduct. The Lawgiver takes the responsibility of stipulating the realities of worship with regard to form, time, place, quantity, method, what is general and what is specific, etc. This is specified by His wisdom and there is no room for the exertion of our own opinions; we are only required to fulfil these obligations. The acts of worship should remain the same as they have been from the era of the Prophet (ṣ) to the end of time, with no difference between our predecessors and the generations to come. Complete compliance has to be shown in this matter, from beginning to end.

However, all other enactments revolve around the public welfare and all the preserved texts and stipulated principles point towards the attainment of this objective. It is not possible to specify the ways of attaining these reforms because of the inherent differences between one generation and another or one nation and another. One may also be able to achieve the same reforms through different methods and, therefore, all alternatives are to be regarded as acceptable. The fact that all enactments concerning conduct are founded upon logical reforms does not diminish the importance of the textual sources that provide the necessary principles and details. These texts can be compared to the concrete foundations that lie underground: one is able to construct the building of one's choice, employing any methods, but one is obligated to depend upon these foundations and recognize their importance.

The breadth of the sphere within which the intellect operates alongside the text in matters of conduct has prompted some to follow the same course with regards to acts of worship. This is a manifest error. As has been shown, the foundation of acts of worship is straight forward compliance. The position is obviously different for other matters; whatever developments take place with regards to these matters cannot correctly be referred to as *bid‘ah*, whether praiseworthy or reprehensible.

Indeed the preservation of the five fundamentals is a responsibility shared by divine legislation and by worldly laws, even though Allah's guidance is obviously far wiser and more reliable. The five fundamentals are: *religion, life, honour, intellect* and *wealth*. The preservation of these fundamental rights is based upon many proofs, but this is not the place to explain them all. One may not find a specific proof, maybe just a statement vindicating these five fundamentals or any one of them. If this proof is respected by the Lawgiver, it is acted upon. For example, the single directive ordering the compilation of the Qur'an into a single volume served to preserve the *sharī'ah* and helped implement Islam. Writing books that explain the Islamic belief system and that refute the scepticism of atheists serves a similar objective. Even though they have not been stipulated by the religion, all these actions serve to promote the general objectives of Islam and are referred to by some as *al-maṣāliḥ al-mursalah* (the public welfare). They are reforms that are the product of sincere reasoning and serve to promote the betterment of people's livelihood, in addition to securing their salvation in the hereafter.

It is incorrect to refer to these actions as *bid'ah ḥasanah* (a good innovation) or as *bid'ah wājibah* (an obligatory innovation), etc. People make such categorizations thinking that these actions are innovations because they did not occur in the era of the Prophet (ṣ). Similarly, they think that they do not fall into the category of reprehensible innovations because they lead to good results. This, in reality, only confuses the meaning of disliked innovation. It confuses what is valid in acts of worship and what is valid in acts of conduct.

Bid'ah is confined only to devotional acts, in which the exertion of opinion plays no part. Matters of public welfare lay in the sphere of conduct, where reason is exerted to arrive at the best general reforms. There is therefore a vast difference between *bid'ah* and *al-Maṣāliḥ al-Mursalah*.

Bida' (pl. of *bid'ah*) are innovations introduced by ignorant worshippers with the intention of gaining closeness to Allah, as they claim. They are innovations that were introduced with the intention of performing the innovated act itself. *Al-Maṣāliḥ al-Mursalah*, on the other hand, are actions that are introduced for the preservation of the general rights of the majority of the community. Therefore, not everything that emerges with the passing of time is to be regarded as an act of *bid'ah* for which punishment is to be expected. As long as an overriding principle has been recognized and approved of by the Lawgiver, it is not regarded as *bid'ah*. There are many examples of this. Conclusions derived by acceptable analogies can therefore not simply be described as *bid'ah*. Examples of these would be actions that fall into the sphere of the promotion of the public welfare approved of by the Qur'an and the Sunnah, as well as various actions that are encompassed by a general command in which a specific illustration has not been defined by established rules. Allah, the Most Honoured and Most High, states: "And do good that you may be successful" (22:77), as well as "Help you one another in virtue and righteousness" (5:2).

There is no harm in creating different ways to do good and to help promote virtue and righteousness. One cannot reject or make any accusations against these methods if they are innovative and broad-based. Allah, the Blessed and Sublime, also states: "And fight in the Way of Allah and know that Allah is the All-Hearer, All-Knower" (2:244). This verse indicates that the methods and spheres of fighting are immeasurable. The expression of creative genius that occurs in this field has no link whatsoever with reprehensible innovation. It is in fact a response to a divine calling.

However, general texts cannot be used to advance arguments for the creation of actions that would conflict with specified acts that the Prophet (ṣ) has stipulated. Allah states: "O you who believe! Remember Allah with much remembrance. And glorify His praises morning and afternoon" (33:41-42). This command to remember Allah profusely and to praise Him constantly does not give one the right to add a cycle (*rak'ah*) to the prayer, or to validate the *adhān* for the Eid prayer, or to write formulae and obligate the community to recite them, etc. All these acts of worship have already been cast in their final forms. No person, no matter what his position, is allowed to add anything new in this regard.

However, there is no harm in implementing orders that concern general matters even if this was not done by our predecessors. This is equivalent to the application of one law to several situations. The protection of wealth, the safeguarding of rights, and the consideration of welfare all form the primary purposes of the *sharī'ah*.

If a ruler sees that he has to mandate certain taxes or implement certain measures to guarantee the safety of his people, then he is obligated to do so even if no such measures were implemented in the era of the Prophet (ṣ). By doing so, he is not regarded as having created a *bid'ah*. The implementation of 80 lashes as a punishment for drinking by the companions of the Prophet (ṣ) is an example. Another example is the provision of guarantees by manufacturers for damaged products, or the implementation of capital punishment upon all the participants in a murder (even if they were a hundred participants) or the introduction of imprisonment. These matters were all dealt with by the companions and their followers, without any repudiation, and were referred to by some as *al-Maṣāliḥ al-Mursalah*, as we have mentioned. The title does not concern us, only the concept. There is no disagreement amongst judicious scholars that Islam has general purposes that are understood from its texts and many directives. It is possible to reach these established general objectives with innovative, progressive means and one is not obligated to adhere to any single method as long as the intended objective is being sought.

Allah has commanded justice and fairness and the supporting of kin; He has prohibited lewdness, evil-deeds and oppression. Whatever leads to the implementation of good and the removal of evil is regarded as an acceptable method in order to pursue development and in submission to the requirements of time and place; it cannot be seen as a prohibited innovation. As a result, we are able to accept the introduction of an attorney-general's office in the legal bureaucracy as a guarantee to ensure legal proceedings and to safeguard the rights of the community. We accept, as well, the current system of courts and their arrangement, even if it was not prevalent in the earlier eras. The creation of as many guarantees as possible to resolve disputes amongst people does not fall into the framework of *bid'ah*. Prohibited innovation involves actions that fall into the sphere of purely devotional acts, in which there is no room for *ijtihād* and the application of reason. In the sphere of conduct, where the Lawgiver has not drawn up clear boundaries that have to be adhered to, innovation that leads to good is not only acceptable but in reality falls under the famous principle: *that without which an obligatory act cannot be fulfilled is to be regarded as obligatory itself.*

The boundaries of compliance

Precise conformity to the teachings of the Prophet (ṣ) requires that we do not disregard anything that he did nor do we do anything that he disregarded. The Sunnah deals with the positive and negative together, i.e., there are certain practices the performance of which is regarded as Sunnah, and others the abstinence of which is regarded as Sunnah.

Adding to reported practices by attaching something new or by filling in a blank where nothing was reported (thereby taking initiatives pertaining to matters that the Prophet (ṣ) had remained silent on) are both regarded as reprehensible innovations; neither is sanctioned by Islam. A person that does something that was ignored by the Prophet (ṣ) is the same as someone who ignores that which was performed by him. We have explained earlier that evolving methods, by their nature, do not fall into this framework. Therefore, waging war with cannons is not regarded as *bid'ah*, or as an action that was disregarded by the Prophet (ṣ). It, in fact, falls under the principle of *that without which an obligatory act cannot be fulfilled is to be regarded as obligatory itself.* The discussion revolves around established objectives and defined obligations.

Therefore, whatever was ignored by the Prophet (ṣ) with the possibility existing of it being performed and without the presence of any inhibitor is regarded as Sunnah; i.e., Sunnah to ignore. To perform such an act is regarded as *bid'ah*.

Muslims of today are in the habit of gathering after someone's death, sometimes in a large tent, to listen to the Qur'an being recited and where refreshments are thereafter served.[24] People seek solace or consolation in this way. There is no doubt that the intention of reward and attaining mercy were ever present amongst our earliest predecessors. In spite of this, we did not see any of the practices we see today when one of the companions passed away. Many of them died and therefore soliciting mercy on their behalf was only natural; there was nothing to stop the companions from putting up tents in which to listen to recitations of the Qur'an and to exchange condolences. This widespread practice is an innovation because the Prophet (ṣ) did not give permission for it and did not resort to it, in spite of the opportunity for doing so existing and the absence of any inhibitor. Therefore, if one thinks that not performing these acts makes one negligent of attaining Allah's pleasure, or of soliciting mercy for the deceased, it would reflect a very bad opinion of the Prophet (ṣ) and his companions. There is, however, no way that we will ever be like them or come even close to their status.

One might argue that 'Umar had gathered the people under one imam for prayers in Ramaḍān, even though this was not undertaken in the Prophet's lifetime.[25] It is, in fact, firmly established that the Prophet (ṣ) did not really wish to have the people join him in this prayer but when they did, he lightened the prayer (i.e., he did not extend it for a long period). This is true, but the secret behind 'Umar's action is that the fear which had prompted the Prophet (ṣ) to want to pray alone was no longer present. When the Prophet (ṣ) saw the dedication of the community in emulating him in the performance of the *tahajjud* (midnight-early morning) prayer, he became concerned that it would be regarded as obligatory and thus did not continue with it. When the Prophet (ṣ) passed away, revelation came to a stop and all doubts and fears in this regard were resolved. The fear of obligation had fallen away and the desire to perform this prayer remained. 'Umar, thus, saw no harm in bringing the community together for the *tarāwīḥ* prayer. In addition, 'Umar was one of the senior Righteous Caliphs, by the command of the Prophet (ṣ) himself, and therefore his practices are part of the guidance of Islam and adherence to them is just another way of following the Prophet (ṣ). Is this not in conformity to the Prophet's command?[26]

Indeed, that which Allah's Messenger (ṣ) had refrained from, with opportunities existing for him to indulge in and without anything inhibiting him, cannot possibly be part of Islam or be regarded as guidance to the straight path; if it were, he would never have refrained from it. We see no comparison between what the Prophet (ṣ) refrained from (due to lack of need in that particular context) and *bid'ah*. The Prophet (ṣ) had legislated the general principles that would lead to the performance of the action when the need arose. In fact, the performance of this action is in conformity with the principles of Islam. For example, the Prophet (ṣ) refrained from pronouncing the *niyyah* (intention) when performing acts of worship, so one learns that to refrain is a Sunnah and to pronounce the *niyyah* is *bid'ah*.

The Prophet (ṣ) did not use the methods and syllogisms of logic in its technical sense—as introduced by Aristotle and others—when debating with his opponents. There would be no harm done if we were to use them, due to the development of our environments and the spread of these philosophies. We would, in fact, be defending the religion with a method that is now suitable. Addressing illiterate individuals is not the same as addressing the People of the Book of the first era, or addressing liberated rationalists.

We fear that the danger confronting the teachings of Islam is that people have started performing acts that the Prophet (ṣ) had deliberately refrained from, with his Rightly Guided Companions following in his example. His companions would have been the first to perform these acts had there been any good in them, or if they were seen as a means of gaining closeness to Allah.

If only those that bounce around at religious dance-parties (called *dhikr*) could direct their efforts at something like football instead, it would be far more beneficial to them, to the rest of us, and to Islam as well. Why should we burden ourselves with what Allah has pardoned us from, or adhere to something that He has made no mention of? The Prophet (ṣ) said: "Indeed Allah has made obligatory certain things, so do not neglect them, and He has appointed limitations, so do not transgress them, and He has remained silent on many matters as a mercy to you—not out of forgetfulness, so do not delve into them."[27]

Ibn Qayyim states in his book *A'lām al-Muwaqqi'īn*: "As to their (the companions of the Prophet) reports concerning that which the Prophet (ṣ) had refrained from, we find that there are two types, both of which are Sunnah. The first is their clear reports that the Prophet (ṣ) had refrained from something, and did not do it, like the washing and praying upon the martyrs of Uḥud, the *adhān* and *iqāmah* for the Eid prayer, and the *tasbīḥ* between the two prayers, when they are joined. The second is that which they did not report; if the Prophet (ṣ) had in fact undertaken a certain action they would certainly have paid attention to it—all or at least one of them. So if they did not report an action, or talk about it in some gathering, one knows that the Prophet (ṣ) did not perform it, like refraining from pronouncing the *niyyah* (intention) when beginning the prayer, or refraining from making *du'ā'* after the prayer, facing the congregation with all of them echoing *āmīn* in response to his *du'ā'*, after *fajr* and *'aṣr*, or after all the appointed prayer times."

Ibn Qayyim then explained that the Prophet's abstentions are a Sunnah, just as his actions are. If we respond by performing an action that the Prophet (ṣ) had avoided, it would be equivalent to responding by leaving out that which he had done; there is no difference in this respect. Ash-Shāṭibī also supports this principle in his book *al-I'tiṣām* (The Refuge).

Someone may ask: if the Lawgiver keeps silent on something, is it not permissible for us to either carry out the act or to refrain from it. Ash-Shāṭibī responded: "The silence of the Lawgiver with regards to a ruling on a particular issue, or his ignoring of a particular matter, is of two types. The first type includes issues on which the Lawgiver remained silent as there was no call or incentive for a response, like issues that occurred after the death of the Prophet (ṣ) and that did not occur in his lifetime. Scholars of the *sharī'ah* therefore needed to consider these issues in the light of the broader principles upon which Islam was founded. All the issues considered by our righteous predecessors are of this type, like guarantees for producers, inheritance of the grandfather with the brothers, support of legal heirs, the compilation of the Qur'an into book form, codification of legislation, etc. These are, in other words, issues for which there was no need of a resolution in the era of the Prophet (ṣ). The scholar would therefore deliberate on issues of this type when the need arose; silence on these issues does not imply that ignoring them is permissible.

"The second type are those rulings on which the Lawgiver remained silent, or when he ignored a certain matter, with the need for it being apparent and a reason for it to be addressed being present in the era of revelation. The Lawgiver did not specify a ruling that would clarify that this was, in fact, an issue pertaining to the religion. This section, specifically, constitutes a reprehensible innovation from the perspective of the law."

He then stated: "The proof for this being a *bid'ah* is that remaining silent on the issue—with the possibility of it being performed existing—is the consensus (*ijmā'*) of all those who remained silent on the issue, i.e., there was not supposed to be any addition to what already was. If it had been proper, from the perspective of the law, they would have carried it out as they were most likely to perceive this and precede us in its performance." This is the position that has been decided upon by the jurists of the *ummah* and the *ummah* is thus obligated to comply.

Bid'ah: original innovations and imitative innovations

We have thus far said that innovation doubtlessly shares a similarity with the *sharī'ah*, but is stimulated by extremism and unfounded additions. The effects of these fabrications vary extensively and therefore *bid'ah* may be divided into various categories. That which differs from Islam in both form and content and has strayed extensively from its clear methodology is not the same as that which is linked to it in some way or borrows from its teaching for some reason or the other.

For this reason scholars have divided *bid'ah* into that which is original (*al-bid'ah al-ḥaqīqiyyah*)and that which is imitative (*al-bid'ah al-iḍāfiyyah*).[28] For example, circumambulating the tombs of the dead—which is done in a manner similar to the circumambulation of the Ka'bah—is an original innovation. The Lawgiver permitted the visiting of graves as a reminder of the final destiny of all human beings and to deflate the intense sense of vanity caused by this life, which dominates the attention of many people. The elevation of graves and the building of domes over them, the sanctification of corpses, special visits and circumambulation of graves two, three or four times as a means of drawing closer to Allah are all practices that are without doubt regarded as original innovations. If the inhabitants of these graves are supplicated to with the hope of some sort of response, then this action is tantamount to transgression and *shirk* (associating partners with Allah).

Such rituals have no basis in the laws and ethics of Islam and were invented by weak-minded people; they are therefore classified as *al-bid'ah al-ḥaqīqiyyah* (original innovations). Examples include the puritanism and celibacy of the clergy and their abstention from wholesome and permissible things as an expression of intense worship of Allah, the rejection of textual injunctions and considered analogies in favour of one's own unique thinking or absolute speculation under the pretext that the intellect—without the assistance of revelation—is able to attain that which would please Allah. In general, *al-bid'ah al-ḥaqīqiyyah* (original innovations) have no justification or proof from the Qur'an, the Sunnah or *ijmā'* (consensus), and have no approval based on considered opinion that is able to link it to the fundamentals of Islam.

What is referred to as *al-bid'ah al-iḍāfiyyah* (an imitative innovation) is far more widespread and enjoys fertile breeding ground amongst people. These are matters that are afflicted by mixed judgment, regarded as Sunnah from one perspective and as *bid'ah* from another. If one considered these matters from a certain perspective, one finds that they are based on a sound principle or a specific text. When considered from another angle, one clearly sees the innovated factor in the form of the fabricated status that encompasses the act. For example, the concluding of the prayer with the recitation of the *tasbīḥ* (glorification, praise, and majesty of Allah)[29] is a practice that is regarded as mandatory (*mandūb*) by scholars—without any difference of opinion—due to the authentic *aḥādīth* that have been transmitted on the issue. The Prophet (ṣ) and his companions used to conclude their prayers in this manner (individually and in silent recitation) until someone came along and systemized these invocations, thinking that one of the worshippers could assemble the people around them in a manner that would bond together the members of the congregation. This led to the appointed person for this *khatam* (conclusion) chanting the invocations and supplications while the congregation of worshippers followed him, reciting *āmīn* before finally departing. The *tasbīḥ* is a Sunnah, but this new form of performing it is an innovation (*bid'ah*). Those who oppose this innovation are of the opinion that the transmitted practices of the Prophet (ṣ) should not be overstepped. Those who indulge in it regard it as a means of joint co-operation in fulfilling a Sunnah, which people in their individual capacities might ignore.

The recitation of Sūrah al-Kahf[30] before the Friday congregational prayer is a similar case. It is well known that the Prophet (ṣ) and his Companions used to strive to perform the obligation of al-Jumu'ah (the Friday congregational prayer). When reaching the *masjid,* they would enter in silence and seat themselves with respect, with unchanging tranquillity and veneration, until they had listened to the sermon and performed the prayer. There is no tradition whatsoever that has been transmitted making the recitation of Sūrah al-Kahf (as is practised by people today) one of the rituals connected with the Friday congregational prayer. However, there are weak traditions that encourage the recitation of this Sūrah, along with others, on Thursday evening or on Friday. Al-Ḥākim reports that the Prophet (ṣ) said: "Whoever recites Sūrah al-Kahf on Friday will have that which is between him and two Fridays filled with light." A similar report mentions Thursday evening instead of Friday.[31] Even if we were to ignore the opinion concerning the weakness of these *aḥādīth* and accept their content, it would not legitimate its observance by gathering people around a reciter in this decisive fashion. The Prophet (ṣ), his righteous companions and the masses of the Muslim community continued practising the rituals of Friday for several centuries without such recitations before or after the prayer. To do what the Prophet (ṣ) had done and to abstain from that which he had abstained from is the Sunnah, liberated from all speculation. Muslims today make the recitation of Sūrah al-Kahf before the Friday prayer a practice that is regulated and systemized, where the best voices are chosen for the recitation, in addition to *fatwas* (juristic opinions) being issued to encourage the practice.

Another imitative innovation is the joining of salutations upon the Prophet (ṣ) with the *adhān* (call to prayer), resulting in lay people thinking that it is part of the *adhān*. The words of the *adhān* are protected, having being specified in authentically narrated texts. In the eras of the Prophet (ṣ), his righteous companions and the communities of our predecessors, the *adhān* was free of any such additions. Salutations upon the Prophet (ṣ) are a separate practice that have their own context, place and rules. When Muslims hear the *adhān* it is mandatory for them to repeat its words, to recite salutations upon the Prophet (ṣ), and to ask Allah to grant him preference, an elevated station and the ability to act as an intercessor. Strange, innovated formulations in salutation of the Prophet (ṣ) have arisen and have been joined with the pronouncement of the *adhān* to bring the two together in a single conjunction. This fabrication has become imposed onto the method of this ritual. Added to this is the dedication shown on the part of the *mu'adhdhin* (caller to prayer) to swaying and chanting while inviting people to Allah. The practice of the *adhān* has thus been transformed into a frivolous tune, having once been a serious, dignified call.

From these examples, we realise that imitative innovations are practices that, in the majority, are taken from established or dubious teachings of the *sharī'ah*, which are then overtaken by actions and fabrications that remove them from their intended framework. The teachings of Islam are like the workings of the body, with its senses and characteristics. If you were to take a leg and put it in the place of a hand, or an ear in the place of the nose, you would cause damage to the body, even if you did not introduce something new from outside the body.

Ash-Shāṭibī summarizes the essence of an imitative innovation as follows: "It has two perspectives: the first is linked to accepted proofs and it is not an innovation in this regard. From the second perspective, it conflicts with appearance, order and position, making it similar to an original innovation. Therefore, because it is not completely independent from any of the above perspectives, it merits being called *al-bid'ah al-iḍāfiyyah* (an imitative innovation)." Indeed, its validity from the perspective of its source is firm, whereas from the perspective of method, conditions and detail, it is not. It may be based on an opposable obscurity or not upon anything specific. This is what makes it objectionable, because all acts of worship are to be rejected if they do not emanate from the Lawgiver.

It is imperative to qualify that the explanation of the general Qur'anic directives by Allah's Prophet (ṣ) by way of his practical actions are not open to any additional considerations, either in principle or form. Ibn Ḥajar was asked about the salutations and greetings after the *adhān* as it is now commonly practised. His reply was: "The principle is a Sunnah, but the method is *bid'ah* (an innovation)." The verse: "O you who believe! Send you salutations and greetings upon him [with the Islamic] way of greeting"(33:56) is not acceptable as a justification for this innovation. We can never be more knowledgeable than the Prophet (ṣ) and his companions concerning the method of acceptable implementation.

Lay people have invented a prayer for the months of Rajab and Sha'bān, which is performed with specific intentions. Some scholars have shown leniency in allowing these prayers, arguing that prayer in general is not a practice that is disapproved of. An-Nawawī said—in condemnation—that these two prayers are, "A spurious, vile and rejected innovation." He then said: "You should not be misled by the fact that they are mentioned in books like *Qūt al-Qulūb* and *Iḥyā' 'Ulūm ad-Dīn*.[32] None has the right to draw evidence for their legitimacy from the Prophet's saying: 'The prayer is the best intention.'[33] This is in specific reference to prayer that does not contradict the law in any way."

Exploiting a general Qur'anic text by using it as a basis for changing an act of worship, enforcing obedience, or portraying devotion in a specific manner contradicts the guidance of Allah's Messenger (ṣ). On this basis, scholars regard the *adhān* inside the *masjid* for the Friday prayers (not the first one over the P.A. system, but the second *adhān*) as an imitative *bid'ah*. The *adhān* in its essence is valid, but in view of the place in which it is being performed, it is an innovation. The raising of the voice while reciting the Qur'an in front of the deceased (*al-janā'iz*) is a similar example. Indeed, invoking Allah and reading His book are part of Islam, but not in this manner or under these circumstances. A similar example is fasting on the 27th of Rajab and the 15th of Sha'bān; the act of fasting is a form of worship but specifying these days is *bid'ah*.

It is apparent that those dedicated to these innovations are blending virtuous actions with vile ones, even if they think that all of their actions are commendable and free from fault. This is only as a result of their ignorance of the position of the Sunnah and their rigidity with regards to what they have learnt through imitating individuals inclined to ignorance and vain desire.

Perhaps what invites the most astonishment concerning such people is the rapidity with which they cast aspersions upon whoever tries to teach them authentic religious practices. If someone tries to strip the *adhān* of the additions that have been joined to it, attempting to return to the practice of the first generation and the Sunnah of the Prophet (ṣ), such a person is accused of expressing dislike for Allah's Messenger (ṣ).

Professor al-'Adawī stated: "One should know that the one who rejects the above-mentioned innovation does so from the second perspective, i.e., the perspective of innovation. What some people say with regards to others, i.e., that he/she rejects the *du'ā'* or *dhikr* or salutations upon the Prophet (ṣ) or the recitation of the Qur'an, are all statements that arise out of ignorance of Islam and ignorance of the intentions of the person who supposedly rejects these practices. They may even be statements that are intended to slander the one who invites to the Sunnah."

He added: "One of my friends informed me about a certain *shaykh* (teacher) who, whenever he wanted to make an example out of one of his peers that taught people Islam, would gather the lay folk and ask them: 'What is your opinion on salutations upon the Prophet?' They would reply: 'It is a part of the religion!' He would then retort that so-and-so (his peer of whom he wanted to make an example) rejected this practice. He would then ask: 'What is your opinion on asking forgiveness and reciting the Qur'an?' They would reply: 'Asking forgiveness is an act of worship and so is the recitation of the Qur'an.' He would then say to them that so-and-so rejected these two practices.

"When the *shaykh* was asked why he had said these things when he, in fact, knew what the person had meant, he replied: 'I want the lay folk to have an aversion towards him so that they do not listen to any of his advice.' This kind of a *muftī* (one who gives legal opinions), in addition to the misguidance and innovation he spreads, is also burdened with the sin of casting accusations of falsehood at people."

Innovations in acts of worship and matters of custom

Our knowledge of the obligatory acts of worship has been conveyed to us by the Lawgiver alone. If there was no revelation pertaining to these matters, we would not have been able to perform them in the clear, ordered manner expounded by the Lawgiver. The five daily prayers, the number of their cycles, their times, their form and manner, are all matters that the religion alone is able to legislate. These, and all other acts of worship, are not open to the dictates of the intellect regarding form and quantity. We may perceive the face of wisdom in many of the required acts of obedience, or come to know the beautiful benefits of performing them as Allah has commanded, but this does not imply the independence of the intellect in judging and speculating on matters concerning worship, whether in general terms or in detail. Deference to the absolute authority of the revealed traditions is required in all of these matters, free from any interference.

Matters of custom, however, have a different status, with reason and experience playing a huge role. Custom was prevalent before the coming of Islam. It may be a great distance away from the guidance of Islam or it may adhere to the limits and ethics propagated by Islam, encouraging the believers to adhere to them as well. Muslims and unbelievers alike engage in eating, drinking, marriage, buying, selling and rental. They also enforce various rules to regulate peace and to administer the development and politics of the state, etc. Even though these examples of customary matters differ from absolute acts of worship in terms of the nature of legislation, Allah has surely not left people to go about them in accordance with the inclinations of personal opinion or desire. Many verses have been revealed in this regard, to guide us to that which protects our interests and prohibits whatever may cause harm.

Islam is a complete, multi-faceted religion. Everything that leaves an impression regarding purification of the self and the safety of society has been exposed and advised on by way of a set of scriptural texts and principles. If the influence of Islam stopped at acts of worship, in which no intellectual exertion is required, thereafter leaving people free to legislate in general or customary matters, it would be like a pathway that does not lead to perfection, failing to protect individuals and communities from injustice, enmity and purposelessness.

Exalted virtues are not forged in the prayer-niche inasmuch as they are forged by refined conduct and lofty traditions. It is no wonder that Islam prescribes many rules pertaining to general customary matters, regarding their implementation as a sign of devotion, just like the implementation of acts of worship. We find thousands of well-ordered statements in the Book of Allah and the Sunnah of His Prophet (ṣ) regarding these general matters, but some people still have the audacity to risk ignoring their value. These directives complement the injunctions on worship, whose teachings are found in other parts of the scriptural texts.

Take marriage as an example. It is a customary matter that all people confront, regardless of their differences in faith. Islam, however, legislates specific rules and religious obligations without which the marriage would not be valid. It is absolutely necessary to have a proposal, acceptance, a bridal-gift, and witnesses. Furthermore, a widowed woman cannot marry in her period of mourning, and if a couple is irrevocably divorced they cannot remarry. In addition, a Muslim woman cannot marry a non-Muslim man, even though a Muslim man can marry Christian and Jewish women. There are also prohibited categories of women with whom a Muslim man cannot contract marriage under any circumstances, as well as ethics regarding sexual relations within marriage that Islam expounds on and that cannot be ignored.

Another example is trade, which is a general practice that everyone without exception is involved in from one perspective or another. Nevertheless, Islam places stipulations upon trade that a Muslim cannot ignore. Contracting parties have to be competent in conducting their affairs, sales have to be clean and beneficial with the items being sold belonging to the seller and fit for sale. There are rulings that prohibit risk, monopoly, usury, and cheating, mapping out for Islamic trade a just and clean path.

People—by their nature—eat, drink and attire themselves. Islam approaches these customary matters by prohibiting certain types of food, drink and clothing. The Qur'an stresses the prohibitions concerning food several times, as well as the disputes with the idolaters, Christians and Jews of the early generation in this regard. The longest verse revealed by Allah in the Qur'an concerns the recording and witnessing of debt. When considering these customary matters, scholars have emphasized that the protection of public welfare is the prime objective and they have relied upon transmitted scriptural texts as well as general principles of legislation for guidance.

Intellectual speculation conforms to the noble law on many common rules of conduct. I have seen texts of classical civil law that have been amended for the needs of contemporary civil law so that—according to the people that have made the amendments—they may be closer to the general welfare. I noticed that sometimes the classical material conformed to the teachings of some prominent jurist, while the adjusted material conformed to the teachings of some other jurist. There is as such no distinction; Muslim jurists—through the strength of their faith in Allah and their desire to achieve His pleasure, as well as their understanding of His Law and their devotion to it for the benefit of humankind—used to judge these customary affairs and deal with them according to the teachings of Islam.

In contrast, men of public law do not pay consideration to the pleasure of Allah, nor do they respect His religion when passing legislation. One therefore notices that the mixing of customs with worship to reflect religious devotion is a part of the nature of our religion. So then, is innovation applicable to conventional practices as it is to acts of worship?

Regarding this, ash-Shāṭibī said:

> It has been entrenched in the principles of the law that all conventional acts are also devotional in some way. This is because any act whose import is not understood in detail—i.e., an act that is ordained or prohibited—is to be regarded as devotional; acts whose import are understood and whose benefits and risks are known are regarded as conventional.
>
> As such, ablution, prayer, fasting and pilgrimage are all acts of religious devotion, whereas buying, selling, divorce, rental and criminal offences are all conventional acts, as their rulings are clearly understandable. However, the latter also consist of a devotional aspect as they are restricted by the law so that the protagonist has no freedom of choice, whether dealing with a compulsory or a voluntary matter. Indeed, even voluntary acts pertaining to devotional matters are binding, just as compulsory acts are binding, according to the proofs laid down in my book, *al-Muwāfaqāt*.
>
> It is thus apparent that there is participation of both divisions, i.e., devotional acts have devotional and conventional aspects. Thus, if an innovation appears in matters of convention,

it would be correct to apply it to conventional acts just as it is applicable to devotional acts. If not, then it would not apply.

Therefore, conventional matters of life have two aspects to them. First, that which is progressive, proceeding in submission to development and change. Islam places no restrictions on this aspect and is not concerned with compliance or innovation. It would be correct to quote, in this regard, the *ḥadīth*: "You know best the matters pertaining to you world."[34] This aspect is not the subject of our research. We do, however, strongly advise Muslims to engage in these matters with all of their hearts and with good intention. If a man follows the best example, he is able to benefit from everything in order to attain his goals. If the Muslim sought the pleasure of Allah through his actions, then all his efforts are acts of worship. His eating, sleeping, playing and marriage are all worship, over and above the burdens of his work if he is employed, or his business transactions or farming if he is a businessman or farmer. These purely conventional matters are overtaken by noble intentions based on piety and goodness as if they were prayer or *jihād* (exertion in the path of religion), in spite of remaining, in essence, free from all restrictions and unqualified by any specific agency or form. Innovation and excellence transform such matters from that which is good into that which is better.

As for the second aspect, the boundaries that are drawn by the Lawgiver, whether narrow or wide, have to be complied with and we have to adhere to whatever has been related to us on these matters in accordance with what the Lawgiver regards as closer to public welfare. This transmitted aspect should not be transgressed upon by disobedience nor corrupted by innovations. Islam does not intervene in ordinary matters of convention such as business, social matters, penal matters or political matters so as to bring hardship to people; intervention is for the express purpose of lifting hardship and to block the path of Satan, thereby protecting the masses from the fluidity of human-made laws that sometimes submit to peculiar impulses.

One might ask: What is the position of innovation in this case? Some people claim that they exaggerate and add to conventions and their transmitted forms so as to draw closer to Allah. Thus, they ask, how could they be creating innovations in conventional matters when the role of the Lawgiver is only to order (or administer) purely civil matters?

In response, it must be said that when people emphasize specific interests (or welfares) as if they were divine ordinances, relying upon them as acts of worship, they thereby guarantee the perpetuation of the acts through the use of Allah's name since it is not possible to perpetuate it in the name of the specific interest or welfare itself. For example, consider the system of monarchy in any nation. It is only the desire of the sovereign to perpetuate this system that causes him to safeguard it in the name of Allah and His Prophet (ṣ). As a result, leadership of the nation is inherited as one would inherit any other legacy. Oaths of allegiance are sworn for this purpose and are regarded as drawing one closer to Allah; abstaining from doing so is regarded as being detrimental to Islam. Since the inheritance of position is not advocated by Islam, how can it be one of its laws? This is an example of a forbidden innovation in matters of convention, as has been determined by scholars.

Another example is the enforcement of taxes and the application of its revenues according to personal whim, after it has been collected from the masses under the pretence of obedience to Allah, His Prophet and those in authority. To portray such acts to the common masses as if they have to be abided by, as one abides by other legitimate requirements of Islam, is the basis for regarding such acts as *bid'ah*.

One might ask: how does one regard such matters if they do not fall victim to such misleading portrayals? Our response is that one should consider such matters in light of what is established in the religious texts and borne out of its principles. If it conflicts with this, then it is sinful, but if not, then it is part of modern matters of convention in which religion plays no role. As a result, we can say that the enforcement of taxes according to personal whim is no different from stealing and looting, but implementing taxes for the welfare of the masses is not blameworthy in any way. We can state further that if a nation was allowed to establish its system of governance on the basis of a monarchy—as in England—where the absolute welfare overrules the monarchy, then one cannot regard its proponents as being obedient to Allah or its opponents as being sinful. This is regarded as a matter of convention that Islam does not oppose.

Professor al-'Adawī said: "Similar to (innovation with regards to convention) is the adornment of *masjids* with colours that distract the hearts of worshippers, or carpets with the kind of patterns that preoccupy the worshipper, or adornments of exorbitant value. If indeed, as many people believe, this is done to elevate the houses of Allah and is regarded as spending in the path of Allah, the Most High, then it becomes an innovation that is despised. Administering the *masjids* by strengthening their buildings and adorning them appropriately, cleaning their walls and painting them in colours that do not distract the worshipper, carpeting them with carpets that are moderately priced, etc., does not stir up controversy and is regarded as maintenance. Those who believe in Allah and the Last day spend of their wealth in this manner."

In a sentence: innovation that enters matters of convention does so from the perspective in which it may carry implications of religious devotion. The matter goes back to the fact that despicable innovations do not prevail in matters that are purely conventional. From this, one is able to establish the rulings on innovation pertaining to matters of eating, drinking, walking and sleeping. These are all conventional matters that have been infused with religious devotion. The Lawgiver has restricted them with ordinances that are obligatory, like the prohibition of lengthening one's garment out of vanity or pride, or the recitation of the name of Allah when commencing eating and drinking and the prohibition of wasting food, or the prohibition of sleeping naked on the terrace, etc. All the matters recollected are conventional; if they become infused by innovations then it is not from the conventional perspective but rather from the perspective pertaining to the directives regarding these matters as established by the Lawgiver. If there is deviation from the legislated practice, which is now also regarded as a religious practice by which one gains closeness to Allah, then this is to be regarded as an innovation. It is, in fact, both a transgression and a *bid'ah*: a transgression because it contradicts the legislated practice of the Lawgiver and a *bid'ah* (heretical innovation) because it is taken as an act of religious devotion in this contradictory form.

Are there established practices (*sunan*) in matters of convention?

When religion intervenes in ordinary matters of life, it does so within limits sufficient to maintain morality and to preserve welfare. It does not aim to limit freedom of creativity or ingenuity, or to impede human activity. Do the civil laws legislated and implemented in courts in the East and West aim to shackle the mind or suppress the desire of discovery? Do the social conventions that are conformed to today with regards to behaviour, visiting, invitations and similar practices aim to cause one to live within the cruelty of fanaticism and coercion? The intervention of Islam in these matters is similar in many ways to these laws and conventions, which are so easily accepted by people. Pronouncements of the Prophet (ṣ) on the ethics of eating, for example, are similar to the table manners practiced by the elite; both share the same objective!

However, some Muslims are mistaken in their understanding of the relationship between their religion and these conventions. There are some who think that everything new after the Prophet (ṣ) is to be regarded as an innovation and must be rejected; others interpret certain conventions that were practised by the Prophet (ṣ) as if they are part of Islam and regard clinging to them as religious devotion or as something that gains one closeness to Allah. Both parties are wrong. Surely it is not permitted to reject or drive people away from conventions that were introduced after the era of the Prophet (ṣ) and his companions; such conventions are not *bidʿah* in the sense that the law rejects.

For example, the first four innovations that reportedly occurred after the death of the Prophet (ṣ) were: the use of sieves (to sift flour, wheat; etc), satiation (i.e., to eat to one's fullest), washing of the hands with *al-ashnān* (a plant that was used as soap is today) after eating, and eating at tables. We do not know why these four acts were mentioned or why they were feared. Abū Ḥāmid al-Ghazālī said in response:

> We do not hold that eating at tables is prohibited (either by way of dislike or in the absolute sense)[35] as such prohibition has not been established. Concerning the view that this was an innovation that occurred after the era of the Prophet (ṣ), it must be stated that not every innovation is prohibited. Prohibition pertains to any *bidʿah* that contradicts an established Sunnah or removes and replaces a legislative ordinance. Innovations are sometimes required in certain circumstances or under changing conditions. A table does no more then elevate food off the ground to make eating easier. There is nothing detestable in this. These four acts, which have been grouped together as innovations, are not all the same. *Al-ashnān* is good because it promotes and facilitates cleanliness and constitutes part of washing, which is a desirable action. It was not used before because people were not used to it or because it was not well known. Sieves are used to improve food, which is allowed, and cannot be considered an excessive luxury. Finally, satiation, which is the most potent of these four, arouses the passions and circulates illness in the body.

In truth, Abū Ḥāmid's defence is unsound, even though it has noble objectives. He affirms the view that regards something that is new by way of convention as *bidʿah*. He then links what comes forth from this with results, either good or bad. In our opinion, this labelling should be rejected from the beginning as we have clearly shown the limits of what is a false innovation in Allah's religion. Abū Ḥāmid is of the opinion that eating on the floor is better than eating at the table, consoling himself with the fact that the Prophet (ṣ) never ate at a table. I regard both situations as equal, as both are conventions that are not related to religious devotion. The path of closeness to Allah is far away from all of these matters. If there was something objectionable about eating at a table there would have been a prohibition against it and if there was something good about eating on the floor then it would have been obligated.

At this point we ask: Are there conventions followed by the Messenger of Allah (ṣ) that are to be regarded as religious matters, where the implementer is rewarded and the abstainer is sinful? Scholars have elaborated on this issue. They have agreed that whatever the Prophet (ṣ) had done within the limits of his own unique nature as a human being does not impact upon the community in any way and we are not obligated to follow his example in these matters. It is known, for example, that Khālid ibn al-Walīd ate lizard. The Prophet (ṣ) felt disgusted by this as it was not customary to do so amongst his people. Yet Khālid—by this action—did not commit anything shameful.[36]

As for the practices of the Prophet (ṣ) that are unrelated to his stated purpose of conveyance of the message from Allah, or the instructing of people, or the confirmation of divine ordinances, it is affirmed that in these matters as well, people are not obligated to do what he did or abstain from that which he abstained from. Before we quote statements of the scholars in this regard, we want to point out that sentiment that is inflamed by love may sometimes obligate upon itself things that Allah does not obligate upon any of his creatures. It is narrated that 'Abdullah ibn 'Umar used to search for the paths that were travelled by the Prophet (ṣ) so that he may travel upon them. He also sought out the places in which the Prophet (ṣ) had isolated himself, so that he might sit in them, and for no other purpose. Ibn 'Umar thus obligates upon himself things that are not obligatory. The majority of the Prophet's Companions did not incline towards such actions nor see in them any means of gaining closeness to Allah!

'Abdullah ibn 'Umar is similar—with regards to these actions—to Mu'āwiyah ibn Qurrah and his father. Ibn Ḥabbān narrated the following from Mu'āwiyah ibn Qurrah, who narrated from his father: "I came to Allah's Messenger (ṣ) in a group from (the place of) Muzaynah and we pledged allegiance to him." The narrator of the *ḥadīth* said: "I never saw Mu'āwiyah or his son—in winter and in summer—except with their mantles unwrapped."[37] No one has ever said that this action is a Sunnah and its application by some of the Companions does not obligate it upon us in any way.

Scholars have expressed conflicting views concerning actions of the Prophet (ṣ) that do not reflect the objective of gaining closeness to Allah. Some scholars say that such acts are mandatory while others say that one is allowed to either perform them or to abstain. Some exaggerate and say that it is obligatory to perform these actions while others abstain from passing any judgment at all. In my opinion, the correct view has been expressed by al-Āmidī—in his book *al-Aḥkām*—which is supported by al-'Adawī in his precise treatise on innovations and established practices. This view holds that: "A straightforward act of the Prophet (ṣ) does not hold proof as an act of piety. All that it indicates is that such an act is simply not forbidden." Therefore, regarding such an act as one of piety is another matter.

The companions were the most learned of people concerning religion and the most devoted to following Allah's Messenger (ṣ) in all acts of piety. They used to observe the actions of the Prophet (ṣ) and whatever appeared to them as acts that were not devotional in intent would not be regarded as part of the religion or as a ritual obligation and they would also refrain from encouraging people to perform such actions. There are many such examples:

When the Prophet (ṣ) migrated to Madīnah he travelled along the coastal route because it was the furthest away from his enemy. If a straightforward act like this indicated devotional piety then everyone travelling from Makkah to Madīnah would have been required to use the coastal road in imitation of the Prophet (ṣ), even if that route is longer! But none of the companions have advocated this, proving that it is not an established religious practice.

The Prophet (ṣ) and one of his Companions had hidden in a cave from their idolatrous enemies. They spent several days in it, worshipping Allah, until they were able to continue their journey. If this straightforward act was to be regarded as mandatory then the companions would have gone to that cave to worship Allah, just as the Prophet (ṣ) had done. Since it has not been transmitted to us that any of the companions went to the cave to worship, we know that worship in that specific cave is not a requirement and that a straightforward act does not imply devotional piety.

It is narrated on the authority of Anas: "The Messenger of Allah used to have straps on his sandals." This is reported by the five authorities of *hadīth* with the exception of Muslim.[38] The report describes the Prophet's shoes. Therefore, is wearing such shoes an established religious practice? Does one regard whoever chooses not to wear them as a rejecter of a Sunnah? Or are there none that express such an opinion?

It is known that, before the Battle of Badr, when the Messenger of Allah (ṣ) had camped at the waterhole nearest to Badr, al-Ḥubāb ibn al-Mundhir said to him: "O Messenger of Allah, has this position been indicated to you by Allah and we therefore have no choice in moving forward or retreating from it, or is it your opinion; and know that war is about strategy? The Prophet (ṣ) replied that it was his opinion and that war was indeed about strategy. Al-Ḥubāb then suggested changing the campsite to a more appropriate position. The Prophet (ṣ) said to him: "You have indicated your opinion," and then the Prophet (ṣ) adopted it.[39]

These examples show that some of the actions of the Prophet (ṣ) are based on his own judgment and are not guided by revelation. Muslims are not expected to conform strictly to such actions. They should express their opinions concerning such matters, and then do what they feel is correct. The Prophet (ṣ) approved of this practice and even implemented it.[40]

Inserting ordinary matters of convention into the sphere of Islam is undoubtedly harmful to Allah's religion as well as to the worldly affairs of people. It harms Islam because it widens the circle of acts of worship in a manner that is based on pure fantasy. Such false acts of devotional piety cannot draw one closer to Allah.

Those who are knowledgeable about Islam know that the aspects of conveyance (*al-balāgh*) and explanation (*al-bayān*) in the Prophet's biography are laden with examples that purify the self and awaken one's determination. Both these aspects cannot accommodate exaggeration. In my opinion, such exaggeration in conventional matters is no more than a covering for short-sighted people who avoid performing obligatory and mandatory acts. You might see someone that is incapacitated when it comes to following the example of the Prophet (ṣ) in purifying the self and striving against the enemy. However, he would leave this clearly established practice (Sunnah) and take the Prophet's love for sweets—for example—as a practice for emulation and to express his extreme love and devotion to following the legacy of Allah's Messenger (ṣ).

Many conventions followed by Allah's Messenger (ṣ) may well have been in submission to the requirements of the environment or context within which he lived. That is, they are actions that apply equally to Muslims and idolaters who happened to live in the same hot climatic region. If white garments are good for repelling heat and if one extends his head-covering at the back to avoid the blaze of the sun, is it then recommended that inhabitants of cold regions wear white and extend their head-coverings to their shoulders because the Prophet (ṣ) had done so? The truth is that these conventions—whether practised or preached—are not part of the message of Islam. People's livelihoods are harmed by such a parochial understanding because worldly matters are founded upon constant change. These changes should be pursued by free inquiry or else they will be touched by shortcoming and neglect. To regard some of these matters as a constitutive part of Islam is a stagnant judgment that leads to intellectual and developmental paralysis that can have dangerous consequences.

The various shackles that Muslims latch upon themselves in the name of Islam is perhaps the main reason for their backwardness in certain fields. They have, thus, become imprisoned by self-imposed shackles, unable to move, while others have progressed without any impediments. Muslims lost their spiritual and intellectual essence, which is the heart of Islam, in the time spent bound by these false shackles. Their bonds with both Islam and worldly matters thus weakened and they were defeated in both spheres.

We will conclude this topic by quoting an all-encompassing study undertaken by Shaykh Maḥmūd Shaltūt, in which he summarized the subject in a learned manner, presenting it with precision and brevity. He states:

We have learnt from the history of Islamic Law that corruption caused by *bid'ah* sets in from three different perspectives:

a. From the perspective of *'aqīdah* (belief), where *shirk* (association with and worship of other deities by supplicating and seeking refuge and assistance from them instead of Allah) has manifested itself;

b. From the perspective of *'ibādah* (worship), where changes in the manner of performing acts of worship by either additions or shortcomings have manifested themselves; and

c. From the perspective of *ḥalāl* and *ḥarām* (lawful and prohibited), where the prohibition of that which is lawful and vice versa, has manifested itself.

The researcher that inquires into the reasons that lead to *bid'ah* (heretical innovation) finds that certain factors result in innovation from the outset, while other factors assist to spread the imperatives of the innovator after the onset of these innovations. We will clarify both matters.

Causes of innovation

1. Lack of knowledge of the sources of religious rulings, or lack of knowledge in terms of understanding these rulings in light of their sources.
2. Following prejudices or biases when deriving religious rulings.
3. Favouring rationalization over established practice in matters of religion.

We will discuss all of these causes briefly.

The first cause—lack of knowledge of the sources of religious rulings

We would like—before discussing the various defects arising from these causes—to establish the following:

a. The sources of legislative rulings—as is well known—are the Book of Allah (the Qur'an) and the Prophetic practice (Sunnah), in addition to consensus (*ijmāʿ*) and analogy (*qiyās*).
b. The general principle for all these sources, which overrides all others, is that Allah's book has the highest priority, followed by the Sunnah, then consensus and, finally, analogy.
c. Analogy (*qiyās*) is not resorted to in rulings pertaining to acts of worship because one of its pillars is that the ruling should be causative (*maʿlūl*), meaning that it is found elsewhere as well; acts of worship are based on pure devotion as they serve the purpose of genuine trial.

The defects arising out of the first cause can be ascribed to four factors:

a. Unfamiliarity with the conventions of the Arabic language.
b. Ignorance of the Prophetic tradition.
c. Ignorance of the rank of analogy.

d.   Ignorance of the position of analogy.

a.   *Unfamiliarity with the conventions of the Arabic language* led to certain texts being understood incorrectly, resulting in the innovation of practices unknown to our predecessors. A few examples follow:

1. The claim by some that only the flesh (*laḥm*) of swine is prohibited and not its fat (*shaḥm*), on the assumption that the Qur'an prohibits the *laḥm* (flesh) only. This is an innovation arising from ignorance of the fact that the word *laḥm* in Arabic applies to fat as well, but not the other way round.

2. Some dialectic theologians claim that Allah has a "side" (*janb*), based on the verse: "Lest a person should say: 'Alas, my grief that I was undutiful to Allah (*mā farraṭtu fī janbbillāh*)'" (39:56). This innovation arises from ignorance of the fact that the Arabs do not define *janb* in this linguistic construction as a reference to that well-known part of the anatomy. When you say: "This is small alongside that," you mean: "in comparison to it". It is unimaginable that such negligence could occur in respect to *janbbillah* (literally, side of Allah), such that it is understood as a reference to a part of body anatomy. It is, therefore, necessary to interpret *janb* as referring to "aspect". Imam ar-Rāzī wrote in his tafsīr: "*Al-janb* is called *janb* because it is an aspect of something. If something is a necessary component or part of something it is an aspect of it. Because of the similarity that occurred between *al-janb* in the sense of anatomical part, and in the sense of being a necessary component of something or a part of it, there is surely no harm in referring to *janb* as 'the right (of)' and 'to enjoin obedience to'."

3. The Prophet (ṣ) said: "If you hear the *mu'adhdhin* (caller to prayer), then repeat his utterances and thereafter recite

salutations upon me."[41] Some people thus hold that this *ḥadīth* requires the *mu'adhdhin* to recite salutations upon the Prophet (ṣ) after the *adhān*. However, they do not ask him to recite it in a manner different from the *adhān*—which is recited aloud, thereby implying that it is permissible to recite it in the same way. They direct the intent of the *ḥadīth* at the *mu'adhdhin* by holding that the address in the Prophet's statement "recite salutations upon me" is applicable to all Muslims including the *mu'adhdhin*. Or, that the Prophet's expression "If you hear" includes the *mu'adhdhin* because he hears himself.

These are a few examples that illustrate how heretical innovation arises due to unfamiliarity with the Arabic language, either in its vocabulary or in its stylistic conventions. The early scholars unanimously agree that knowledge of the intricacies of the Arabic language—upon which understanding of the Qur'an and Sunnah depend—is an essential prerequisite for exercising *ijtihād* (reasoned opinion), as well as for dealing with and approaching legal texts.

b. *Lack of Knowledge of the Prophetic tradition* encompasses the following:

1. Lack of knowledge of authentic *aḥādīth*; and
2. Lack of knowledge of the position of the Sunnah in legislation.

The first leads to the proscribing of rulings that have been established by such *aḥādīth* and the second results in the proscribing of authentic *aḥādīth* and the failure to implement them. They are then substituted by innovations that have no basis in legislation. The following *ḥadīth* draws attention to this: "Surely Allah does not withdraw knowledge by snatching it away from people. Rather, He withdraws knowledge by seizing the scholars. When there are no scholars left, people take as their leaders the unlearned who, if they are questioned, answer with no knowledge, thereby misguiding themselves and others."[42]

Another *ḥadīth* relates: "Every messenger that is sent forth by Allah has, from amongst his people, disciples and companions that imitate his way and follow his ordinances. After them come people who say that which they do not do, and do other than that which is ordained. Whoever strives against such people with his hand is a believer; whoever strives against them with his tongue is a believer; whoever strives against them with his heart is a believer. Beyond this there remains not even the equivalent of a mustard seed in faith."[43]

c. *Lack of knowledge of the rank of analogy (qiyās) in the sources of legislation. Qiyās* comes after the Sunnah, but it may happen that people use analogy even though an established Sunnah addresses the issue at hand. By failing to draw upon the established Sunnah, they are led to innovation (*bid‘ah*). Anyone familiar with the discussions of the jurists will find many examples of this type. The clearest example relates to the view expressed by some who draw an analogy between the *mu'adhdhin* and the listener on the issue of salutations upon the Prophet (ṣ) after the call to prayer. They thus insist that the *mu'adhdhin* should recite the salutations aloud as well, in spite of the fact that the Sunnah—which should be given priority over *qiyās*—does not validate such a position.[44] In addition, the *ḥadīth* "when you hear the *mu'adhdhin*" indicates by way of its style of expression that it refers to the listeners specifically, and requires them to recite salutations after the *adhān*.

d. *Lack of knowledge of the position of qiyās (analogy) in legislation.* This came about as a result of jurists from the later eras drawing analogies from acts of worship. They thus established acts that had no precedent in the Sunnah and which were never before reported to have been carried out even though there were no impediments blocking their implementation or the possibility of their implementation.

A good example is the innovation of omitting the prayer by drawing an analogy with the permissibility of compensation for missing the fast, for which there is a textual precedent. These jurists did not stop at the point of permissibility; they expanded this and legislated juristic ploys that stripped prayer of all its spirit and effect. This innovation is one of the strangest and is appropriately referred to as a compound innovation (*al-bid'ah al-murakkabah*), pertaining to an essential ruling but containing a ploy to drop the mandatory status of the ruling for the innovator. It then regards both matters—the innovation and the ploy—as part of Islam, even though they cancel an obligation and place it beyond the sphere of obligatory responsibility but still regard it as being open to the reward that Allah has prepared for those who believe and do righteous deeds.

The second cause—following personal prejudices or biases when deriving rulings

This is brought about when the person researching rulings succumbs to his own biases, resulting in the verification of a ruling that fulfils his own objectives by seeking proofs that he is able to rely on and argue by. In reality, this validates prejudice as a principle. It infringes upon proof and judges against it, thereby overthrowing legislative proceedings and corrupting the objectives of the Lawgiver with respect to the setting up of evidence. The principle position is to derive rulings from evidence or proof and not to decide upon rulings and then search for supporting evidence.

Following personal prejudice causes deviation from Allah's straight path: "And who is more astray than one who follows his own prejudices, without any guidance from Allah?" (28:50). It is also narrated in an authentic tradition that the Prophet (ṣ) said: "None of you (truly) believes until his personal prejudices submit to that which I have come with."[45] Most of the innovations arising from this cause are introduced by greedy individuals who serve kings and heads-of-state, with the intention of gaining worldly wealth. Perhaps most of the associated subterfuges—from which Islam is completely absolved—can be traced back to this cause. The *adhān* of the Sultan and similar innovations that we do not see except in prayers for kings and sultans is not a far-fetched example. Other examples include innovations such as portable thrones and gatherings on commemorative nights[46] sanctioned by the ruling authority and which are probably due to the wishes of a king or a recommendation of someone close to him. These practices were then inherited by the coming generation and passed on, generation after generation. It thus became common practice amongst the masses, who came to regard it as a part of the religion and rejected whoever denied these practices.

In reality, the following of personal prejudice is the worst attack against religion as it kills all good. Innovations arising from it are the most sinful in the sight of Allah and the greatest transgression against the truth. How much corruption has personal prejudice brought to laws? How much has it transformed religions? And how far has it carried human beings into clear misguidance? The innovator who succumbs to personal prejudice is undoubtedly affiliated with those who Allah describes in the following verses: "And buy not with my verses a small price. And mix not truth with falsehood, nor conceal the truth while you know (it)" (2:41-2).

"Verily, those who conceal what Allah has sent down of the Book, and purchase a small gain therewith (of worldly things), they eat into their bellies nothing but fire. Allah will not speak to them on the day of Resurrection, nor purify them, and theirs will be a painful torment. Those are they who have purchased error at the price of guidance and torment at the price of forgiveness. So how bold they are (for evil deeds which will push them) to the fire. That is because Allah has sent down the Book (the Qur'an) in truth. And verily, those who disputed as regards the Book are far away in opposition" (2:174-6).

The third cause of innovation—favouring rationalization in matters of religion

Allah has placed a limitation upon the mind and has not made it possible for it to perceive everything. Certain things remain completely incomprehensible whereas others are comprehended on the surface, without full grasp of the essence. In spite of this innate shortcoming, the mind is able to perfectly comprehend realities that Allah has given it the ability to grasp. Perceptive abilities amongst individuals vary to a large degree. For this reason, it is necessary—on issues that are incomprehensible to the mind and on which perceptive abilities vary—to be able to refer to a truthful informer who compels the mind to submit to his miraculous authority. Such a person is none other than the Prophet (ṣ), assisted by Allah, who knows everything and has absolute knowledge of what He has created.

In accordance with this principle, Allah has sent forth his prophets to make clear to humankind that which pleases their Creator and which guarantees their happiness. It also ensures for them a great share of the goodness of this life and of the hereafter. In spite of this, people have deviated from this principle. They have elevated the mind above the level that has been predetermined by Allah. They have, in fact, made the mind Allah's authoritative source over his servants and use it to judge matters of revelation that they did not fully comprehend. They then employed it in matters of legislation and rejected anything in the transmitted traditions that they were not able to gain familiarity with by way of their intellects. They then went further, regarding the intellect as one of the sources of divine legislation. As such, they made permissible by way of their intellects that which Allah did not permit and what we have no way of knowing will ensure His pleasure.

They introduced innovations in acts of worship that were supported by their scrutinisation of the hidden underlying intentions and wisdom of the divine legislation as explained by other scholars. They thus alleged that these underlying intentions were what motivated Allah in legislating a ruling. As such, they legislated other acts of worship as a means of realizing the same underlying intentions and which were derived from what had already been legislated by Allah. Much innovation has occurred by this means.

By the judgment of this limited intellect, many matters of the hereafter that have been mentioned in authentic *aḥādīth* (traditions) have been rejected, such as the *ṣirāṭ* (path), the *mīzān* (scale), the resurrection of the body, bodily punishments and pleasures, beholding Allah, and other such examples that cannot be encompassed by the intellect because it has not been created to be able to perceive these matters.

Similarly, by the judgment of this limited intellect, many of the rulings of the Sunnah have been discarded in pursuit of other rulings that are sounder—in their opinion—for fulfilling the required objectives of religious obligation. Also, by the judgment of this limited intellect, many acts of worship and practices, which were unknown to the most devoted of worshippers, have been established.

Just as innovations are caused by the shortcomings of the intellect, or under the pretence that underlying intentions motivate and justify legislating innovations, so too are they caused by the desire to repel a forbidden action or transgress upon an established norm. As such, innovations arise that preoccupy people and prevent them from revolting against forbidden acts under the assumption that an innovation—based on a permissible act—is better than committing a forbidden action. Examples include the recitation of the Qur'an in the *masjid* and the recitation of supplications (*du'ā'*) in front of the funeral bier (*al-janāzah*) in a loud voice to prevent—as they claim—people from chattering about worldly matters in the *masjid* and graveyard. Innovations introduced with the intention of acquiring extra reward from Allah are also of this category. The underlying assumption is that the sought-after reward burdens the person with a similar difficulty as the actions by which the person worships Allah. The first variation is to link that which is not enacted to that which is enacted, because it augments the objectives of the legislation. Examples include:

a. To fast without *suḥūr* (i.e., eating before sunrise) because it increases the challenge of overcoming one's desires, which is the objective of the legislation of fasting.

b. Religious devotion through denying oneself permitted adornments or beautification—which are not allowed by Allah—because it augments the intended wisdom behind the prohibition of adorning oneself with gold and silk.

Other examples of this variation are:

a. To choose the more difficult of two choices in the case of conflicting narrations, even though the practice of the Prophet (ṣ) was to choose the easier of the two choices when such a case arose.

b. To regard all of the actions of the Prophet (ṣ) as devotional—therefore meriting emulation—even though many of them are conventional and therefore do not require emulation.

The second variation includes choosing gruelling acts of worship that the Lawgiver has not commanded, like continuous fasting, instituting celibacy or abstaining from marriage and adherence to recommended acts and practices as if they were obligatory. The Prophet (ṣ) warned against all of this: "What is wrong with people that go beyond my actions. I swear by Allah that I am more knowledgeable than them concerning Allah and more fearful than them of Him."[47] He (ṣ) also said: "None is able to add to this religion without finally being overcome."[48]

The Prophet (ṣ) also retorted "Do not be too strict upon yourselves as Allah may then be strict upon you,"[49] in response to Ibn 'Umar and a group of believers that were arguing about worship practices and wanted to burden themselves by excessive devotion. People have neglected these warnings and have invented for themselves acts of worship, methods of worship, and specific devotions for worshipping Allah. They teach these practices to their followers as if these were a very important part of the religion and ignore the fact that devotion to Allah is only achievable through compliance to Allah's laws and codes. Devotional practices are restricted to that which He has legislated and which has been transmitted by his faithful Messenger (ṣ). By undertaking such actions, these people are guilty of *bid'ah* (heretical innovation) and transgression and have prevented themselves from attaining the rewards for righteous deeds. They are thus guilty of wrongdoing.

All the causes of *bid'ah* that we have recollected thus far are addressed in the following *ḥadīth*, where the Prophet (ṣ) said: "This knowledge is carried in every generation by the most fair-minded; they refute the corruption of extremists, the impersonation of fabricators and the interpretation of the ignorant."[50] The *corruption of extremists* refers to strictness and extravagance. The *impersonation of fabricators* refers to favouring rationalization over established practices in matters of religion and succumbing to personal prejudices. The *interpretation of the ignorant* refers to lack of knowledge of the sources of legislation and the conventions of understanding them in light of these sources."

We have explained this in sufficient detail earlier so as to draw the attention of the believer and to help him avoid such practices.

Notes
1. *Ṣaḥīḥ Muslim*, Book of Friday Prayer, ḥadīth no. 1435.
2. *Sunan Ibn Mājah*, Introduction, ḥadīth no. 45.

3. *Sunan at-Tirmidhī*, Book of Ethics, ḥadīth no.2662.
4. *Sunan at-Tirmidhī*, Book of Qur'anic Exegesis, ḥadīth no. 3020.
5. *Ṣaḥīḥ Muslim*, Book of Alms, ḥadīth no.1691.
6. *Sunan ad-Dārimī*, Introduction, ḥadīth no. 219.
7. *Musnad Aḥmad*, ḥadīth no. 16356.
8. *Sunan Abū Dāwūd*, Book of Prophetic Practice, ḥadīth no. 3995.
9. *Sunan Abū Dāwūd*, Book of Prophetic Tradition, ḥadīth no. 3996.
10. *Ṣaḥīḥ Muslim*, Book of Alms, ḥadīth no. 1691.
11. *As-Silsilāh aḍ-Ḍaʿīfah*, al-Albānī, ḥadīth no. 533.
12. *Sunan ad-Dārimī*, Introduction, ḥadīth no. 512.
13. *Musnad Aḥmad*, ḥadīth no. 21326.
14. *Riyāḍ aṣ-Ṣāliḥīn*, an-Nawawī, critically appraised by al-Albānī, ḥadīth no. 1841. Also included in an-Nawawī's *Forty Hadith*, no. 30.
15. *Sunan ad-Dārimī*, Introduction, ḥadīth no. 143.
16. *Sunan ad-Dārimī*, Introduction, ḥadīth no. 206. See also *as-Silsilāh aṣ-Ṣaḥīḥah*, al-Albānī, 5/115.
17. *Kitāb al-ʿIlm*, Abū Khaythamah, critically appraised by al-Albānī as correct.
18. *Ṣaḥīḥ al-Bukhārī*, Book of Reconciliation, ḥadīth no. 2459.
19. *Ṣaḥīḥ Muslim*, Book of Judgements, ḥadīth no. 3243.
20. The Gold Coast was a British colony in West Africa from 1821 to 1957. It became the independent West African state of Ghana in 1957 [Translator].
21. "And those who take helpers besides Allah (say): 'We Worship them only that they may bring us near to Allah'" (39:3) [Translator].
22. *Musnad Aḥmad*, ḥadīth no. 15115.
23. The obligatory limitations that are however expressed are a right of Allah, decreed by Him, with no room for the exercising of personal opinion in the matter.
24. This practice—as described—is still prevalent in the Arab world and is referred to as *Taʿziyyah* (lit. condolence or consolation). In other parts of the Muslim world it may take different forms [Translator].
25. *Ṣaḥīḥ al-Bukhārī*, Book of the *Tarāwīḥ* Prayer, ḥadīth no. 1871.
26. Shaykh al-Ghazālī probably has the following *ḥadīth* in mind: "Follow the example of these two after me, Abū Bakr and ʿUmar." It is narrated by at-Tirmidhī, in the book of virtues (see also *Tuḥfah al-Aḥwadhī*, vol. 10, p. 102, *ḥadīth* no. 3906) [Translator].
27. *Riyāḍ aṣ-Ṣāliḥīn*, an-Nawawī, critically appraised by al-Albānī, ḥadīth no. 1841. Also included in an-Nawawī's *Forty Hadith*, no. 30.
28. *Al-bidʿah al-ḥaqīqiyyah* literally translates as *real innovation*, while *al-bidʿah al-iḍāfiyyah* would be literally rendered as a *relative innovation*. The latter term's literal translation is especially problematic since "relative" may be construed as not so bad, which

is exactly the opposite of what is intended. I have therefore chosen to render *al-bid'ah al-ḥaqīqiyyah* as an *original innovation*, and *al-bid'ah al-iḍāfiyyah* as an *imitative innovation*. These terms capture the intended meaning far more accurately, as is apparent from the way they are defined by the author [Translator].

29. By reciting the invocations: *Subḥānallāh*, *Alḥamdulillāh* and *Allāhuakbar* [Translator].

30. The 18th chapter of the Qur'an [Translator].

31. *Sunan ad-Dārimī*, Book of Virtues of the Qur'an, ḥadīth no. 3273. Ibn Kathīr states in his Tafsīr: "Reported by Ibn Mardawayh and Sa'īd ibn Manṣūr. This *ḥadīth* is probably *marfū'* (attributed to the Prophet, but not actually his pronouncement); in the best of conditions, this is a statement of Abū Sa'īd al-Khudrī."

32. *Qūt al-Qulūb* is a famous tract by Abū Ṭālib al-Makkī and *Iḥyā 'Ulūm ad-Dīn* was written by the 12th century reformer, Abū Ḥāmid al-Ghazālī [Translator].

33. *Musnad Aḥmad*, ḥadīth no. 20572.

34. *Ṣaḥīḥ Muslim*, Book of Virtues, ḥadīth no. 4358.

35. *Nahī Kirāhah* and *Nahī Taḥrīm*—are jurisprudential categories of prohibition, the first translates literally as prohibition by way of detestation or dislike and the second as absolute prohibition [Translator].

36. *Ṣaḥīḥ al-Bukhārī*, Book of Foods, ḥadīth no. 4972.

37. *Sunan Abū Dāwūd*, Book of Clothing, ḥadīth no. 3560.

38. *Ṣaḥīḥ al-Bukhārī*, Book of Clothing, ḥadīth no. 5460; *Sunan at-Tirmidhī*, Book of Clothing, ḥadīth no. 1695; *Sunan Abū Dāwūd*, Book of Clothing, ḥadīth no. 3605; *Sunan Ibn Mājah*, Book of Clothing, ḥadīth no. 3604; *Sunan an-Nisā'ī*, Book of Adornments, ḥadīth no. 5273.

39. Narrated by Ibn Hishām from Ibn Isḥāq, critically appraised by al-Albānī: see Shaykh al-Ghazālī's (1997) *Fiqh-U-Seerah—Understanding the Life of the Prophet Muhammad* (IIPH: Riyadh), p. 237.

40. Paraphrased from al-'Adawī's treatise.

41. *Ṣaḥīḥ Muslim*, Book of Prayer, ḥadīth no. 577.

42. *Ṣaḥīḥ Muslim*, Book of Knowledge, ḥadīth no. 4828.

43. *Ṣaḥīḥ Muslim*, Book of Faith, ḥadīth no. 79.

44. *As-Sunnah at-Tarkiyyah* is a category of Prophetic Practice that is derived from acts that the Prophet (ṣ) explicitly did not do. Jurists regard such explicit abstentions as encompassed by the term *sunnah*.

45. *Al-Arba'īn an-Nawawiyyah*, an-Nawawī, ḥadīth no. 41. See also *Fatḥ al-Bārī bi Sharḥ Ṣaḥīḥ al-Bukhārī*, Ibn Ḥajar al-'Asqalānī,

commentary on ḥadīth no. 6764, *Ṣaḥīḥ al-Bukhārī*, Book of Holding Steadfastly to Allah's Book and the Prophetic Practice.

46. Sometimes also referred to as a Big Night, which is given some religious significance, like the birthday of the saint or a historical event.

47. *Ṣaḥīḥ al-Bukhārī*, Book of Holding Steadfastly to the Book of Allah and the Prophetic Practice, ḥadīth no. 6757.

48. *Ṣaḥīḥ al-Bukhārī*, Book of Faith, ḥadīth no. 38.

49. *Sunan Abū Dāwūd*, Book of Ethics, ḥadīth no. 4258.

50. *Mishkāh al-Maṣābīḥ*, critically appraised by al-Albānī, ḥadīth no. 239.

4

Heretical Innovations and Doctrine

*M*onotheism (*tawḥīd*) is the essence of Islam; it is its form, its kernel, its outer-layer, the support-structure of all its teachings—in fact, the framework of its structure; it is the colour of its surface and the nodal point of its principles and branches. However, Islam is not unique in its propagation of monotheism. All the messengers of Allah were sent to propagate this pure belief. They brought people together on the basis of monotheism and warned them against every pollutant that soils its purity or taints its lustre: "And We did not send any Messenger before you (O Muḥammad) without revealing to him that none has the right to be worshipped but Allah, so worship none else" (21:25). Nonetheless, large masses of people strayed from this path and clung to foolish beliefs that distanced them from Allah and led them to ruin.

Every past prophet came with the truth and urged people to turn to it, right up to the appearance of Muḥammad ibn ʿAbdullah (ṣ), the final prophet. He crumbled the edifice of polytheism and nurtured in the hearts of people the belief in the One and Only Allah. The Qur'an is and has always been the universal call to this certain truth and the strongest detractor of any doubt or falsehood and error that it is exposed to.

It is lamentable that Muslims have also been touched by the affliction of past nations and have wronged their sublime religion by corrupting the doctrine of monotheism, exposing it to heretical innovations and superstitions. These heretical innovations and superstitions are similar to those that led earlier nations astray or are a repetition of earlier nonsense, and following in the same footsteps: "So said the people before them words of similar import. Their hearts are alike; We have indeed made plain the signs for people who believe with certainty" (2:118).

Heretical innovation may advocate something and its opposite at the same time, thereby corrupting the balanced doctrine. For example, by equating the Creator with creation, one commits a transgression that corrupts the doctrine of monotheism. Similarly, advocating the idea of annihilation of creation and its incorporation into the Creator is a misguided idea that has no place in Islam, even if on the surface it appears to be an overzealous appraisal of Allah and an exaggeration of the principle of *tawḥīd* (in the sense of unity).

Unity of being (*waḥdah al-wujūd*)

We were under the impression that the superstitious belief in unity of being (*waḥdah al-wujūd*) came to an end with its demise in early Sufism. However, we find that when small groups of sinful Muslims of our time leave their lives of decadence and desire to return to Allah, they become afflicted by strange and foolish ideas. They think that the only way to express their repentance properly is to make the essence of Allah prevail over all people and all things that they are exposed to. You see them going beyond all bounds, and stripping the world of its normal characteristics. They may repeat the words of al-Ḥallāj, who, when asked what was in his clothing, replied: "Allah".

Because it is impossible to construct any rational behaviour on the basis of this idea, those who incline towards it accept a kind of determinism that paralyses the will, and they submit to whatever happens around them. Furthermore, to speak about a god that is within all things is to completely surrender oneself and to disappear. Many Muslims have been afflicted by this superstition, which had suspended the development of concrete logic in the lands of Islam, with all sorts of issues becoming intertwined with theology for no reason whatsoever.

The world is something apart from Allah—in spite of what a certain group amongst the Sufis say. Allah, the most Honoured and Sublime, is characterised by His Essence and names and His rights, which are explained in detail in His revealed books. There is a huge difference between *unity of being* (*waḥdah al-wujūd*) and *unity of witness* (*waḥdah ash-shuhūd*). A person may become engrossed in contemplating a certain issue to such an extent that he becomes oblivious to all that is around him. He may be called—while drowning in contemplation—and does not hear the call. Does such preoccupation imply the annihilation of everything around the person simply because the person is lost in thought? When the sun rises, its glaring rays overwhelm its surroundings and one is not able to see any stars over the nearest or furthest horizon. When night falls, and its darkness spreads, the hidden stars once again re-appear, individually and in groups. Does the overpowering nature of the sun's rays mean that to the one who does not see them, the stars do not exist?

Verily, some of the best believers live in an elevated status in Allah's Light, entrenched in the station of goodness, until they come to constitute its brilliant status. The station of goodness, as it is defined by the Messenger of Allah (ṣ) is: "To worship Allah as if you see Him, and if you are unable [then with the consciousness] that He sees you."[1] It is correct for us to describe this level of intimacy as *unity of witness* (*waḥdah ash-shuhūd*). This is an orientation that is completely different from *unity of being* (*waḥdah al-wujūd*), even if the two are sometimes confused by the short-sighted.

Most people that embrace a certain idea, or are driven by a specific emotion, compare their life's experiences in light of these ideas or emotions. In the words of a poet:

> I do not see the world in the light of day
> I rather see the world by the light in my eyes.

It is, therefore, not surprising to see believers whose feelings are overcome by religious emotion, who restrict all their activities to that which pleases Allah, and whose outlook is restricted to this specific viewpoint only. The following well known Prophetic tradition pertains to this context. The Prophet (ṣ) stated that Allah had said: "Whosoever shows enmity to one of My close friends, I make war against him permissible. Nothing endears My servant to Me more than doing of that which I have made obligatory on him. And My servant continues to seek closeness to Me through additional voluntary acts, until I come to love him. When this happens, I become the ears with which he hears, the eyes with which he sees, the hand with which he grasps, and the foot with which he walks. If this servant of mine were to ask of Me I would give him, and if he were to seek My help I would assist him."[2]

This Prophetic tradition alludes to such a level of devotion in seeking Allah's pleasure that the senses and limbs of the seeker become completely subjected to the obedience of Allah alone. It does not imply—in any way whatsoever—that addictive worship will result in incarnation or union with Allah as is believed by certain naïve people, or that it may result, in certain instances, in a supernatural status that transcends the laws of nature as is believed by certain Sufis who refer to a false tradition that states: "My servant has obeyed Me; I will grant you divine status so that if you pronounce anything, so shall it be!"

Intermediaries

Another practice prevalent amongst the masses is the visiting of the graves of pious people to request from them that which should only be requested from Allah, the Sublime and Honoured. This deviant behaviour is, perhaps, explained by the fact that people see themselves as inferior and thereby not worthy of supplicating

Allah directly. They, therefore, approach persons that are of a "purer" status than they are in order to put forward on their behalf what they cannot present with their own hearts and tongues. This explains why people migrate away from Allah to his servants, those servants who have the capacity to hear and those that do not hear, and those that are able to reason and those that do not have the capacity to reason. The many explanations for these actions appear to express added veneration of Allah, but are, in fact, a violation of Allah's sanctity. The Makkan polytheists, men and women, used to circumambulate the Ka'bah naked, under the pretence that it was not proper to perform the ritual in clothing that was worn while committing transgressions.

The fear of approaching Allah without any intermediaries was a sin of the ancient idol worshippers. The Qur'an portrays their excuse for associating objects of worship with Allah in the following verse: "We worship them only that they may bring us near to Allah" (39:2). This very excuse is repeated by the custodians of ignorance in our era, in defence of those that visit graves seeking healing, success, assistance, and deliverance.

It is obvious that there is no place in Islam for intermediaries between Allah and his creation. Every Muslim, no matter what his status, is accountable before Allah and should be certain that his supplications are heard by Allah, the Merciful, without the interference of any other. The primary form of worship in Islam—the five prayers spread throughout the day and night—are founded upon this certain reality about which there is no doubt. How else is it possible that Allah would obligate his servants to stand in His presence and ask of Him—as a matter of duty—to be guided along the straight path and to prostrate before Him in reverence and to ask of their needs? How else is it that failing to perform these prayers is regarded as an act of disbelief and is tantamount to neglecting a duty due to Allah, only to thereafter allow a certain individual to say: "I am in need of an intermediary to convey to Allah my needs"?

There is no explanation for this, except a desire to associate partners with Allah, whether blatantly or subtly. If a person seeking an intermediary was asked who he would choose to speak to Allah on his behalf, and he was to choose a person characterised by virtue to supplicate Allah for him, the matter would not be as complicated. Is it not strange, however, that he chooses from among the dead? Is it not strange that he chooses someone whose links with the world have been cut, and who only has with him his own deeds from his lifetime? The deceased person has no awareness of this ignorant seeker that has come to him. What does the seeker seek of this person? To ask of him for something or to seek his intercession?

Islamic thought had fallen into this scandalous pit a long time ago and many superstitions have evolved around saints (*awliyā'*) and allegiance to saints (*wilāyah*). At a certain point in time, people even believed that the keys of creation were in the hands of a select group of these mortals who manipulated them—as Allah's intermediaries—as they pleased. Matters became vaguer when it was claimed that the abilities of these "friends of Allah" (*awliyā'*) transcended the laws of causation. Consequently, the way in which Muslims perceived Allah's laws of creation became confused, and they began to believe that these laws could be manipulated by anyone who devoted himself to worship.

The fate of our unfortunate community of believers was such that it lost its place in a world that came to rely on factual knowledge of nature and the laws of existence. The Muslim community also lost its status before Allah, having associated with Him as equals people that were not able to accrue benefit or harm to themselves or to anyone else. Allah says of such people: "Do then those who disbelieve think that they can take My slaves as *awliyā'* (lords, gods, protectors, etc.) besides Me? Verily, we have prepared hell as an abode for the disbelievers" (18:102).

Why should Islam acknowledge the right of "certain people" to intercede between Allah and his creation? Why should Islam acknowledge the ability of these people to transcend the laws of nature and to commit supernatural acts? Why is affirmation of the rights of these people (and their vast abilities to impact upon the outcome of things) to be regarded as a part of the branches of faith, along with belief in Allah, His prophets and the day of resurrection? In truth, this is all a repulsive mix of confusion, and to insist upon it is to incline towards ignorance.

Islam has not been absolved from such impostors, who defend such fallacies and try to soil the purity of monotheism—which is the spirit and substance of Islam—with tumultuous nonsense that is neither rational nor sincere, while claiming that reliance upon intermediaries does not contradict the teachings of Islam. This is not strange if one considers that the Christians regard the Trinity as an expression of monotheism. "But human beings are ever more quarrelsome than anything" (18:54).

Metaphysics

Islam is a message of righteousness and reform; righteousness for the individual and reform of the general society. When the noble Qur'an was revealed, and the Prophet (ṣ) began gathering people around its clear guidance, people were committed to both these aspects. The believers would polish themselves with the ethics of Islam and regarded it as their obligation to place life within a framework of perfection and to push this world—voluntarily or by compulsion—towards truth and goodness. The burdens of this message are tremendous and do not leave any space for idle inactivity or the self-indulgence of the intellect. As a result, in the era of the pious ancestors, Islamic history showed no record of any deliberations on issues of theology or any leniency in understanding religious directives. That generation preoccupied itself with a far greater matter, namely, delivering the correct message of Islam. Therefore, diligent practice and integral output was their first and last concern.

When the intensity of this amazing activity had weakened and people retired to their gatherings in tranquillity, they turned their attention to the principles of Islam and its branches, making out of its interrogation and dissection an activity whereby they sought closeness to Allah. One may even say they undertook this activity to fill their spare time. This intellectual pastime exposed Islam to much evil, especially after Greek philosophical problems had been translated into Arabic and received much attention from Muslim scholars.

Some scholars saw no harm in mixing the principles of Islam with the methodology of Greek theology. As a result, the sphere of disputation was considerably broadened and the discipline that dealt with the subject matter of doctrine came to be known as dialectical theology (*'ilm al-kalām*). Muslim scholars became preoccupied with some of the following issues:

- Is creation the essence of existence or an outward characteristic?
- Are the characteristics of concepts essential or not, or something else?
- Is the Qur'an Allah's eternal speech or is it created?
- Is it possible or impossible to see Allah?
- Are the same human bodies physically resurrected after death, or are they similar bodies?

Is...? Are...? We are not interested in establishing the truth in response to these questions inasmuch as we are interested in showing that all these inquiries are nonsensical chatter. Muslims devoted themselves wholeheartedly to these issues only after they became confused about their legitimate purpose in life and after their constructive involvement with people was reduced.

Does this imply that deep intellectual inquiry is frowned upon and that abstaining from thinking—so as to avoid speculation on these issues—is recommended? Or that paying attention to these matters is a heretical innovation? In response, it must be said that knowledge is of two types:

1. Experimental, inductive knowledge, based on research pertaining to physical matter, within the realm of the observable world. None should place any limit or restrictions on this type of knowledge. Preoccupation with it is seen as an act of obedience to Allah and His Prophet, and as the steadfast grasping of the truth, as well as following the guidance of the Qur'an.

2. Knowledge pertaining to metaphysics, that is, to the unseen world. The only source of knowledge pertaining to this world comes to us by revelation from the Heavens; the intellect has no role to play here, except to hypothesise and speculate. Most of the philosophies dealing with metaphysics are irrational and confused. This is because they do not submit to methods that are determined by the sound intellect or that conform to its overriding logic.

With regards to unseen realities, we are required to submit to that which has come to us from the Legislator and to give the intellect the opportunity to ponder and inquire over the wide sphere of creation. Is it not foolish for a person to inquire into the manner in which Allah, the Merciful, sits upon his throne when he knows nothing about the laws pertaining to simple matters or about the laws of reflection or refraction? Assume that he has some knowledge of these matters by virtue of the physical instruments in his possession. What instruments would he use to gain insight into the reality of how Allah sits on His throne?

There is no doubt that the preoccupation of the Islamic intellect with these metaphysical inquiries has helped result in its severe and shameful shortcomings in dealing with inquiries pertaining to the physical sciences, in addition to its shortcomings in fulfilling its practical mission, as we have explained earlier. Therefore, why bother with theological matters of this sort, which are innovated heresies that have harmed Islam and its followers, past and present?

Between the seen and the unseen

Allah, the Sublime and Honoured, has placed in things specific characteristics that do not normally unravel. People come to know the characteristics of various elements as they build and develop their environment and try to benefit from these as best as possible. Modern civilisation has been very successful in discovering the specificities of matter and has been able to benefit from them in many spheres. Gaining knowledge of these specificities is left to human beings, to the extent of their experience and learning.

If the possible characteristics of something have come to be defined through sound means, then the Muslim is expected to respect this definition and not—in the name of Islam—to belittle or exaggerate it. Furthermore, it is not acceptable to ignore such knowledge under the pretence that one should place one's faith in Allah or to add one's own elaboration to such knowledge under the pretence that these details are as a result of one's relationship with Allah. Placing one's faith in Allah does not negate the law of cause and effect, nor does it affect the forces that Allah has granted to various elements since pronouncing, "Our Lord is He who gave to each thing its form and nature, then guided it aright" (20:50). One of the characteristics of fire is that it burns; to ignore this is stupidity and is not something advocated by religion. Faith requires acknowledging this characteristic as the nature that Allah has placed in this matter. There is not a single atom in the heavens and earth that does not owe its existence and movement to its inherent nature, which is derived from Allah, the Eternal and Sublime.

What, then, is the relationship of this obligatory observation with the suspension of the laws of existence? The believers that seek to ignore these forces and effects—under the pretence that they place their trust totally in Allah—do a severe injustice to themselves. Islam is totally absolved from their actions. Such practices are indicative of a deficiency in learning and not a heightened sense of certainty.

It is also absolute nonsense to add fallacious characteristics to the characteristics of things as they have been defined by the natural sciences. Idols, for example, are stones that could be used as building blocks in the construction of a home or as paving stones to make a pathway. Over and above this, no other unique characteristics should be attributed to them as is proclaimed by those who worship them. Benefit can be extracted from the cows of the Hindus by deriving milk from them or eating their flesh; there is no place for attributing sacred characteristics to cows or for using them as a means to draw closer to the Creator. The same applies to all the elements created by Allah. Their characteristics are not extended or restricted in accordance with the beliefs of ignorant people; they remain constant, within the parameters defined by the highest power and as has been elaborated by the genuine sciences. Allah's religion affirms these realities.

The one who hangs up a trinket, or keeps with him an amulet, believing that these objects help to prevent illness, bring sustenance, or give one long life, is no more than an idol-worshipper who, by his sick logic, follows the thinking of those who truly worship idols and cows. However, there are specific elements that can be used for medicinal value, as has been indicated by the genuine sciences.

It is narrated that 'Abdullah ibn Mas'ūd saw an amulet around his wife's neck and snatched it, breaking it off. He then said: "The family of 'Abdullah is free from associating with Allah things that Allah has not attributed any authority to." He then said: "I have heard the Messenger of Allah (ṣ) saying: 'Incantations (ar-ruqā), amulets (at-tamā'im) and at-tawlah are a form of associating partners with Allah (shirk).'" He was then asked: "O Abū 'Abd ar-Raḥmān, we are familiar with incantations and amulets, but what is at-tawlah?" He said: "It is something concocted by women, which they use to endear themselves to their husbands."[3]

Aḥmad relates from 'Imrān ibn Ḥuṣayn that the Messenger of Allah (ṣ) saw a yellow bracelet around a man's arm and said: "Woe unto you! What is that?" The man replied: "It is for protection against feebleness." The Messenger (ṣ) replied: "It will only increase you in feebleness! Cast it aside, for if you were to die with it on you, you would never achieve success."⁴

There are people that use the Qur'an as a talisman, claiming that it protects them against bankruptcy if they are traders, or that it protects them from the anger of their bosses if they are employees. This is an unhealthy blunder, and if these naïve people regard it as an expression of faith in Allah and veneration for His book, they are truly misguided. The Muslim's relationship with the Qur'an should be based on reflection and the practice of its teachings. If he is a trader or an employee, then his success lies in the performance of his duties, his first and last responsibility. He should undertake his work as best as possible without any shortcomings, constantly maintaining uprightteousness. Being neglectful of his duties should not motivate him to use a copy of the Qur'an as a talisman. The Qur'an and the Prophetic traditions are an excellent source of noble supplications, which the believer may rely upon to address his Lord if he is troubled by a matter or overcome by affliction.⁵ These supplications are clear in meaning, insightfully expressed, and can be repeated by the believer with passion and the hope that Allah will deliver him from his affliction and encompass him in His all-embracing Mercy. This is the type of incantation that we affirm because it has been taught to us by the Legislator. It is a natural effect of creation.

If one who is in need asks from the All-Powerful for that which is in accordance with general wisdom, to receive a response is not unnatural; it is, rather, a relief that one should acknowledge and be grateful for. When the Prophet (ṣ) visited a sick person, it was his habit to supplicate for him as follows: "Lord of humankind, dispel the affliction, heal him, You are the Healer, there is no healing like Your Healing, which leaves no trace of illness."⁶

When Prophet Ayyūb was afflicted by sadness, he turned to his Lord, seeking deliverance. "And remember Ayyūb, when he cried to his Lord: 'Verily, distress has seized me, and You are the Most Merciful of all those who show mercy.' So We answered his call, and We removed the distress that had overcome him, and We restored his family to him (that he had lost), and the like thereof along with them, as a mercy from Ourselves and a reminder for all who worship Us" (21:83-84).

Allah's servants should stand before Him and ask of Him. They should, however, understand that supplication does not contravene the laws of Allah's creation or dismantle the laws of cause and effect. A bachelor will not be blessed with children, even if he supplicates for a thousand years. Allah's response to one's prayers takes the form of making a person conform to the right conditions, avoiding any impediments that may arise. If there is something particular to the highest power, with no role therein for man, then the response may come by the manifestation of the truth in accordance with Allah's Mercy and Wisdom.

Whenever people are exposed to crises they turn to Allah in humility and seek assistance. However, they quickly return to wrongdoing as soon as they have been delivered from their predicament. This is confirmed by the Qur'anic verse: "No! Verily, man does transgress all bounds. Because he considers himself self-sufficient" (96:6-7).

This type of incantation (i.e., supplication) is not blameworthy; it is, in fact, an expression of true faith. It is not like the *shirk* that Ibn Mas'ūd warned against. He warned against false incantations, that is, the mutterings of the magicians and the amulets (*ta'wīdh*) of the sorcerers and similar superstitions that lead people to believe in strange things that, supposedly, are able to produce supernatural outcomes and achieve whatever they desire.

Strangely enough, Muslims have indulged in these nonsensical practices and have transformed their religion into belief in talismans that achieve the impossible, at a time when they have become incapacitated by the challenges of everyday life. As a result, they bumble through life while others have taken possession of the keys to the heavens and the earth, by natural and easy means. Do you think—alongside this degradation—that we have pleased our Lord, or shown respect to our religion?

The discord sown by the early scholars of dialectic theology on the relationship between cause and effect injected a deadly poison into the thinking and practices of Muslims. There is an opinion that is held by a few people but is claimed to represent the orthodox belief (*'aqīdah ahl as-sunnah wa al-jamā'ah*). However, it has no basis in religious thinking or in rational thought. These people claim that fire does not cause burning by itself, and that burning results when Allah approaches the fire. They similarly claim that water does not quench thirst, nor does the knife cut. Matters continued along this trend, where the properties of things—properties that were created by Allah—were rejected. A pedagogical poem on doctrine stated:

> Whoever speaks of an inherent force
> He is a heretical innovator who should be ignored

Why is the opinion that there exists an inherent force a heretical innovation that "should be ignored"? Shaykh al-Islām Ibn Taymiyyah came along and interrogated this opinion in great depth and then denounced it. He was surprised that an intelligent person could claim that fire does not burn by itself, and that Allah brings about the burning in it! He then quotes statements from the Qur'an in similar contexts, such as: "And He caused rain to descend upon you from the sky, to clean you thereby, to remove from you the evil suggestions of Satan, and to strengthen your hearts, and make your feet firm thereby" (8:11).

Ibn Taymiyyah[7] wrote:

> The rightly guided people and those who attain success affirm Allah's knowledge, His power, His will, and His absolute Uniqueness, and that He is the Creator, Possessor and Lord of all things. In spite of this, they do not reject what Allah has also created in terms of cause and effect.

Allah States: "When [the winds] have carried a heavy-laden cloud, We drive it to a land that is dead, then We cause rain to descend thereon. Then We produce every kind of fruit therewith" (7:57).

"Wherewith Allah guides all those who seek His Good Pleasure to ways of peace" (5:16).

"By it He misleads many, and many He guides thereby" (2:26).

Allah, the Sublime and Honoured, thus informs us that He does these things.[8] Whoever claims that he only does what he wants when these causes are in effect and not by their very nature, has contravened the Qur'anic teachings and has rejected the forces and properties that Allah has created in things.

Why should the literal import of these and other verses be rejected in favour of interpretations? Why should one hunt for fallacious hypotheses in this manner so as to support the belief in monotheism. The Muslim masses look down upon the value of cause and effect after it became common among them to believe that its natural impact is false. They have come to believe that desired results may either come about as a result of the law of cause and effect, or by themselves! After the powerful relationship between cause and effect had been broken, another superstitious belief took hold of the masses.

They came to believe that supernatural occurrences are commonplace and to be expected, and that Allah causes these occurrences to happen by day and night, by the hand of any of his chosen servants, whether pious or sinful, a believer or a disbeliever. If a supernatural act occurs by the hand of a prophet it is seen as a miracle (*mu'jizah*), if it occurs by the hand of a saint (*walī*) it is also a miracle of sorts (*karāmah*), and if it occurs by the hand of a sinner it is seen as a form of assistance (*ma'ūnah*) or persuasion (*istidrāj*).

These ideas have been linked to the principles of faith, and if someone is sceptical of a supernatural act performed by a certain individual, people begin to question his faith and virtue. These ideas should be distanced from the principles of doctrine and its branches of study—except that which relates to prophecy and prophethood, and should be inquired into by other disciplines of study, whether religious or secular. Muslims should know that they will not achieve success in matters pertaining to religion or life if they conduct their affairs in a manner not affirmed by revelation or supported by reason.

Ibn al-Jawzī wrote in his book *Searching the Conscience (Ṣayd al-Khāṭir)*:

I was overcome by a certain illness and, in my heart, I turned to Allah alone, in full knowledge that none was able to bring me assistance or protect me from harm except Him. I then began searching for the causes of my illness and was confronted by my sense of certainty, which said to me: "This is a slanderous compromise of placing full faith in Allah (*tawakkul*)." I responded that that was not the case because Allah had stipulated certain rules that had to be adhered to, or else my illness would not be lifted, as its presence pointed to a cause.

How is this so? All causes in the religious law adhere to the principle set out in the following verse: "When you (O Muḥammad) are among them, and lead them in prayer, let one party of them stand up (in prayer) with you, taking their arms with them" (4:102). Allah also says: "Leave (the corn) on its cob" (12:47).

The Prophet (ṣ) made use of armour and consulted doctors when he was ill. When he passed Ṭā'if, on his way to Makkah, he realised that he would not be able to enter Makkah without protection. He, therefore, called for al-Muṭ'im ibn 'Adiy and asked for the protection of his tribe. The Messenger of Allah (ṣ) could not simply enter Makkah, placing his trust in Allah but paying no attention to the circumstances. If the religious law itself has linked all matters with their causes, my turning away from the cause of my illness would be contrary to wisdom. That is why I regarded seeking medical assistance as an obligation.

The founder of the school of thought that I adhere to, Imam Aḥmad ibn Ḥanbal, had advocated not seeking medical assistance as a better option, but due to the lack of supporting evidence, I reject his view. It is related in an authentic Prophetic tradition: "Allah has not sent upon us any ailment without also sending with it a cure; so seek the remedy."[9] This expression is in the emphatic form, suggesting a command, implying that it is either obligatory to do so or it is highly recommended. The expression is not preceded by an admonition, which would have made it a permissive command. 'Ā'ishah used to say: "I learnt medicine due to the Prophet's many sicknesses and their causes." The Prophet (ṣ) said to 'Alī ibn Abī Ṭālib: "Eat of this, for it is more beneficial to you than that."[10]

Those who support the view that it is better not to seek remedies base their claim on the following statement of the Prophet (ṣ): "Seventy thousand people will enter paradise without being held to account." He then described them and said: "They do not rely upon cauterisation or incantations or omens, but place their faith in Allah alone."[11] This does not negate seeking remedies because people did resort to cauterisation to prevent disease and did invoke incantations to avoid calamities.

The Prophet had cauterised Sa'd ibn Zurārah and allowed certain incantations, as is evident from authentic traditions.[12] We can, therefore, conclude that the prohibition was for the reasons alluded to above. If you were afflicted by diarrhoea, you would eat al-Ballūṭ[13] or drink tamarind water and you would be cured. This is medicine. If I do not drink what will cure me and say: "Dear God, cure me," reason would remind me: "Think first then place your trust in God." Drink and then say "Dear God cure me," and do not be like the one who finds a small elevation of earth between his fields and the river but is too lazy to dig an irrigation channel, resorting, instead, to praying for rain.

This is no different from the case of one who travels as an experiment. He does so in order to see if his Lord, the Honoured and Sublime, will provide him with sustenance or not. If those in his company begin gathering their provisions for the journey, and tell him to do so, and he refuses, then he has perished before he starts! If the time of prayer approaches and he does not have water with him he would be reprimanded for his negligence. It may be said: "Do you not take water along with you before you enter the desert?"

Be warned against the actions of people who split hairs in argumentation and then renounce the status of religion, thinking that true religiosity lies in transcending nature and going beyond the natural state. Were it not for the power of knowledge and the manner in which it strengthens, I would not have been able to explain this matter nor understand it. So understand what I have alluded to; it is more beneficial to you than sanctimonious preaching, and strive to be with people of understanding and not with those who are prone to verbosity and empty speech.

Faith is the soul of existence

The primary requirement of faith (*īmān*) is to affirm the Major Reality, to acknowledge the Higher Existence, and to be aware of the restricted capacity of human beings before an All-Encompassing Lord, in Whose Hand is the power of all things, Who provides sanctuary and from Whom none can offer sanctuary. Alongside this, there is an additional function that cannot be separated from faith: it is the driving force behind good deeds. This is the force by which a person turns to Allah in terms of his actions, in terms of what he abstains from, and, in fact, in terms of all matters of life. Just as the stomach contains secretions that help to digest food and which help to extract that which is most beneficial to the body, similarly, religious doctrine has characteristics that transform common actions into acceptable forms of worship and give it a specific meaning by which one's status is elevated in the sight of Allah. If the heart is devoid of this faith it would mean that all actions that stem from a person are of no avail, and are of a status that does not warrant any reward from Allah.

Faith in Allah is a precondition for virtuous deeds and for the acceptance of one's efforts. "O my people! Truly, this life of the world is nothing but a (quick passing) enjoyment, and verily, the hereafter is the home that will remain forever. Whosoever does an evil deed will not be requited except the like thereof, and whosoever does a righteous deed, whether male or female, and is a true believer, such will enter paradise, where they will be provided therein (with all things in abundance) without limit" (40:39-40).

Nonetheless, the heavy current of life strains all human endeavours—by day and night—and it cannot be controlled by faith alone. Most human endeavours are informed by self-interest and personal desire, and most people remain unmindful of their Creator. Islam is governed by decisive rules for measuring actions and these are judged by their intentions. Only actions that are undertaken for Allah's pleasure are accepted. Actions that are motivated by other intentions, no matter how noble, are rejected.

People have created norms and standards—other than those revealed by Allah—which they have established as a basis for judging good and bad deeds. This is not the place to inquire into and evaluate these many norms. The discipline of ethics deals with some of them and the nature of everyday life deals with others; there is much critical evaluation in circulation. In this day and age, criticism is a commodity of inflated value, but, if properly assessed, is of very little worth. Similarly, most of these norms—promoted by some people, only to be rejected by others—are also of very little worth.

There are efforts being made to legitimate nationalist inclinations over religious beliefs in the political and social spheres, and in the psychological and educational spheres as well. These efforts are amplified whenever they are directed at eliminating Islam from its general position of influence. Love of the nation is an undeniable impulse and defending it is an unquestionable obligation. This should, however, not be at the expense of a person's relationship with his religion and his devotion to his Creator. I do not know why some people insist upon emptying our hearts of faith in Allah, only to fill them with faith in a piece of Allah's earth that we find ourselves inhabiting.

The nationalist inclination

The worst affliction to overcome Islam—during the last incursion upon its lands—was the partition that separated its people, dividing them into hostile factions and turning their lands into emirates and kingdoms so numerous that one is astounded by their number. The demons of colonialism divided the Arabs and Muslims into separate nations, whereas they had been a single nation before; set them along different paths, when they had been moving together in unison. Can one imagine a coherent body telling its constitutive organs to exist separately, with no concern for the whole! The hand is expected to be a state, the leg another state, the eye a state, the nose another state. No relationship between the heart and head, or the heart and the limbs. Can this be the work of a doctor that wants to preserve life, or is it the work of a butcher that seeks to kill?

European politicians constructed and implemented their plans in this destructive manner. Whenever the survival instinct would move these dismembered limbs towards unity, or closer together, colonialism would renew its efforts to keep the Muslims apart, in constant enmity, with some claiming not to be in need of others, and demanding that they could exist independently. Such devotion to separation is no more than suicide! The hidden affliction behind this sad condition is the awakening of tribalistic inclinations and narrow nationalistic partisanship; this is the internal wound that has been inflicted upon Islam.

Although exclusivist partisanship is a general human illness, it is a grave sin in Islam, especially these days, considering its weakened state. It is, in fact, the shortest route to abandoning Islam and for surrendering all of its territories to the foreign usurpers. And, in whose name is this done? In the name of partisanship to a single state!

The neo-colonisers—unlike the Crusaders of old—have realised that the most successful ploy for foiling Islam, breaking its strength, collapsing its sovereignty and overshadowing its future is to fill the hearts of Muslims with stupid nationalistic partisanship, after emptying it of the certainty of faith and consciousness of the rights of Allah, to the extent that a patriot shouts out:

Speech of the nation is what is foremost in the heart
And whispers of the nation are the last words on my lips.

If this is the case, then what is left for Allah? The collaborative efforts to turn Muslims towards this thinking and sentiment were orchestrated by the dirty politics of colonialism, extremely vehement towards us, extremely hostile to our past, present and future. It tried to mislead people by propagating nationalist fanaticism and regional discord and was able to achieve its goals, unlike before.

Religion was tolerated as a fixed component of western nationalisms, especially as part of its colonial campaigns in the East. In contrast, in the Islamic countries religion was completely eliminated from the nationalist movements. For example, Muslims in Algeria were obliged not to be saddened or to take action if Muslims in Tunisia were being humiliated. Muslims in Iraq were asked not to revolt or take action if the Islamic existence in Egypt was under threat. In this way, damage is inflicted upon Islam and Muslims, in the name of patriotism and liberation from the old.

It is only fair to allude to the opinion of a Western intellectual—who is also a committed Christian—on this purely nationalist trend. Emery Reves dealt with this issue in his book *The Anatomy of Peace*.[14] He deals with it from a purely humanistic perspective and makes its value clear in terms of ethical and behavioural principles. He warns the world of the consequences of clinging to nationalism in a chapter entitled "The Failure of Religion":

> What was divine and civilizing in Christianity was its monotheism, its universalism. The doctrine which teaches that all men are created equal in the sight of God and are ruled by one God, with one law over all men, was the one really revolutionary idea in human history....
>
> At the moment modern nations began to crystallize and national feeling in the Western world began to prevail over Christian feeling, the Christian churches, already divided among

themselves, split into a number of new sects, each supporting the rising ideal of the nation.

Nationalism soon became identified with Christianity and in every country nationalist policy was recognized as Christian policy...

Since the abandonment of universalism by the Christian churches—Catholic—as well as Protestant—they have diverged from the original fundamental doctrine of Christianity to which they adhere no longer except in name. In thousands of churches today, Catholic priests and Protestant preachers of all denominations are praying for the glory of their own nationals and for the downfall of others, even if they belong to the same church. This is indeed in violent contradiction to the highest religious ideal mankind ever produced—Universal Christianity....

The same development can be observed in the second great monotheistic creed, in Islam. The great unity which had been maintained by the Koran for so many centuries among peoples of different stock, from the Atlas to the Himalaya Mountains, has been visibly splitting up into nationalist groups within which allegiance to the new nationalist ideal is more powerful than loyalty to the old universal teachings of Mohammed.

There is Pan-Turkism or Pan-Turanism, aimed at the union of all branches of the Turkish race living in the region extending from the Dardanelles to the Tigris and Euphrates.

To the south, the rising Pan-Arab movement is advocating the federation of all the Arab tribes into one nation.

Farther to the east—in India—the believers in Islam are inflamed by a strong Indian national feeling, expressed in the slogan: "I am an Indian first, a Muslim afterwards."...

Not only Christianity and Islam with their vast numbers of believers are being completely absorbed and dominated by neo-pagan nationalism. Even the originators of monotheism, even the Jews, have forgotten the fundamental teaching of their religion: universalism.

They seem no longer to remember that the One and Almighty God first revealed Himself to them because He chose them for a special mission, to spread the doctrine of the oneness of the Supreme Lawgiver, the universal validity of monotheism among the people of the world....

With glowing passion they desire nothing more than to worship their own national idol, to have their own nation-state. No amount of persecution and suffering can justify such abandonment of a world mission, such total desertion of universalism for nationalism, another name for the very tribalism which is the origin of all their misfortunes and miseries.

It is of utmost importance for the future of mankind to realize the apostasy and failure of all three of the monotheistic world religions and their domination by disruptive and destructive nationalism, as without the deep influence of the monotheistic outlook of Judaism, Christianity and Islam, human freedom in society—democracy—could never have been instituted and cannot survive....

Unless the Christian churches return to this central doctrine of their religion [universalism] and make it the central doctrine of their practice, they will vanish before the irresistible power of a new religion of universalism, which is bound to arise from the ruin and suffering caused by the impending collapse of the era of nationalism.

The above is a correct, well-advised judgement. We therefore draw it to the attention of Muslims and ask them to understand it well and to take cognisance of two stark realities:

1. It is not becoming of Muslims to return to the former age of ignorance by promoting blind partiality to the nation, to skin colour or ethnicity; this is a form of thoughtless idolatry; and
2. Such a reversion is a true defeat for Islam and its followers and a certain victory for the neo-European invasion.

Indeed, the way in which Muslims have been deceived is truly scandalous. Israel was established as a tyrannical state after transforming religion into an exclusive form of tribalism, and the world accepted this while simultaneously prohibiting Muslims from uniting in the name of their religion. Thereafter, Israel even instructed some Egyptian Jews, in the name of Jewish nationalism, to conspire against Egypt so that it failed in its noble struggle to save Palestine. The Egyptian government rewarded these traitors with hanging, which was a just punishment, because it is a dirty crime to abuse nationalist inclinations to give life to subliminal hatred and ancient bigotry.

The methods devised by the global neo-Crusaders to conspire against Islam and to conspire against its future—under the banner of exclusivist nationalisms—are no less devious or dangerous than the machinations of Zionism. Muslims have finally begun to realise this and to take heed, due to their prolonged and ongoing suffering.

Notes
1. *Ṣaḥīḥ al-Bukhārī*, Book of Faith, ḥadīth no. 48; *Ṣaḥīḥ Muslim*, Book of Faith, ḥadīth no. 10.
2. *Ṣaḥīḥ al-Bukhārī*, Book of Upliftment, ḥadīth no. 6021.
3. *Musnad Aḥmad*, ḥadīth no. 3433.
4. *Musnad Aḥmad*, ḥadīth no. 19149.
5. Shaykh al-Ghazālī has written a brilliant book that outlines these supplications. It has been translated into English by Yusuf Talal DeLorenzo, entitled *Remembrance and Prayer of the Prophet* (Islamic Foundation: Leicester, United Kingdom) [Translator].
6. *Musnad Aḥmad*, ḥadīth no. 3433.
7. From his *ar-Risālah at-Tadmurriyah*.
8. Effects are real tools, and natural means; to ignore them is senseless and to place one's confidence in them to achieve certain goals is a religious imperative.
9. *Ṣaḥīḥ al-Bukhārī*, Book of Medicine, ḥadīth no. 5246.
10. *Sunan at-Tirmidhī*, Book of Medicine, ḥadīth no. 1960.
11. *Musnad Aḥmad*, ḥadīth no. 2800.
12. *Musnad Aḥmad*, ḥadīth no. 22123.
13. It is a kind of fruit that causes constipation, and is prevalent in the forests of Lebanon. Its properties—according to the dictionary—are that it is cold, dry, heavy, rough and suppresses urination.
14. Emery Reves (1945). *The Anatomy of Peace*. New York and London: Harper & Brothers Publishers. Orville Prescott of the *New York Times* wrote: The logic of *The Anatomy of Peace* is simple and

eloquent.... It might be a good thing for the world if ten or twenty million persons read and discovered it.

5

Heretical Innovations and Acts of Worship

Dhikr (remembrance) or forgetting?

*W*hat are known as "religious dances" or "remembrance gatherings (*ḥalaqāt adh-dhikr*)" have slowly begun disappearing. The disappearance of these innovated acts of worship is not because of the prevalence of the correct teachings of religious jurisprudence but, rather, due to rebellion against religion in general, against both that which is true therein and that which is false and foreign. Wherever the correct teachings of Islam (or even general knowledge) are not widespread, one finds the masses addicted to these types of ignorant gestures and their accompanying chanting that incorporates the names of Allah, the Sublime and Honoured, being repeated with a passion of unknown source, with no beginning or end.

In a place called Zarwah, close to Sudan, I saw large groups that were affiliated to various Sufi orders practising these superstitious rituals after the obligatory Friday prayer, with reverence and determination. Both young and old were sweating from exertion, from the extended periods of jumping and shaking, left and right, croaking out expressions that they regarded as *dhikrullah* (remembrance of Allah). Their actions, however, were more an expression of complete forgetfulness and an ungracious obscurity.

When I left the *masjid* and reached the city-centre, I saw Europeans seeking their livelihood with determination and hope, in towering business premises, surrounded by wealth, strength and beauty. I shook my head in sadness and shame and remembered the popular saying: "Arab poverty walks on a street of gold." I asked myself why those worshippers, after having performed the obligatory Friday prayer, did not disperse and seek the bounties of Allah, as Allah commands?[1]

Those who have invented these *adhkār* (pl. of *dhikr*—ritual recitations) have led Muslims astray from two perspectives. First, they have led them astray by adding poisonous, bloated additions to that which Allah has commanded, and, second, they have also deviated attention away from other works which are better for Allah's religion and more beneficial to people in general.

The leading scholars of Islam had rejected these additions at the very earliest period, when they appeared to be more beneficial than harmful.

Ibn Kathīr narrates the following on the authority of Ismāʿīl ibn Isḥāq:

> Aḥmad ibn Ḥanbal once asked me, "Can I see al-Ḥārith al-Muḥāsibī when he visits your home?" I replied in the affirmative and was gladdened by his request.
>
> I then went to al-Ḥārith and said to him: "I would like you to spend the night at my home, you and your companions." He replied that they were many and that I should have dates and provisions for them. They came before the evening meal and the time of the late evening prayer, but Imam Aḥmad had arrived before them and sat in a room where he could see and listen to them, but they could not see him. After having performed the late-evening prayer, they did not perform any additional prayers but sat in the company of al-Ḥārith in silence, shaking their heads, as if there were birds perched on them.
>
> When it was close to midnight, one of them questioned al-Ḥārith on a particular issue and he began to speak about it and related matters pertaining to asceticism, piety and good counsel, causing those around him to weep and sob. I then went to Imam Aḥmad and found him weeping, on the verge of losing control, and he remained in that state until morning.

When the guests had left, I asked him: "What is your opinion of these people, O Abū 'Abdullah?" He replied: "I have never seen anyone speak about asceticism like this man, and I have never seen the likes of his companions, but in spite of this, I do not advise you to keep their company."

Ibn Kathīr explained: "He did not approve, because they preached the kind of austerity and strict behaviour that was not recommended by Islamic teachings, as well as scrupulousness and exaggerated accountability that was not commanded either."

It is for this reason that, when Abū Zar'ah ar-Rāzī came across al-Ḥārith's book, entitled *Guardianship (ar-Ri'āyah)*, he regarded it as a heretical innovation. He said to the person who brought him the book: "You should rather adhere to the teachings of Mālik, ath-Thawrī, al-Awzā'ī and al-Layth. Ignore this book because it teaches heretical innovation." This is the opinion of the early imams concerning certain acts of worship innovated by the Sufis in the days when Sufism was a form of knowledge tainted by extreme dedication, not ignorance overpowered by superstition, as is the case with most of its adherents today.

The truth of the matter is that many Muslims today practise types of *dhikr* that are far removed from the teachings of the Qur'an and the Prophetic tradition. *Dhikr* is the opposite of forgetfulness and is a trait of the heart, not the tongue. A person may have a clear recollection of something, which fills his entire being, without even moving his lips, or even a single muscle of his body. In fact, the tranquillity of his body is more conducive to reflection and remembrance. The more settled and focused he is, the easier it becomes for him to grasp the thoughts he is pondering in his mind. The moving of the tongue—in such a case—comes as an unintended result of the exhaustion of the conscience and what it encompasses. The quiet person, from whom you do not hear a sound, is the one whose heart is overflowing with the remembrance of Allah. The person speaking about Allah with his tongue, whose heart is far removed from Allah, and isolated from

Him, is like a recording of the Holy Qur'an, repeating it as it has been revealed, but gaining no reward in return.

I do not deny that Islam has recommended many *adhkār*, which a believer recites with his tongue and not only his heart. However, the *dhikr* pronounced by the tongue is not perfect or exalted if the tongue is not the key to the heart, which stirs it from its idleness. The recitation of specific expressions that are mentioned in authentic Prophetic traditions brings one many rewards. However, these transmitted recitations are not suited for fervent anthems, composed by people in this era for singing the praises of one's country and to create a strong sense of patriotism. The masses of students and workers who raise their voices singing these anthems, trembling and with sparkling eyes manifest— through this outpouring of sentiment—an expression of love for country that deserves appreciation.

However, none of these individuals seems to understand that their service to their country ends with this singing, no matter how sincere. The student's primary responsibility to his country is to study earnestly, attend classes regularly, and be devoted to his books. The worker's primary responsibility to his country is to master his duties, and to be devoted to his work. Singing the national anthem has no relationship to these obligations and is undertaken in times of rest, after one has expended one's energies fulfilling one's obligatory tasks. If a student expresses love for his country only by singing the national anthem two or three times, people would regard him as an idiot.

Similarly, Islamic teachings recommend certain supplications and recitations that encompass exalted expressions in praise and honour of Allah, which emphasise His divinity and shake the conscience of the believer, bringing tranquillity to his heart. The wisdom behind recommending these supplications is to strengthen the bonds of the heart with Allah in a direct and emotionally charged manner. It is pleasing to see a Muslim steadfastly practising these *adhkār*, and to see their effects imprinted upon his personality. It is, however, a tremendous error to devote all one's energies to this, thinking that these recitations absolve one from entrusted duties that should occupy most of one's time.

It is, of course, permissible for a Muslim to remember Allah with his tongue, on condition that he does not forget Allah in his actions and affairs. Genuine, obligatory *dhikr* is to remember Allah when one sees poverty and to give generously, or to offer assistance when one encounters misery. If one forgets Allah in these two instances, then he is truly the loser, as is related by Allah in the Qur'an: "Let not your properties or your children divert you from the remembrance of Allah. And whosoever does that, then they are the losers" (63:9). Indeed, they are losers, even if they shouted *dhikr* until the skies were rent asunder.

In addition, for remembrance to be accompanied by understanding and reflection, it cannot be undertaken by repeating single expressions hundreds or thousands of times. Remembrance is speech, and speech—if it is to be understood—must be constructed of complete sentences. Say, for instance, that you wanted to remember a person called 'Umar. Would it be sensible to do so by repeating: "'Umar, 'Umar, 'Umar," and so on? When Allah commands: "O Mankind, remember the grace of Allah upon you!" (35:3), is it acceptable to carry out this order by repeating certain graces that we are familiar with, so that one would say: "bread, bread, bread, meat, meat, meat"?

To understand the pronouncements of people in this uncouth manner is to abandon thinking altogether. How have these kinds of understandings taken possession of the speech of Allah, the Lord of humankind, so as to lower its esteem instead of being elevated by it? One finds masses of common people dancing to disconnected words, claiming that this perplexing behaviour is *dhikrullah* (remembrance of Allah). We do not give any human being—no matter what his status—the right to invent expressions to be regarded as *dhikrullah*, and to obligate people—many or few—to recite them. It is not even permissible to delimit fixed times and patterns for the legitimately transmitted expressions of *dhikr*, as long as the Legislator has left them open-ended, free of such limitations. If an individual establishes for himself a programme of recitation, supplication and *dhikr*, according to his specific needs, it is not permissible to regard that as a general practice and to obligate others to follow suit. This has not happened in poetry, so why should it be allowed to happen in religion.

The great Arab poet, al-Ma'arrī, had composed a collection of poems that he called "Obligating that which does not require obligation" and structured its reflections around specific letters of the alphabet. Arab poets—whether in short or long compositions—do not make a rule out of this. Therefore, al-Ma'arrī's actions are unique to him, and poets are not obligated to follow suit. Nonetheless, commonsense in the sphere of poetry is transformed into stupidity in the sphere of religion. One thus encounters adherents to Sufi *ṭarīqahs* who have created specific recitations for morning and evening, and have attached them to the five obligatory prayers, as if they were a religious obligation.

I am not saying that *dhikr* is not praiseworthy, or that practising it in abundance is repulsive or worthy of condemnation. *Dhikr* is truly praiseworthy, and to practise it in abundance—within the limits which Allah has specified—is something we advocate and cannot imagine any Muslim opposing. The *dhikr* that Allah has specified is broader than the repetition of the tongue or the regurgitation of words.

The *dhikr* that Allah is pleased with as an expression of religious faith, which He accepts from His servants as a means of drawing close to Him, has a deeper effect and is worthy of abundant reward, unlike the rituals that have been fabricated by the adherents to Sufi *ṭarīqahs*, whereby people are led astray.

Allah's wisdom informs all acts of obligation, and He has restricted acts of worship within specified limits. The Muslim cannot do less than what is required, nor go beyond what has been specified. It is reckless to think that consuming a specific product in abundance is recommended simply because it is a medicine. Do not one or two tablets of Aspirin cure a headache? In fact, one would consume an excessive amount of these tablets if one wanted to commit suicide.

We have noticed that those addicted to these *dhikr* supplications and gatherings are not successful in the spheres of knowledge acquisition and education. We see how their Islam has impeded them in the spheres of production and capacity. The reason for this degeneration is that these people have deviated from the teachings of the Messenger of Allah (ṣ) and from the straight path.

The true nature of worship

It is not possible to understand any behaviour if one ignores the reasons that have led to it, or the factors that have brought it about. Scholars of ethics dwell on environmental and genetic factors when trying to explain behaviour, objectives and goals, or similar matters. We are, however, not concerned with this. Behaviour—from the psychological perspective—is an effect of the third aspect of the three aspects of consciousness in a living being. The aspects of consciousness—as defined by psychology—are: perception, emotion and impulse (desire). If one wanted to understand a certain inclination and to comprehend the various actions that accompany it, one has to understand the aspects of consciousness that precede it, so as to construct one's understanding upon sound foundations.

Some view the various forms of worship as actions with no unity or link between them, or as obligations that a person has to fulfil, whether they are liked or disliked, or as a commodity that a servant has to buy from the market. People who view worship in this manner are absolutely ignorant of religion. Many worshippers engage the well-known acts of devotion as if they are metaphorical acts derived from an environment beyond the one they live in; as if they were imposed metaphors empty of any meaning. In reality, the worship that Allah has commanded—and for which He has created everything—is far above this. It embodies a consciousness that is made up of all its elements: it begins with rational knowledge, and is followed by emotional excitement that leads to a behavioural impulse. The final state is therefore the fruit of what preceded it.

This is the correct status of establishing prayer, of giving charity, of perfecting one's character, of speaking the truth, and of all the remaining acts of worship. The primary act of worship in Islam is to be acquainted with Allah through sound knowledge. The mind that is illuminated by such knowledge is a conscious guide for upstanding behaviour and a firm foundation for sound conduct. When this knowledge vanishes from the core of a person, he will not be able to give expression to his religion, or to establish anything of virtue. Having sound knowledge of Allah weakens the errors that a person may become entangled in, because they are passing errors, or superficial scars.

However, ignorance of Allah is an unforgivable error, which makes the performance of meaningful actions impossible. As a result, Allah states in the Qur'an: "Verily! Allah does not forgive setting up partners in worship with Him, but He forgives other than that from whom He pleases. And whosoever sets up partners in worship with Allah has indeed strayed far away" (4:116). Associating partners with Allah (*shirk*) is evidence of tremendous ignorance of Allah, the most Honoured and Sublime. Is there anyone more ignorant than a man living in a towering apartment building, who thinks that the garbage collector is the one who built his building? Is this not similar to superstitious idol-worship, which attributes aspects of greater existence to certain solid objects, animals, or people?

Reliable knowledge is derived from its unique sources, that is, from Allah's works and pronouncements, from His creation of the universe, and from His speech expressed in revelation. There is no knowledge beyond this. An idiotic person cannot be equated with someone who knows his Lord, someone who lives between the heavens and the earth, aware of the signs of creation, and able to uncover its mysteries.

Allah has clarified—according to what has been revealed to His messengers—that true faith is based on intelligent reflection about this world and through extensive travel across its vast horizons: "Verily, in the creation of the heavens and the earth, and the alternation of night and day, there are indeed signs for men of understanding. Those who remember Allah standing, sitting and lying down on their sides, and think deeply about the creation of the heavens and the earth, (saying): 'Our Lord! You have not created (all) this without purpose'" (3:190-191). Motivated reflection about knowledge of Allah is the secret of showing veneration to Him and the basis of God-consciousness, which is why these "men of understanding" finally declare: "Glory to You! Give us salvation from the torment of the fire" (3:191).

Thinking people are those who ponder over Allah's creation and benefit from their reflection by coming to revere Allah, which is why they ask for salvation from His wrath. God-consciousness (*taqwā*) is not the exclusive product of the mind, or an intellectual edifice; it is, rather, the product of a mature awareness of life and what it entails. This is what is meant by the Qur'anic verse: "It is only those who have knowledge amongst His slaves that are conscious of Allah" (35:28).

Seeking to know as much as possible about Allah is the primary act of worship. To come to know Allah through His vast creation is to adhere to that which He has commanded in His revealed books. The physical sciences give rise to findings that cannot possibly contradict revelation, which transcends the physical world, as both come from Allah. The contradiction that some short-sighted individuals claim exists between religion and science is nothing but a minor superstition that has arisen from the mistakes committed by those working in both the fields of religion and science. I have read studies by scholars of astronomy, which correct errors committed by their colleagues who have either purposely maligned religion or done so unintentionally. I am able—for those working in the field of religious studies—to clarify the position of Islam regarding the physical sciences and to confirm that its inquiries and findings are a necessary precursor for true certainty, and is the only means that the Qur'an is pleased with for coming to know Allah. Therefore, to ignore this type of knowledge is the most blatant transgression committed against Islamic civilisation. In fact, Muslims have wronged themselves and their religion by such negligence.

If the early Muslims had stuck only to the trend of studying nature and creation—instead of the theoretical Greek philosophies— it would have been to their greater benefit and to that of people in general. Aṣ-Ṣalāḥ aṣ-Ṣafadī relates that when al-Ma'mūn had concluded a truce with the ruler of Cyprus, he wrote to him requesting that the library of Greek books in their possession be sent to him. These books were stored in an abandoned house, so the ruler gathered his advisers and consulted them on the matter. All the advisers indicated that the books should not be dispatched. One lone patriarch differed from the others. He said: "Send it to him. Never have these sciences entered an established state without leading to its corruption and sowing discord amongst its scholars." The cunning patriarch's expectations were fulfilled and the Muslims integrated these sciences with the teachings they had inherited from the Qur'an and the prophetic tradition. They then began understanding their religion in light of these foreign sciences and whatever stagnant teachings they incorporated. This condition developed further and these sciences were regarded as religious teachings and their proponents were regarded as scholars of Islam, even though they had only very little knowledge of the teachings of the Qur'an and the prophetic traditions, having devoted so much effort to triviality and tales of adventure.

A person cannot be regarded as a scholar of religion until he acquires knowledge of what Allah has revealed and he cannot be regarded as a scholar in this regard until he has some knowledge of creation. His knowledge and reverence of the Lord of all Creation is dependent upon his knowledge of existence and living creatures.

If this knowledge is not the essence of virtue, it is most definitely the guide to virtuous behaviour, which makes people special, so that they are able to be elevated by their actions as well as their thinking. Anyone who is familiar with his Creator and that which He has created will be obligated to seek perfection in whatever he does and to guard against error at every moment of his life. Islam obligates every person that enters into its fold to strive to do good deeds. These good deeds are not restricted or defined in any way. Complete open-endedness is intentional in many Qur'anic verses that append "good deeds" to genuine faith.

What are good or virtuous deeds? They are the goodness that is mentioned in certain Qur'anic verses, in response to those who regard paradise as the exclusive right of specific factions: "And they say, 'None shall enter paradise unless he be a Jew or a Christian.' These are their own desires. Say, 'Produce your proof if you are truthful.' Yes, but whoever submits his face (himself) to Allah and does good deeds, his reward is with his Lord, on such shall be no fear nor shall they grieve" (2:111-112). Allah also says: "It will not be in accordance with your desires (oh Muslims), nor those of the People of the Scripture (Jews and Christians), whosoever works evil, will have the recompense thereof, and he will not find any protector or helper besides Allah. And whoever does righteous good deeds, male or female, and is a true believer, such will enter paradise and not the least injustice will be done to them. And who can be better in religion than one who submits his face (himself) to Allah and does good deeds" (4:123-125). The virtuous deeds that have been specified by the Legislator are but a small portion of comprehensive goodness that Allah has ordained in all actions: "So whosoever believes and does righteous good deeds, upon such shall come no fear, nor shall they grieve" (6:48).

Whosoever believes that religion is restricted to specific actions performed in specific places is clearly confused. An individual's faith is not completed until the capacity develops within him, which allows him to be able to undertake whatever is required of him, the comprehensive capacity that is able to fulfil a command to its fullest, dislikes shortcomings, and is mindful of corruption.

The two expressions "believe" and "do good deeds" characterise a people that love good deeds in all forms and are not familiar with corruption in anything they do. They manage their social and economic concerns with skill, awareness, good taste and sensibility. That which is "good" is any action that is supported by thinking and order, and which avoids recklessness and vanity. From the moment that a person wakes and faces the requirements of everyday life, he has to deal with matters that are unending, surrounding him from all sides; he has to take decisions and leave his mark. The right that Allah has over the Muslim is that he should be good and virtuous in all matters, whether he is a farmer, businessman, writer, accountant, employer or employee, student or teacher.

An instrument that has been created to perform a certain task is able to do so by its very nature under various circumstances. Similarly, genuine faith guides a person in a manner that makes general goodness the nature of his heart and essence. Therefore, the Muslim's permanent duty is always to improve himself and to improve the lives of others as well. The restriction of religion to a fixed number of duties is the worst affliction to have affected it. Ignorant people think that if they fulfil these duties they have fulfilled their obligations and nothing more is required of them. This faulty understanding has made life distressing, creating categories of worshippers, those that may pray and those that may fast. But matters of everyday life are corrupted in their hands as they do not see them as matters of faith. If one were to assume that they will perform these matters in an acceptable manner, one cannot expect them to master these matters or to compete with others to improve their abilities. We are not criticising their praying and fasting, as they may be performing these correctly in their outward form. There is, however, no doubt that their religious commitment is abnormal, and that their minds and hearts are sick.

The faculty of goodness by which they are supposed to judge their faith is obviously malfunctioning. Their knowledge of Allah may, perhaps, even be tainted by uncertainty and haphazardness. The virtuous heart transforms common actions into elevated acts of devotion that accrue great rewards. The matters of the world and the spheres of life are numerous and vast. However, the believer is able to control both in a polished, steady system and is able to transform them into pure acts of devotion just as the stomach is able to transform food into energy and life.

Allah has made clear in the Qur'an that the expulsion of one's enemy, the confiscation of his possessions and bringing harm to him may be regarded as a "good deed", stating: "That is because they suffer neither thirst nor fatigue, nor hunger in the cause of Allah, nor take any step to raise the anger of the disbelievers nor inflict any injury upon an enemy but it is written to their credit as a deed of righteousness. Surely Allah does not allow the reward of those who do good to be lost. Nor do they spend anything—small or great, nor cross a valley, but it is written to their credit, that Allah may recompense them with the best of what they used to do" (9:120-121).

Some may claim that the above verses are in the context of *jihād*, that not all the actions of a person in the general sphere of life can be regarded as *jihād* and are therefore less important than the *jihād* mentioned in the above verses. This, however, is not the case, as has been narrated in the prophetic traditions concerning actions that are closer to seeking pleasure and fun than to serious endeavours, as long as the person seeks to do good by these endeavours. Restricting good deeds to specific acts of worship has caused those who seek to attain piety to devote extended periods of their time to repeating these limited acts, as if they do not regard any other acts as a means of gaining Allah's pleasure. They hold on to these acts steadfastly, performing them over again as soon as they are done.

Ash-Sha'rānī said: "When I would begin a *dhikr* session after the late evening (*'ishā'*) prayer, I would not bring it to a close until the time of the early morning (*fajr*) prayer. I would then perform the early morning prayer and, thereafter, continue with *dhikr* until morning had broken and then perform the voluntary mid-morning (*ḍuḥā*) prayer. I would then continue with *dhikr* until the time of the noon (*ẓuhr*) prayer and then perform the prayer. I would then continue with *dhikr* until the late-afternoon (*'aṣr*) prayer, and then until the early-evening (*maghrib*) prayer, then until the late-evening (*'ishā'*) prayer, and so on.

"I continued in this manner for about a year. I would recite a quarter of the Qur'an in the time between *maghrib* and *'ishā'*; I would then recite the remainder in the *tahajjud* prayers before *fajr*, and would perhaps even recite the entire Qur'an in one cycle of prayer. I would only rest if overpowered by sleep, when my head would collapse from exhaustion. If I felt that I was being overpowered by sleep, I would lash my thighs with a whip. In the winter, I would soak my clothing in cold water to prevent me from dozing off."

This way of living is not Islamic. We do not reject it only because of its extremism and contradiction of the prophetic tradition, as is well-known by the scholars of Islam, but also because it suggests that devotion is addiction to *dhikr*, recitation and prayer in this repetitive and boring manner. Does one think that a judge who is immersed in trying to settle a dispute, staying awake at night researching and deliberating over the case, pleases Allah any less than the one who devotes his time to reciting the

Qur'an? Does one think that the teacher, who is preoccupied with fighting ignorance, staying awake at night to prepare his lessons, is of a lower status than the suffering *dhikr*-addict mentioned above? No. In fact, the latter two are closer to the truth and to righteous behaviour. Also, the worker who is in a deep slumber due to having exerted himself during the day sleeps and awakes under Allah's watchful eye, as long as his heart is clean and his conscience is clear.

By erring in the way we understand worship, our civilisation and culture has strayed and we have come to accept ignorance as learning and learning as ignorance. This has impacted decisively upon us as a community of believers and has led to our collapse. Recently, I have even encountered young religious devotees who follow this disastrous path. When they join these Islamic groups, they regard it as an act of devotion to Allah to take on the responsibility of preaching and to read encyclopaedic works of jurisprudence and Qur'anic exegesis and the like, while they are failures as doctors or are uncommitted engineers. I am at a loss to understand what would distract a doctor from such a noble profession! How is it that he does not understand that when he undertakes a successful surgical operation or prescribes curative medication, his actions are the best of deeds, which Islam regards as a cornerstone of success and a precondition for salvation? Such acts are no less valuable than the performance of prayer or the giving of charity.

We have inherited the false idea that regards the religious sciences as virtuous and neglects the importance of the physical sciences, whereas all of these point equally to Allah and equally serve His religion. Another false inheritance is the failure to pursue productive scientific studies. The low percentage of Muslims on important technical scientific bodies—until recently—is indicative of our appalling backwardness and the progress of others.

When the Jews confronted the Arabs in the first skirmishes in Palestine, the Israeli side included an army of specialists in the fields of engineering and mathematics, agriculture and electricity, on the nature of land and on the sources of water, enabling them to know everything about every inch of the land. This silent army worked in the service of the gangs that fought the seven member states of the Arab League, who were quickly swept aside and whose forces were liquidated. They did not benefit from flowery sermons and enthusiasm that was devoid of experience and honesty. Our resources—in terms of men and action—were far less than that of our enemies. To gain mastery over world affairs is a necessary precondition for the strengthening of Islam, and there is no place in this world for someone who is ignorant of its ways.

Professor Ṭāhā ʿAbd al-Bāqī wrote, in his defence of genuine Sufism and of ash-Shaʿrānī: "ash-Shaʿrānī had advocated the merging of worship and work, regarding them as the support structures of life. He gathered evidence proving that the pious adherents of Sufism were insistent upon avoiding living off the charity of well-wishers. Ash-Shaʿrānī preferred those who worked in the manufacturing industry over those devoted to worship, because the former contribute to the well-being of others while the latter benefit only themselves. He also used to say: 'There is nothing better than the tailor using his needle as his prayer rosary (*tasbīḥ*) or the carpenter that uses his saw as his prayer rosary (*tasbīḥ*), as this is a beneficial and acceptable form of counting the praises of Allah.'"

Ash-Shaʿrānī promoted the life of the body over the life of the spirit as the latter is derived from the life of the body and is affected by the difficulty and ease that the body experiences, such that when the body is weakened the mind is confused and one's thinking is distracted. That is why Abū Ḥanīfah used to say: "Do not seek the advice of a person who does not have flour in his home." This is valuable advice that should be adhered to. If Sufism is understood in this manner then it is Islam; the rest is nonsense.

God-consciousness (*taqwā*) does not entail renouncing the world. Rather, *taqwā* is to take possession of the world, and to ensure, if you are a servant of Allah, then you and all that you possess are at Allah's service. Those that flee from the world are not real men, nor are they true believers. It is foolish for some people to claim that devotion to Allah is expressed by the diligent practice of certain acts of worship, while ignoring others. Worshipping Allah in the markets and other places of work is no less valuable than worshipping him in *masjids* and prayer niches. Indeed, this world may represent a threat to the faith of less-committed and easily influenced people, just as food can be dangerous to certain groups of people afflicted with illness. Does this imply that all people should be prohibited from eating and that praise poems should be sung encouraging abstinence?

The Indian poet, Muhammad Iqbal, makes the point very well:

The disbeliever dissolves in the world
But the world dissolves in the believer.

It is true that the world is a danger to the small-hearted, but it is no more dangerous than prayer and fasting if they breed arrogance and pride in a person or fail to cleanse him of malice or suppress his whims.

We are, therefore, not actively opposed to these acts of worship in as much as we are opposed to not benefiting from them. We take the same position against those who are swayed by the passions of life and sell themselves to the devil, instead of taking advantage of the world so as to worship Allah, the Merciful. Showing absolute goodness to everything that one touches is to strive to improve this life and to maintain the link with Allah, the Most-High. This is the true meaning of worship that conforms to the all-encompassing message contained in Allah's pronouncement: "Believe and do good deeds" (2:25), which is repeated more than 70 times in the Qur'an.

We are expected to accept the acts of devotion that the Legislator has obligated as they have been conveyed, with clarified frequency, form, beginning and end. We are not allowed to interfere by making modifications, additions or subtractions.

If these were performed as stipulated by the Legislator, they would guarantee much goodness for all, individuals and groups. Unfortunately, interfering with these acts of devotion—in form and in substance—has stripped them of most of their benefits and has allowed corrupt individuals to undermine them completely.

I have discussed the spiritual aspects of worship in some detail in my book *Fiqh-u-Seerah*[2] and have explained that worship is the submission of one drowned in love and adoration and not submission based on coercion or dislike. The spiritual dimension of worship received admirable attention in the time of the early Sufis. They filled the heart with warm emotions through their relationship with Allah, causing it to overflow with a noble sentiment that made the performance of obligatory acts of devotion feel like listening to beautiful music. This is not surprising, since most of the early Sufis were sensitive, artistic people, overpowered by the imagination. They were able to lead the masses and spread their teachings in most of the Islamic lands.

Sufi teachings are a mixture of the realities of religion, the teachings of philosophy, long commentaries on the principles of ethics, the ailments of the soul and the bonds of the group. The primary criticism against the Sufis is that emotion has overpowered the intellect in their culture and that they judge Islamic practices and teachings in light of their own personal sentiments. Their teachings, both correct and incorrect, continued to persist primarily because the scholars of jurisprudence—who devote their attention to studying the *sharī'ah* and its related disciplines but who are not necessarily deeply entrenched in religious practice or popular amongst the masses—pay more attention to the literal teachings and outward manifestations of Islam.

If scholars of jurisprudence discuss the disciplines of monotheism (*tawḥīd*) or ethics (*akhlāq*), they muster textual evidence and draw principles in accordance with Aristotelian logic and thereafter engage in an ocean of futile disputation that knows no end. If a person were to go to the *masjid* and hear all of this in the religious lessons presented in the study circles, he would not believe his ears. He would rather pay attention to the Shaykh that performed the *dhikr* in praise of Allah with tears in his eyes, even if he did so accompanied by the beating of a drum or the whistle of a flute. This is why—after foreign influence and jest had taken a foothold—scholars of jurisprudence became unpopular and the authentic discipline of jurisprudence went into decline. The Sufi *ṭarīqahs* spread and their fascinating ideas, insane sentiments and emotions continued to develop, passing judgement without any consideration to the intellect or to the teachings of Islam.

The lamentable conditions that one sees manifest in the Islamic world today is what has been left behind of the generations that have developed in the absence of Islamic jurisprudence and the Islamic spirit. That is, in the absence of sound perception and taste. This great tragedy came about as a consequence of the shortcomings of the scholars of jurisprudence in the fields of education and worship and as a consequence of the shortcomings of the Sufis in the fields of knowledge and the religious sciences. Islam can only be established by those who are firmly entrenched in all of the above aspects of learning. On account of this, there circulated amongst us many different terminologies and innovated teachings, which were tremendously harmful to our religion and our community.

Adam Metz wrote in *Islamic Civilisation:*[3] "The Sufi Movement had established three principles in Islam that had a tremendous impact: complete and firm confidence in Allah, belief in saints (*awliyā'*) and the veneration of the Prophet (ṣ). These three principles are still the most important and influential factors upon Islamic life. It is perhaps the popularity that was achieved by these Sufi principles that explains the animosity of the scholars towards the Sufis."

This is indeed a strange pronouncement, because confidence in Allah and the veneration of His Prophet is not a Sufi invention!

What then would characterise Islam? What the Sufis did indeed invent, and attacked this religion and its followers with, is their belief in saints. European dishonesty places this superstition in between two sound principles, to give it the advantage of strength, in this way mixing truth with falsehood and monotheism (*tawḥīd*) with associating partners with Allah (*shirk*).

Perhaps the writer intended by "firm confidence in Allah" to mean false reliance that does not encourage action or seeking one's livelihood. If this is what he means, then it is indeed a real and ignorant Sufi innovation that was not known to the first generation of Muslims. It appears as if this is what he is alluding to.

About the Sufi way, Ibn Khaldūn said: "Its essence is devotion to worship, turning to Allah, the Sublime and Honoured, turning away from the adornments and beauty of this world, and showing abstinence from things of pleasure, wealth and fame, which most people seek. This was common amongst the Prophet's companions and the early predecessors. When people started turning more towards the world in the second century and thereafter, getting involved in its affairs, those who chose to turn towards Allah were referred to as Sufis."

Ibn Khaldūn's position is confusing and disturbing because the position of Islam concerning this world and practising asceticism or on monasticism and wealth and how to spend of it was well known. A Muslim must know that religion needs the world just as the soul needs the body and that any teaching that belittles the material strength of the community and empowers anything else over it is an act of treason against Allah and His prophet. If it is not an act of treason of the heart, then it is, at least, an act of treason of the mind.

The Noble Qur'an grants equal importance to economic *jihād* (striving) and military *jihād* (striving). It gives permission to the *mujāhidīn* (strivers) in both spheres to shorten their recitations during the prayers because paying attention to their tasks at hand is more important than lengthy recitation. Sa'd ibn Abī Waqqāṣ used to perform only one cycle of prayer for the *witr ṣalāh*, because he was preoccupied with fighting the enemy. "And Allah measures the night and the day. He knows that you are unable to pray the whole night, so He has turned to you (in mercy). So, recite of the Qur'an as much as may be easy for you" (73:20).

All types of knowledge and actions that serve the truth are a means of drawing closer to Allah and are no less important than prayer and recitation of the Qur'an. I do not know how a message carried by people that are way behind other communities in matters of everyday life will be able to succeed when they regard carrying prayer beads as a form of worship and carrying an axe or a hammer as a profane individual activity? The Messenger of Allah's companions in Makkah and in Madīnah were no less understanding of the responsibilities of life and matters of this world than the idolaters of Makkah and the disbelievers of Madīnah. In fact, their ingenuity in devising the plan of digging a trench around Madīnah during the Makkan siege reflects a flexibility and freshness of thought that put them ahead of the disbelievers and idolaters.

When they had entered Islam, the Arabs were no less mature or experienced than their enemies. While they were equals in many matters, the Arabs gained excellence by virtue of their new religion and its dynamic and adventurous spirit. However, if the Muslims of today are compared with others in the fields of science, technology and civilisation, or even in agriculture or sheep and cattle farming, they would be found to be embarrassingly backward. This is due to ignorance of their religion and attachment to repugnant heretical innovations, as well as confusingly following misguided paths which have distanced them—from very early on—from the straight path. Obligatory devotional acts have been exposed to many heretical innovations and we will now discuss some of these.

Extravagant adornment of *masjids*

No specific location is required to undertake the worship of Allah. Two Prophetic traditions in this regard state: "Be conscious of Allah wherever you may be"[4] and "The Earth has been made a place of prayer and purity for me."[5] Allah, the Sublime and Exalted says: "O my servants who believe! Certainly, My earth is spacious. Therefore, worship Me (Alone)" (29:56). The Prophet (ṣ) taught us to pray the voluntary (*nawāfil*) prayers at home, so that these prayers could bring life and light to the home. Such convenience pertaining to worship does not prohibit the establishment of specific places for Allah's remembrance and for prayer gatherings, where a person would go to find tranquillity, far from the clamour of life, where one would meet one's brothers in faith, who are also seeking Allah's mercy, with pure intentions and in awe of one's Creator.

The cause of truth is assisted when one sees others running towards it and actively participating therein. The whisperings of weakness that an individual may be prone to are dissipated in group participation and activity. For this reason, the frequenting of the *masjid* is seen as a sign of piety, and fondness of doing so is a sign of the love of Allah. Striving to visit the *masjid* acts as an expiation of bad deeds, adds to one's good deeds and elevates one's standing.

Masjids are, however, neither museums for showing off the aesthetic arts nor exhibitions for the wonders of engineering. There is no place in their construction and building for such burdens, expenses and vanity. It is narrated that when the second Caliph, 'Umar, had ordered the building of a *masjid*, he simply said to the builders: "Make sure that the people are protected from the rain and be warned against adorning the building in red or yellow."[6] This was also the precedent set by the Noble Prophet (ṣ) when building his *masjid*. He made it of a solid structure, a place of tranquillity and a model of simplicity. There is no harm in extending the *masjids* so that they are able to accommodate thousands of people, or to strengthen them in a manner similar to a fortress. This is not similar to wasteful adornment and embellishment that serve only to capture one's eye.

The impetus to construct fashionable *masjids* and to adorn them extensively seems to derive from the desire to compete with the Christians, who go to extremes in building their churches and spend fortunes on carvings and paintings. We find it more appropriate to adhere to the spirit of Islam as it is informed by constant consciousness of Allah.

Building *masjids* on grave-sites

The building of *masjids* on grave-sites has become a common practice in many countries and is seen as a means to remember the dead as well to draw closer to Allah—as some claim—by showing love for the deceased and by placing them in close proximity to Allah. However, the religious texts prohibit this practice in no uncertain terms and strongly censure those that commit it. Those undertaking such building should rather ponder the deeds of the dead and restrain their activities to what Allah has commanded, without transgressing His teachings.

This heretical innovation penetrated Muslim practices through Christian influences, after they had been corrupted. It has been authoritatively narrated by 'Ā'ishah that Umm Salamah informed the Messenger of Allah (ṣ) about a church she had seen in Abyssinia, referred to as "Māriyah". She described what she had seen in it and the Messenger of Allah (ṣ) responded: "They are a people that build places of worship upon the grave-sites of pious persons, when they die, and draw in it those pictures that you saw! They are the worst of creation in the sight of Allah."[7]

This heretical innovation entered Christianity from early paganism. Ibn Jarīr narrated on the authority of Ibn 'Abbās and others of the first generation that Wadd and Suwā'a and their siblings had been righteous people from the community of the prophet Nūḥ. After they had died, people continued to be attracted to their grave-sites. Thereafter, statues were carved of them at the grave-sites and, with the passing of time, people began worshipping these statues. This is how idol-worship began.

So as to close this door of corruption and block the path that leads to deviation, the Prophet (ṣ) had emphatically warned Muslims against these practices and had encouraged them to let go of the dead and turn to life, with all their strengths and desires, without dependence upon pious people, whether living or dead. A person derives benefits from his Creator only for his own pious deeds.

In guiding towards this clear teaching, the Prophet (ṣ) said: "Do not pray to the graves and do not sit upon them."[8] He also said: "All of the earth is a place of worship, except the grave-site and the toilet."[9] Finally, he said: "Allah cursed the Jews and the Christians because they have taken the grave-sites of their prophets as places of worship. Do not take grave-sites as places of worship; I forbid you to do this."[10] Ibn 'Abbās related that the Messenger of Allah (ṣ) had said: "Allah has cursed those who frequent the grave-sites, taking them as a places of worship and lighting lamps upon them."[11]

The Prophet (ṣ) also prohibited the whitewashing or plastering of graves and construction upon them.[12] He had advised his army—when he was expelling paganism and idolatry from the Arabian Peninsula—to destroy every idol and to flatten every elevated grave-site.[13]

Ma'rūr ibn Suwayd reported: "I prayed the morning prayer with 'Umar ibn al-Khaṭṭāb—on the way to Makkah—and he recited: 'Have you not seen how your Lord dealt with the owners of the elephant' (105) and '(It is a great grace and protection from Allah), for the taming of the Quraysh' (106). After having completed the prayer, he saw people dispersing and asked: 'Where are they going to?' He was told: 'O Leader of the Faithful! To a place of worship where the Messenger of Allah (ṣ) had prayed, to pray there as well.' He responded: 'Those before you were destroyed because of similar actions. They used to follow in the footsteps of their prophets and establish synagogues and churches on those sites! Whosoever finds himself in such a place at the time of prayer, let him perform his prayer and whosoever does not, let him continue on his way without intentionally stopping there and waiting for the time of prayer.'

The Messenger of Allah (ṣ) prayed to his Lord that his grave-site should not become a place of celebration—a pilgrimage site—which delegations intentionally come and visit.[14] People well-versed in the reality of religions and the nature of human beings understand the wisdom behind Allah and His Messenger's prohibition against taking grave-sites as places of worship. The hope of being blessed is the first thing mentioned by those who violate or distort the religious texts which contain these prohibitions. These so-called blessings are quickly transformed into veneration of the dead and people turn to them with supplications and vows and shout out to them in times of difficulty and misfortune. If this is not pure idolatry then it certainly leads to it, no matter how much those who indulge in these practices may deny it. I have seen many written grievances being thrown into the grave-site of Imam ash-Shāfiʿī; some were even sent by mail! I have also seen hundreds of ignorant people panting with compassion and shouting out for help at the grave-sites of Imam Ḥusayn and others. There are none more ignorant than these people, except those who defend them, like the Sufi dervishes and similar individuals who lay claim to special knowledge.

The only way to cure these despicable heretical innovations is to spread knowledge and virtuous behaviour and to purify our minds and habits. The Prophet (ṣ) was only able to destroy the idols after he had devoted 20 years to nurturing a community that believed in Allah and rejected idol-worship.

An official *fatwā* (juristic opinion)

A few Islamic societies in India sent questions to Shaykh Aḥmad Ḥusayn al-Bāqūrī, the Minister of Endowments in Egypt, seeking answers to the question: "Is it religiously permissible to adorn graves and to build mausoleums on them? Is it permissible to build installations next to grave-sites, like a pathway, *masjids* (places of worship) or places of relaxation? What is the ruling on planting flowerbeds on graves, or illuminating the grave-sites during the evenings on religious festivals?"

Shaykh al-Bāqūrī began his reply by responding to the issues of adorning graves and building mausoleums on them. He said that this was a pagan practice equivalent to the worshipping of individuals and that Islam has prohibited it. The Prophet (ṣ) also forbade this practice and had encouraged people to abandon it. It is narrated that Jābir said: "The Messenger of Allah (ṣ) has forbidden the whitewashing of graves, or sitting on them, or elevating them through construction."[15] 'Alī advised one of the companions of the Prophet (ṣ): "Shall I delegate to you what the Messenger of Allah had delegated to me? Destroy every idol you encounter and flatten every grave."[16]

Muslims today utilise the grave-site as a place to show pride and prominence and thereby follow the same deviations as before. Some of them establish mausoleums on graves to show that the deceased person is a saint (*walī*), or from the lineage of an important family, exploiting such links at the expense of Islam. All of this is strictly prohibited.

Regarding establishing other installations next to the graves, like pathways, *masjids* or places of rest, know that Islam frowns upon overcrowding the grave. This is only tolerated if these installations are on the private property of the developer. However, if they are on public burial grounds, then it is prohibited, from a religious perspective, to establish any other sites except grave-sites. Such installations can be established on ground alongside or close to the grave-site.

There is no harm in planting flowerbeds on or around the graves. However, trees carry the same ruling as the installations mentioned above. They are not encouraged on private grave-sites,

and are definitely prohibited on public grave-sites as they crowd
the graves. It is not permissible to overcrowd the dead, so as to
bring some tranquillity to the living.

The question of illuminating the grave-site, as a eulogy to it
and the deceased, remains. This is not a practice upheld by Islam
in any way. The only thing that is able to illuminate the grave is
the actions of the deceased person and whatever good deeds he
has accrued in his lifetime, not candles and lamps that have been
lit by living relatives, usually from the wealthy classes.

The Islamic perspective

Shaykh al-Bāqūrī thereafter digressed to reveal the Islamic
perspective on these issues. He stated:

> Islam is a religion that advocates equality amongst the living, so
> why should it then discriminate amongst the dead in terms of
> grave type and appearance? Furthermore, Islam affirms that the
> grave is an endowment to the deceased and those that bury the
> deceased person are obligated to mark the grave with the name
> of the deceased so that no transgression is committed by the
> living upon their fellow-brother's grave-site and it is left for him
> alone after he has left this world and everything in it and has
> settled in this small hole.

If wealthy people decide to construct mausoleums and domes
on the graves of their departed and illuminate the site, surrounding
it with gardens and trees, this will have no standing in the sight of
Islam. They will, in fact, be held accountable for their extravagance,
the wealth they have wasted and for their audacity towards Allah
by expressing these false and misleading appearances of closeness
to Him. While the construction of these mausoleums and domes
may have been a leisurely pastime for the wealthy, they have
resulted in causing a shift away from the essence of religion and
an emphasis upon appearances. Domes and mausoleums have
sprouted all over the Islamic world, with minarets competing to be
the highest and *mawlid* celebrations being held in honour of the
deceased. All this is done as recompense to Allah for not having

performed prayers, or fasting or pilgrimage, or not having given charity.

This has resulted in Muslims venerating deceased persons whose grave-sites have mausoleums or domes on them and paying little attention to the deceased buried in common graves. We see evidence of this in Egypt, with specific regard to some of the companions of the Prophet (ṣ) that are buried there, like ʿAmr ibn al-ʿĀṣ and ʿUqbah ibn Nāfiʿ. Muslims do not pay the kind of attention to their grave-sites as they do to the sites of those that have mausoleums and high domes! This, in spite of the fact that the Prophet's companions are of a much higher status and are far closer to Allah, as is attested to by the sayings of the Prophet (ṣ) and the consensus of the learned people of Islam.

While this is the situation in Egypt, it is not much different in other countries. The colonisers and occupiers of Muslim lands are aware of this weak point and have paid attention—primary attention—to establishing mausoleums and domes all over the country. The populace thus became complacent towards them and obeyed without difficulty. We are all aware of Napoleon's strategy and how he had duped the Egyptian people with his famous declaration after his occupation of Cairo so that he could get to us by acting as if he respected Islam. His plan was devised by General Menou, who announced that his name was Abdullah Menou. We will also not forget the swindling of Lawrence,[17] who was able to reach the heart of Arab character by exploiting the appearance of Islam and thereby managing to capture most of the Arabian Peninsula.

Similarly, I remember a prominent Easterner speaking to me about some of the methods of colonisation in Asia, particularly about how important it was for the colonisers to change the caravan route from India to Baghdad to a new direction that served their purposes. No amount of propaganda was able to convince the caravan to follow the route preferred by the colonisers. Finally, they devised a plan to establish several mausoleums and domed grave-sites in close proximity to this route. It was only a matter of time before rumours spread about the saints (*awliyā'*) buried at these sites and the miracles witnessed there; this route quickly became popular and developed.

I want to make an earnest appeal, for Allah's sake, to all Muslims, in the East and West, to desist from glorifying grave-sites as it is a fanatical devotion and an invitation to selfishness, and an aristocratic abomination that has killed the spirit of the East. We should return to the all-encompassing embrace of religion that treats all people equally, the living and the dead. There is no preference of one over the other, except in God-consciousness and in terms of the deeds that one has undertaken, solely for the pleasure of Allah.

Employment positions in the *masjid*

Praying in congregation is a pious act that every Muslim strives to fulfil, seeking only the reward of the hereafter. It is irrelevant whether he leads others in prayer or is part of a congregation that is being led by someone else. Leading the *masjid* congregation in prayer is not a type of formal employment for which one receives a salary, big or small. However, it has been noticed that it is to the benefit of the community to appoint persons to carry out this task.

Exercising authority, education, administration and law are all types of general worship that have to be undertaken by people of sufficient capability and experience. The state should provide for such persons[18] in a manner that does not oblige them to seek other employment so as to support themselves. This is the nature of things, as has been determined by societies that are founded upon religious as well as other systems.

It is well known that the *masjid* occupies a very important position in Islam and it is therefore not proper to leave its supervision to chance. What do we mean by this? The *masjid* is a space in which Muslims meet day and night, men and women, young and old. They listen to the verses of the Qur'an during the obligatory prayers, to sermons during the Friday congregational prayers and on the occasion of Eid, to educational lessons that tie Muslims to their religion and help them to adhere to its morals and teachings. Therefore, in order to guarantee good results from these activities, it is important to appoint persons that are capable of undertaking these tasks well. Schools and *masjids* are equal in terms of this requirement. Islamic society is in extreme need of such persons of capability. Its spiritual leadership was undertaken in many of the past eras by the shaykhs of the Sufi *ṭarīqahs*, some of whom excelled and others who did not perform as well. If only the *masjid* imams were able seriously to engage their congregants and the youth, providing them with direction and guiding them to good deeds and a love for Allah, they would have fulfilled their mission in the best of ways.

It is true that Islam does not recognise a clergy class. There are none in this massive community that can be rightfully referred to as "men of religion". There are, however, those that are referred to as the people who know (*ahl adh-dhikr*) or those who posses authority (*ulī al-amr*). These people's opinions have the right to priority and they are qualified to give counsel. The common masses are obligated to seek their counsel on problems and difficulties that they encounter. Allah, the Honoured and Sublime, states: "When there comes to them some matter touching (public) safety or fear, they make it known (among the people), if only they had referred it to the Messenger or to those charged with authority among them, the proper investigators would have understood it from them (directly)" (4:83). It is not left to the ignorant masses to follow their naïve sentiments or to take recourse to their narrow understandings with regards to matters concerning general society, in terms of war and peace or anxiety and safety. Directives of prudent and insightful leaders should be sought. This is how Islam guides the short-sighted to the correct path. The cure for ignorance is to ask: "So ask of those who know, if you know not" (16:43).

Therefore, the *masjid* imam should be a person of vast knowledge, someone who understands religion and matters of this world, who is familiar with societal ills and their cures, with politics and economics, and who is conversant in matters of psychology from a Muslim and non-Muslim perspective. It pains us to admit that such a person is only rarely encountered. One, unfortunately, finds lacklustre examples of imams in hundreds of *masjids*; individuals that fall short of fulfilling their duties and from whom one hears nothing inspiring.

Religious advice

The short sermon is an established practice in Islam. The Prophet of Allah (ṣ) rarely prolonged his speech or over-elaborated when offering advice. His preserved speeches at gatherings and special occasions, as well as his addresses to individuals and groups, did not extend more than a few minutes. His proverbs too were short and wise and the words in them can be counted on one's fingers. The prolonging of sermons in *masjids* in the manner now established by imams and preachers is contrary to the guidance of Islam. Many preachers have become accustomed to addressing their audiences for an hour or two, sometimes even three! Three hours is long enough for a person to recite a quarter of the Qur'an, which was revealed in portions by Allah over a period of 23 years!

I have listened to some of these preachers and have found the substance of their speeches to be empty, far-fetched, repetitive, exaggerated and far off the topic. It is lamentable to see that the common masses have become like hardened alcoholics. Long speeches no longer move them because of the persistent drumming on their ears. This is an inevitable result of disorderly speeches and advice that occupy the space of sermonising and counselling in our communities. Preachers of understanding are in a minority in our *masjids*. Most preachers do not know how or what to say.

Notes

1. Shaykh al-Ghazālī refers to the penultimate verse of Sūrah al-Jumuʻah: "When the (Jumuʻah) prayer is finished, you may disperse through the land, and seek the bounty of Allah, and remember Allah much, that you may be successful" (62:10) [Translator].
2. Published in English in 1997 as: *Fiqh-u-Seerah: Understanding the Life of Prophet Muhammad* (Riyadh: IIPH) [Translator].
3. The full title of the book is *Islamic Civilization in the Fourth Century of the Hegira*. Shaykh al-Ghazālī probably used the Arabic translation: Muḥammad ʻAbd al-Hādī Abū Riḍā (translator), (1957). *Al-Ḥaḍārah al-Islāmiyyah fī al-Qarn ar-Rābiʻ al-Hijrī*, Cairo: Lajnah at-Taʼlīf wa at-Tarjamah wa an-Nashr [Translator].
4. *Musnad Aḥmad*, ḥadīth no. 20392.
5. *Ṣaḥīḥ Muslim*, Book of Mosques and Places of Prayer, ḥadīth no. 811.
6. *Difāʻ ʻan al-Ḥadīth*, al-Albānī, 43.
7. *Ṣaḥīḥ al-Bukhārī*, Book of Prayer, ḥadīth no. 416.
8. *Ṣaḥīḥ Muslim*, Book of Funerals, ḥadīth no. 1614.
9. *Sunan at-Tirmidhī*, Book of Prayer, ḥadīth no. 291.
10. *Musnad Aḥmad*, ḥadīth no. 10298.
11. *Musnad Aḥmad*, ḥadīth no. 2829.
12. *Sunan at-Tirmidhī*, Book of Funerals, ḥadīth no. 972.
13. *Musnad Aḥmad*, ḥadīth no. 1012.
14. *Musnad Aḥmad*, ḥadīth no. 7054 quotes the Prophet's prayer as follows: "O Allah, do not make my grave-site an idol and curse those people that took the grave-sites of their Prophets as places of Prayer" [Translator].
15. *Sunan at-Tirmidhī*, Book of Funerals, ḥadīth no. 972.
16. *Ṣaḥīḥ Muslim*, Book of Funerals, ḥadīth no. 1609.
17. British officer Lieutenant Colonel Thomas Edward Lawrence, popularly known as Lawrence of Arabia [Translator's note].
18. Shaykh al-Ghazālī is, of course, referring to countries in the Muslim world [Translator's note].

6

Heretical Innovations and Customary Practices

Prevalent traditions

Easterners have certain unique traditions that are not observed outside of their countries. While observing Muslims steadfastly practising these traditions, some people mistakenly conclude that they have emerged from the principles of Islam, the directives of Allah or, at the very least, that they affirm and do not contradict well-established practices of our religion. This is a mistake that contradicts the truth.

Eastern traditions are not the principles of Islam, nor are the actions of people the commandments of Allah. Customary Practice (*'urf*)—no matter how well established—is to be placed upon the scales of judgement and not be used as a justification for passing judgement. Traditions too—no matter how well consolidated— may be absolutely false or a mixture of truth and falsehood. The arbiter in these matters is the Qur'an and the Prophetic traditions.

The person who proceeds through life stripped of volition, and unthinking, for no reason other than that his feet follow in the footsteps of those before him, is a person far-removed from Islam, both intellectually and practically. And have not the earlier generations gone astray simply by imitating bad traditions and customs? "Verily, they found their fathers on the wrong path, so they (too) made haste to follow in their footsteps! And, indeed, most of the men of old went astray before them. And, indeed, We sent among them warners (messengers). Then see what was the end of those who were warned (but heeded not), except the chosen servants of Allah" (37:69-74).

Easterners have unique ways of expressing their happiness and sadness, sometimes inclining towards overstatement and extravagance. They also have their own way of engaging with friends and guests. They have specific inclinations in engaging with women, in interacting with them, in looking after them. They have a unique ethic in viewing life, the value of time, engaging in work, organizing celebrations, gatherings and separation, and so forth. Some aspects of this ethic encompass good, some encompass bad, some are palatable and some are not.

It is unfair to blame Islam for the many burdens of the various elements of our behaviour; the way of life that Islam enjoins transcends the traditions of both the East and the West. There are matters that are delved into in the name of religion that are actually alien to it. For example, common people sometimes believe that Arab dress is advocated by Islam, that some forms of dress are actually an expression of one's Islam, such as the robe and the turban, or the way that the scholars of al-Azhar dress. This is nothing short of superstition. Clothing that we describe as Arab or as Western are no more than garments of varying utility and worth; some are comfortable and some cause discomfort, some are to one's taste and some are not; some types of dress are suitable to a specific group or function. Even the reason behind choosing the colours of clothes is relevant. Elaborating upon these matters is not our concern here. I know people that have abandoned Arab dress in favour of Western dress so as to make a transition from austerity to liberalism. Changing one's dress is one matter and changing one's intention is another matter altogether. If someone were to wear the cloak of the Prophet (ṣ) with a bad intention, he would not be saved from Allah's reproach.

The manner in which Western public amenities are built is very different from the way in which Arab public amenities are built. Both—in my view—have their advantages and their shortcomings. There is, however, no reason for saying that this one is Islamic and that one is unIslamic. The general population amongst us is offended by using toilet paper for cleaning purposes, as they claim that the stones used by Arabs and rural people are far more effective. This is wrong. Using toilet paper together with water is undoubtedly the best. The earlier generation did not use paper because it was not widespread. If it is abundant in our generation there is no reason not to use it.

I notice many different construction techniques in our country. Some are Pharaonic, some are Arabic and some are European. The engineering techniques vary both aesthetically and in terms of sophistication in these ancient and modern methods. It is not appropriate to describe one as Islamic and the other as unIslamic; that would be stupid. I personally find a simple window in an ordinary house closer to good taste than a window made with complicated engravings and coloured glass in the wall of a church.

We have already explained the Islamic position on innovation regarding worldly matters; it leaves the mind free to explore as it wishes and to keep on innovating within its vast expanse as is required. It, in fact, displaces the impediments that challenge free thinking and inclines towards creation and invention. Every person enjoys absolute independence in terms of his work efforts. Every person has a wide scope that allows production and innovation. He is free to form opinions and establish principles in line with certain conventions without any impediment. Islam does not require anything of a person engaged in these endeavours except to follow pure reason and correct insight.

People are most knowledgeable in matters pertaining to their livelihoods. It is also well-known that such productive activities are not left alone and that all societies exploit them. In general, whatever brings about economic progress or academic excellence is utilized in various ways, some praiseworthy and some detestable. This is where the role of noble teachings comes into play, to exploit the energy of life for pious objectives and good deeds. Islam affirms that every action in this world that is undertaken with noble intentions and sincerity, seeking the pleasure of Allah, Lord of the Worlds, is a prayer, a form of charity and an accepted devotion, even in response to the hunger instinct that seeks satiation or the sexual instinct that seeks fulfilment.

However, such flexibility regarding the realities of the physical world is balanced by the strictness that controls the realities of religious expression. It is therefore imperative to adhere to the established tradition, and it is forbidden to introduce any additions, which are then appended to what has been enjoined by Allah and His Prophet (ṣ). Nothing can be supplemented to Allah's revelation: "So, after the truth, what else can there be, save error? How then are you turned away?" (10:32).

What we require is compliance in religious matters and innovation in worldly matters. This is the only way that we can be rightly guided. Nevertheless, some Muslims are reflected in the above verse and you see them coming to a halt when they should be moving, or exploring when they should be showing restraint. This carelessness has placed Muslims in positions that have limited their worldly capacity and has compromised their religion. The effects of corrupt religion are only felt in the hereafter. However, the effects of a corrupt understanding of this world are felt very quickly, and such short-sighted people face continuous defeat in all spheres of life.

The true Muslim is left in grief witnessing the backwardness of his people, especially in fields that they had once excelled in. They are now surpassed not only by the followers of the other heavenly religions, but also by adherents to false, earthly religions. Why? Because their shortcomings in understanding Islam seeped into their understanding of life itself, and their failures led to their degeneration.

It is not enough to only cleanse the acts of worship and devotion from the heretical innovations that have spoiled them. Any community may be able to worship Allah correctly, in accordance with what has been revealed to them, but it places various restrictions upon itself by its own reckoning, and restrictions upon its other endeavours in life, which paralyse its movement, destroy its health and darken its future.

Heretical innovations pertaining to funeral ceremonies

Muslims have traditions that incur burdensome liabilities when paying honour to their lost ones and dealing with their grief. These liabilities are not only monetary; they are an ethical and physical burden as well. Such traditions are a compound of heretical innovations and sinful behaviour. In spite of the difficulties encountered, people still adhere to these traditions and regard them as obligatory. I have seen poor people, who were themselves short of food, incurring debt to carry out these traditions, which had become so entrenched in their understanding that they regarded them as a part of Islam, or even more important!

As soon as someone amongst us dies, relatives immediately busy themselves with these traditions so as to preserve their honour and to honour their relationship with the deceased. They set up pavilions or premises to host the mourners for a night or two, and people are hired to recite the Qur'an even though very few listen to the recitation and even fewer understand what is being recited. After the immediate mourning is concluded, the grave-site is visited after a week or two and alms are distributed. These burdensome expenses are once again incurred after 40 days. A commemoration is offered after the passing of the first year since the person's demise and then again after the second year, and so on.

These traditions are not only rejected by a correct under-standing of worldly affairs, but also by a correct understanding of Islam. Germany lost close to 10 million people in the Second

World War. How did they respond? They covered their deceased with sand in silence, and thereafter resumed their struggle for life in all earnestness and were able to recoup their losses in a short number of years. As far as we are concerned, we follow up on a single death in the manner described. What would we do if we were drawn into a war that killed thousands of victims? How many pavilions would we set up for mourners? How many visits to the grave-sites? How many commemorations after the first week, after the first 40 days, after the first year? These traditions that are practised by Muslims are undoubtedly extremely foolish.

It is all the more lamentable to see commoners and educated people undertaking such foolishness through vague religious practices. Some preachers have endorsed these gatherings, wanting to give them legitimacy or to make their existence more acceptable, and have added general religious admonition to the recitation of the Qur'an. This solution only complicates matters further. The only cure for these afflictions is to practise the correct teachings of the Prophet (ṣ) and to abandon these false traditions altogether.

The Islamic position in relation to these matters is that a person should confront what Allah has ordained with patient perseverance. He should not allow despair to overcome his heart, nor should he allow himself to be overtaken by grief, except very briefly. As soon as he feels sorrow taking grip, he should free himself from it and continue with his life, having greater understanding of his Lord, in total submission to His decree and seeking His beneficence only. The Messenger of Allah (ṣ) said: "Whoever is able to recover from a calamity, Allah will grant him solace, improve his condition thereafter, and grant him a recompense that will please him."[1]

It is not permissible for a Muslim, male or female, to adopt a specific form of dress to indicate grief or to show grief by placing insignia on one's body or on one's person, home or place of work. The passing on of someone to the Hereafter does not give one an excuse to spread chaos and disruption in matters of everyday life. The reality is that the deceased has died and the living should go on living.

Because women are more responsive to grief, Islam has ordained for them a fixed period of time for mourning. The Messenger of Allah (ṣ) said: "It is not permissible for a woman that believes in Allah and the Day of Reckoning to mourn for a person for more than three nights, except for her husband, [for whom the mourning period is] four months and ten days."[2] The relatives of the woman are all the same in that she may not mourn them for more than three days. Mourning here refers to the practice of abandoning her usual adornments and the use of henna and perfume. As far as the husband is concerned, his relationship with his wife and the drastic change she faces for the future deserve a longer mourning period, after which she may go back to wearing adornments and engaging in unreserved speech.

There is no place in Islam for noisy processions that follow the bier. The raising of voices—even for the recitation of the Qur'an or the remembrance of Allah—is not permissible. It has become a custom amongst the commoners to bring people along for the specific purpose of creating this detestable racket. The author of *al-Madkhal*[3] wrote:

> This is contrary to the practice of the Prophet (ṣ), his companions and our pious predecessors, and it should be prohibited by those who have the capacity to do so by means of stern warning and punishment! Some add the wailing of women, the slapping of the cheeks and similar actions to these processions. All of this is in opposition to the manner in which our predecessors carried out their burials. Their burials were characterized by quiet contemplation and reverence where one could not even distinguish the grieving individuals from other mourners. Everyone appeared sad and was contemplative and preoccupied as they were reminded in the procession of death that this was the destination that they were also ultimately approaching.

Al-Ḥasan said: "The deceased of tomorrow carries the deceased of today." Ibn Masʿūd responded to a man who had said during a funeral, "Seek forgiveness for your brother (the deceased)" by telling him: "No! May Allah forgive you. It is disliked for one to raise his voice during the funeral." If this was their response in rejecting any disruptive noise that followed the funeral procession, what should we make of the noise and disruption that is created by the crowds today, or of their noisy recitations and recitals of poetry?

The offering of condolences approved by Islam occurs in the course of events and the family of the deceased does not make special preparations, nor do they gather in an appointed venue. This was the practice of our pious predecessors. They would go about their affairs, and if they met an individual who had experienced a loss they would console him and offer their condolences.

The situation has become extremely confused among people now, and those afflicted by loss are obligated to prepare a venue for mourners offering condolences and to prepare food and drink for visitors. This, in spite of the fact that the prophetic practice is to offer assistance to the household that has suffered a loss, and to prepare food for the family, not for the family to prepare food and drink for visitors in addition to dealing with their calamity. When Jaʿfar ibn Abī Ṭālib had died, the Messenger of Allah (ṣ) said: "Prepare food for the family of Jaʿfar for they have been visited by that which preoccupies them."[4]

The scholars of jurisprudence have affirmed that the food that is prepared by the family of the deceased for those that gather around them is detestable (*makrūh*) as it supports a heretical innovative (*bidʿah*) practice. Imam Aḥmad regarded this practice as an act of the time of ignorance (before Islam), and strongly disapproved of it. Strangely enough, this pre-Islamic practice is at the centre of the prevalent practices common in this day and age.

Graveyards are not places for distributing charity. I have seen many endowments where the deceased have stipulated providing food and drink at their grave-sites and the adornment of their graves with flowers and sweet basil! This type of charity has its origins in the practices of the pre-Islamic age of ignorance, where people would slaughter sheep at the grave-site, seeking mercy for the deceased. With the onset of Islam, these practices were prohibited.

The Messenger of Allah (ṣ) said: "There is no animal sacrifice in Islam."[5] It seems as if Muslims have substituted sacrifice with the distribution of cooked meat and sometimes bread and fruit along with it! All of these are innovated practices that have no basis in Islam.

The reason for these practices, in my opinion, is weak faith in the principle of *individual responsibility* in the afterlife. Therefore, one sees attachment to practices that infer that the deceased benefit from the actions of the living. Correct Prophetic practices that apply to this context should not be understood as a negation of the affirmed principles that indicate accountability in the hereafter; they have explanations that are well-known to people of knowledge. In spite of this, commoners still insist on hiring individuals to recite the Qur'an for the deceased so that they may gain benefit therefrom. I do not know any other community that has treated their holy book in this manner, ignoring it when they are living, but reading it for the dead!

Heretical innovations pertaining to joyous occasions

Muslims have certain bad customs pertaining to celebrating joyous occasions: they incline towards extremism and overburden themselves, and very rarely do they lean towards simplicity and balance. They exploit Islam's permissiveness towards good things and go to extremes, reaching the limits of extravagance not approached in other religious traditions. I have attended functions on various occasions: to celebrate the birth of a child, to welcome an employee, to honour a friend, or to celebrate the joy of marriage. Open extravagance was a general characteristic of all these celebrations, whether in Egypt, the Levant or Ḥijāz.

It is even possible to suggest that non-Muslims are closer to moderation in these matters than we are. They are indeed closer to moderation in their indulgence in worldly pleasures, those that are permissible and those that are prohibited. Drunkards amongst us carry on sipping to the point of collapse, while their drunkards drink as much as would allow them to maintain their balance! A non-Muslim woman will be satisfied with an inexpensive, elegant dress, whereas a Muslim woman will not be satisfied until she covers herself in the most expensive cloth.

These contrasts are expressed in a time in which the Islamic State has collapsed, its power has been expended, its territories trampled upon, and where occupiers have spread throughout its corners, roaring like conquering lions. It would be only natural for the vanquished to turn away from the simple pleasures when the victors indulged in these and other pleasures to their fullest. But to see the victors show restraint and the vanquished engaging in excess is truly calamitous. In the pre-Islamic age of ignorance, the vanquished tribes would abstain from the joys and indulgences they were accustomed to so as to reflect upon their loss. If they were able to extract their revenge or erase what they saw as a blemish they would resume their earlier indulgences. One of their poets said:

> Drink has become permissible for me, whereas before
> I would almost choke on the waters of the Euphrates.

We have seen that Abū Sufyān—after the defeat at Badr—had sworn neither to approach his wife nor to touch perfume until he was able to erase the defeat of the idolaters in this battle, and he did not find peace until he had fulfilled his promise.

As a priority, Muslims should shed the burden of these traditions—as well as other material and moral vices—that turn their celebrations into competitions of ostentation and boastfulness. They should rather adhere to the teachings of their religion and be cognizant of their current situation. Simplicity in all matters is the Islamic way. Ibn 'Umar said: "Being over-excessive is prohibited to us."[6] Ibn Mas'ūd reported that the Messenger of Allah (ṣ) had pronounced: "Indeed, the extravagant ones will perish,"[7] repeating it three times.

Extravagance is to overstep what comes naturally by being excessive and over-scrutinizing. Al-Fuḍayl ibn 'Iyāḍ said: "People are driven away by extravagance; someone invites his brother and goes to extremes, thereby cutting him off so that he does not feel like coming back." It has been reported by Anas ibn Mālik and other companions: "They used to serve to their brothers whatever was at hand, like dry nuts and dates. They would say: 'We do not know what is the greater offense: the one who detests what has been served to him, or the one who detests that which he has to offer.'"

These teachings show that a person should be appreciative of what he has, and not be ashamed by it, causing him to resort to excess to deceive people. It does not, however, imply that one should sink into a pit of stinginess and serve something insignificant when one is able to serve something pleasant. One has to only examine the life of the Prophet Ibrāhīm, the Friend of Allah, to see the embodiment of nobility. As soon as guests had arrived at his home, he asked his family to slaughter and roast a calf, offering it to them without even inquiring or knowing whether they were hungry or not: "Has the story reached you of the honoured guests of Ibrāhīm? When they came to him and said: 'Peace,' he answered: 'Peace,' and said 'You are a people unknown to me.' Then he turned to his household, who brought out a roasted calf. He placed it before them (saying): 'Will you not eat?'" (51:24-27).

Wedding celebrations are generally most deserving of exertion and some excess. However, Islam does not condone extravagant food and wastage with the joy of the occasion that is being celebrated. Asmā' bint 'Umays reported: "I was with 'Ā'ishah on the night of her wedding to the Messenger of Allah (ṣ) and there were other women with us as well." She then said: "By Allah, we did not find anything on offer accept a cup of milk, from which the Messenger (ṣ) drank. He then passed it on to ʿĀʾishah, but she was shy. I said to her: 'Do not refuse the hand of the Messenger of Allah (ṣ). Take it from him.' She took it from him with humility and drank from it. He then said: 'Pass it on to your companions.' We said: 'We are not hungry.' He replied: 'Do not join hunger with dishonesty.' Asmāʾ then said: 'O Messenger of Allah, if one of us had to say concerning something they desired, "I am not hungry", is that regarded as a lie?' He then replied: 'Every lie is recorded and even small lies are recorded as such.'"[8]

When the Messenger of Allah (ṣ) married off his daughter Fāṭimah, the food that he presented to the invitees was a plate of unripe dates. In one narration the Prophet (ṣ) said: "Allah had commanded me to marry Fāṭimah to ʿAlī ibn Abī Ṭālib, so bear witness that I have married her for a dowry of 400 pieces of silver, if this is acceptable to ʿAlī." He then called for the plate of unripe dates and said: "Indulge."[9]

This is how the wife and daughter of a prophet were married! It was in a ceremony that was neither extravagant nor financially burdensome. Just look at what Muslims do during their wedding celebrations and how they are burdened by expenditure to prepare large functions, where neither the hungry nor the needy are fed.

Marriage and family ties

There is a large gap between the ethics of Islam pertaining to the relationship between a man and a woman and the traditions of modern civilization that have developed in the East and the West. There is an equally large gap between the ethics of Islam itself and that which ignorant people expect of Islam concerning the function of women in society. Women are left behind a wall of ignorance and blindness, where half of the *ummah* is dying and the other half is becoming ill. The entire *ummah* is affected by women that are left to temptation and desire, where Satan interferes in their affairs.

The Islamic *ummah* is divided into two spheres: a sphere where women have no place—like Yemen and the Gulf—and a sphere where the place of women is misconstrued, where her place is confused and inequitable—like in Egypt. One cannot tell when we will be rid of these contradictions and be guided to the truth.

The sexual drive is perhaps the most active drive running in the veins of humans. It even seems as if the sustenance of development on the face of this earth has been entrusted to it alone. Taking account of this drive is not forgotten in the fields of economics and education. Its material and ethical underpinnings are equal in terms of precaution and care. This drive cannot be ignored—from the time it is awakened during the teenage years—except by a person that has closed his eyes to reality and deafens his ears to its screaming.

The natural dispensation of the human being (*al-fiṭrah*)—from which the rulings of Islam also emanate—has guided this drive along the straight path. It has neither killed it with asceticism nor allowed it to dominate with complete permissibility. It has allowed it to breathe and to fulfil its intended function, which is not only the perpetuation of human life, but also the granting of serenity through love, collaboration and mercy.

Modern Western civilization concords with Islam in its recognition of this drive. However, it contradicts *all* religions by making broad sexual liberalization the cure for its insatiable desire. Europe has undoubtedly pampered the capricious beast flowing in the veins of people. It has facilitated unrestricted mixing of the sexes and has coolly accepted all of its consequences, even advocating silence in response.

The laws of Allah, which were revealed to Mūsā, ʿĪsā and Muḥammad (Peace be upon them all), are far too sublime to affirm this condition or to make it permissible. It is not surprising to see religious people showing apprehension to this condition, nor is it surprising to see them reacting with added fanaticism and caution, going to extremes that seek to confine women, questioning their behaviour and restricting their movement. This is not a practical solution to this entrenched problem. The solution[10] can be found in the methodology reflected in the Book of Allah and the Prophetic tradition; it is a unique and sensible solution that governs the temporary and permanent relationships between males and females.

Marriage is the only solution to the problem of sexuality. It is the noblest relationship known to humanity for the creation of a family and the nurturing of children in a pure and chaste environment. Society is responsible for nurturing its economic affairs and general traditions, so as to make marriage easy and simple, not something that inspires fear or embarrassment.

Islam is a religion that places modesty and well-being on the same level as enjoining *tawḥīd* (monotheism). Does it not equate murder and the violation of honour with polytheism? Does it not mention the best of believers by saying: "And those who invoke not any other god along with Allah, nor take the life that Allah has forbidden, except for just cause, nor commit illegal sexual intercourse—and whoever does this shall receive the punishment. The torment will be doubled to him on the Day of Resurrection, and he will abide therein in disgrace; except those who repent and believe, and do righteous deeds" (25:68-70)? Whenever Islam fights against the greatest sin (to associate partners with Allah—*shirk*) and the second greatest sin (to take life, which Allah has protected), the sin of lewdness has to also be fought against. Fighting against it does not require absolute suppression or the advocation of asceticism for years on end, which is quite impossible. These alternatives only make our community more deranged. Our community is silent in the face of the lewdness practised by deranged youth. Society promotes the idea that the youth may spend several years engaged in prohibited pastimes before finally turning to a virtuous marriage. It accepts the expression of these abhorrent acts but does not tolerate any negligence with regards to hosting extravagant parties to celebrate marriage.

Many Islamic communities see no harm in delaying marriage and extending the period of sexual chaos that precedes it, so that an exorbitant dowry can be paid. This behaviour proves that those who guard these inherited traditions and sought-after values are more influential amongst people than those who pay attention to Islam and seek Allah's pleasure. Can one doubt this, knowing that we kill a woman for committing adultery and let a man go free without any harm being inflicted upon him. The act of killing in this context is not that of a believer aroused to uphold the rights of Allah. It is, rather, the anger of a person moved to defend his personal reputation. If the matter was about rejecting a person soiled by a filthy transgression, the family would have been as angry at their sinful son and would have disciplined him just as they are extremely angered by the transgression of their daughter, finding no salvation for her except in death. However, these Eastern traditions (or rural traditions, to be more precise) are beginning to vanish due to the modern imported form of ignorance in the form of sexual liberalism, moral abjection and everything else being flung at us by Western civilization.

In all frankness, the Muslim that dislikes the establishment of doubt and suspicion in his community is obligated to guide it to the teachings of Islam in this regard. In order to encourage marriage—instead of lewdness—a Muslim should remove all the artificial obstacles before it and the community and the state should cooperate to make it a desired union for all parties concerned, not a catastrophe that has to face crises and strictures.

I have witnessed exorbitant dowries being asked for in the Ḥijāz and Palestine where a man cannot marry without presenting his wife with a huge price. What has been the result of this? It has been the spread of wrongdoing all around. Ignorant people should not try and convince us of the religious permissibility of claiming exorbitant dowries! Even if this was an acceptable voluntary act, it would not be correct to proceed in this manner because one cannot perform voluntary acts until one has fulfilled the obligatory acts. If the obligatory acts are already being trampled upon, where is the room for voluntary acts? If abstinence has been lost and permissiveness has taken its place, only an arrogant imbecile will uphold the permissibility of asking for an exorbitant dowry. Muslims have made a difficult slope out of religiously sanctioned marriage, and many have consequently slipped thereon.

The marriage of Mūsā deserves to be contemplated. He left Egypt, sad and exiled, seeking stability and tranquillity, and headed for Madyan seeking a home better than the one he had just lost. He turned to Allah, that he perchance be guided and taken care of: "And when he went towards (the land) of Madyan he said: 'It may be that my Lord guides me to the Right Way.' And when he arrived at the water of Madyan he found there a group of men watering (their flocks), and besides them he found two women who were keeping back (their flocks). He said: 'What is the matter with you?' They said: 'We cannot water (our flocks) until the shepherds take (their flocks). And our father is a very old man.' So he watered (their flocks) for them" (28:22-24).

Mūsā's heart was softened by the sight of two girls undertaking the task of their father and he hastened—with noble intent—to carry this burden on their behalf. He did not miss noticing the virtuousness and modesty in their manner. They refused to stir up the crowd around the water. Assistance came to them as they waited for the shepherds to finish so that they could water their flock. The behaviour of these two women represents the high morality that all virtuous women should aspire to, in all ages.

The behaviour of Mūsā is also a great precedent for commendable chivalry. After performing his good deed "then he turned back to the shade, and said: 'My Lord! Truly, I am in need of whatever good that You bestow upon me!' Then there came to him one of the two women, walking shyly. She said: 'Verily, my father calls you that he may reward you for having watered (our flocks) for us'" (28:24-25).

Mūsā followed the girl, but not to collect the reward of his good deed; he was far too noble for that. He only sought succour in this strange land and to find shelter with the head of this household, to share with him what troubled him: "So when he came to him and narrated the story, he said: 'Fear you not. You have escaped from a transgressing people'" (28:25).

The pious old man proposed that Mūsā marry one of his daughters so that he may find security in his present circumstances and in the future. He also offered Mūsā the opportunity to work for him after one of his daughters expressed her positive opinion of him: "And one of them said: 'O my father! Hire him! Verily, the best of men for you to hire is the strong, the trustworthy.' He said: 'I intend to wed one of these two daughters of mine to you, on condition that you serve me for eight years, but if you complete ten years, it will be (a favour) from you. But I intend not to place you under difficulty. If Allah wills, you will find me one of the righteous.' He (Mūsā) said: 'That (is settled) between me and you, whichever of the terms I fulfil there will be no injustice to me and Allah is Surety over what we say'" (28:26-28).

I am sure that if the girl that had pronounced her opinion about Mūsā had been the daughter of a man from Ṣaʿīd (in the Egyptian countryside), her father would have murdered her!! How could she describe a strange man in such terms? In fact, if the father was a man from the present generation of Muslims, he would have flatly refused to send his daughter to summon a man she did not know in the first place.

In spite of this, what was achieved was the fulfilment of a noble marriage, joining two magnanimous individuals, opening the path to pure morals and noble traditions. This is exactly what we seek in our present environment, but do not find! The society that we admire is founded, before anything else, upon alert consciences, strong values, extreme attention to public opinion and to the rule of law.

Perhaps the most unsuccessful means of education is one that is based on the incarceration of women within a prison of intellectual and ethical isolation. It is, in fact, wrong to even regard this as a means of education. However, failure to regulate sexual relations within the boundaries that have been ordained by Allah, and using this failure as a pretence for allowing animalistic passion to find expression as it wishes, is a breakdown of the natural dispensation of humanity and of morals, and rebellion against Allah and all of His commandments.

If only Muslims would study how relationships were conducted in the Prophetic era, how all the members of the family would come together in the courtyard of the *masjid* at various times of the day and night. In fact, men and women had fought together to elevate the word of Allah. Scholars of jurisprudence agree that if Islamic lands are attacked, every Muslim man and woman is obligated to respond to the call to arms and to go out to fight, sacrificing themselves and their possessions.

It is possible—in light of these relationships that are affirmed by the teachings of Islam—to imagine the environment in which the family is born, is sustained, and lives, fulfilling its mission to the fullest. There are many teachings in the Qur'an and Prophetic traditions pertaining to gazing, seeking permission, relaxing one's dress, covering up, leaving the face unveiled, the returning of a man to his home after a long absence, the attitude of a woman towards her and her husband's relatives, the rights of one's parents, the rights of children, and so forth. These teachings are explained in detail and a Muslim should adhere to them and ensure that his family and close relatives adhere to them as well.

There are, however, types of general conduct for which Islam does not mention specific teachings and over which people in the East and West differ. It is clearly noticeable that foreigners give their children lots of freedom. Their children may engage—in the presence of their parents—in a manner we may regard as contrary to proper decorum but which their parents do not find offensive. In addition, as soon as their children transcend childhood, they begin carrying the burdens of life and are questioned about their earnings, which they are expected to use to build their futures. In European societies, both spouses seek employment and household expenses are shared.

We do not affirm any specific conduct from the Western lifestyle but encourage careful inspection of our traditions and theirs, especially those that are not sustained by that which is not based on friendship and kindness and which has no relationship to belief and disbelief or obedience and transgression. If we encounter that which is good, we can transmit it to our societies, if not, we can ignore it. We should take into account that the spirit of consciousness and independence that has allowed Western states to ascend and take control goes back to that which is fed into the blood of their children from a very young age, through nurturing boldness and self-reliance. Weak sensibilities have enticed us to become complacent and dependent on others, and we have become isolated in our own countries so that outsiders have infiltrated them. These foreigners—men and women—extract the goodness of our lands at our expense.

To draw benefit from traditions that we are not familiar with— if they appear to be good—does not compromise our attachment to our religion, nor to establishing its practices. When the early Arabs had begun recording their history and settling in foreign lands, in the process retaining the administrative systems of the Roman and Persian civilizations, they did not, however, thereby abandon their religion.

We should also know—and I take careful account of what I am saying—that women in Islamic countries are seen as sources of consumption whereas in other societies they are sources of production; they are a burden here and a form of assistance there. This is practically and ethically unacceptable! Israel has a population of about five million, but its army comprises the entire population, men and women, with the exception of children. Have any of the Islamic countries, which have far larger populations than Israel, achieved that which the Jewish military has achieved, or do women and children in those countries—I mean our countries—live only for eating and pleasure?

Birthday celebrations

An established tradition among foreigners is the celebration of their birthdays and the welcoming of the New Year with celebrations that fill their lives with joy, vigour and hope. These customs—if they are free from extravagance and prohibited actions—can be retained without any offence. If we were to emulate their traditions to take better account of time, to establish what we have achieved in the past and to see how we can gain more from time in the future, it would be to the benefit of those inclined to do so.

However, this is not what Muslims reproduce through the celebration of their births. Their customs dictate that when someone they regard as pious dies they establish a mausoleum on his grave-site and build an honorific dome over it, turning it into a place of holy pilgrimage (*mazār*) where the deceased person's birthday is celebrated once or twice a year. This practice is a mixture of sin and heretical innovation. There is no doubt that it is a major transgression of the teachings of Islam.

The birthday celebrations of the pious have become common-place, stretching across the length and breadth of our countries. They have become common market occasions and well-known calendar events. It is said that the first people to introduce this practice in Cairo were the Fatimids in the fourth century (AH). They had innovated six birthday celebrations: the celebration of the Prophet's birthday (*al-mawlid an-nabawī*), the celebration of Imam 'Alī's birthday, the celebration of our lady Fāṭimah's birthday, the birthdays of Ḥasan and Ḥusayn, and the birthday of the Caliph of the time. These birthday celebrations remained as stipulated until they were abolished by al-Afḍal ibn Amīr al-Juyūsh, but were re-established during the caliphate of al-Ḥakim bi Amrillāh in 524 (AH), after almost having been completely forgotten by the population.

The first person to introduce the celebration of the Prophet's birthday in the seventh century (AH) in the city of Irbīl (present day Iraq) was the King al-Muẓẓafar Abū Saʿīd. These celebrations became commonplace thereafter in all places, with many adherents. People went to extremes in embellishing and giving prominence to these celebrations so that the word *mawlid* became a symbol for chaos and mockery.

To seek the favour of Allah by participating in the *mawlid* is an act of worship that has no basis. To take the grave-sites of the pious as sites of congregation for these celebrations is a sin committed against Allah and His Prophet, even if it is solely for the intention of gaining Allah's favour. The Messenger of Allah (ṣ) said in this regard: "Do not turn your homes into grave-sites, and do not turn my grave-site into a place of celebration; convey your greetings upon me from wherever you may be, for your greetings reach me, wherever you may be."[11]

Suhayl ibn Abī Suhayl stated: "Al-Ḥasan ibn al-Ḥasan ibn ʿAlī ibn Abī Ṭālib saw me at [the Prophet's] grave-site. He called out to me—as he was in the house of Fāṭimah having supper—and said: 'Come to supper.' I said: 'I do not want [supper].' He then asked: 'Why do I see you at the grave?' I said: 'I have conveyed my salutations to the Prophet (ṣ).' He asked: 'Did you enter the *masjid* for this?' He then said that the Messenger of Allah (ṣ) said: 'Do not take my home as a place of celebration and do not take your homes as grave-sites, and convey your salutations upon me. Indeed, your salutations reach me wherever you may be.'"[12] If the Messenger of Allah (ṣ) disapproved of people taking *his* grave-site as a place of assembly and a point for pilgrimage, what about the sites of others, whether we know who they are or not?

On the other hand, the *masjids* that one should exert effort and expense to visit are well known. These are—as has been enumerated by the Messenger of Allah (ṣ): the Holy *Masjid* in Makkah, the Prophet's *Masjid* in Madīnah and the al-Aqṣā *Masjid* in al-Quds[13] (Jerusalem). The elevated status of these *masjids* is not due to what they contain, or to honour those who may be buried there, but, rather, due to their special significance. This is, however, not the place to elaborate upon this issue further.

People who think that they are pleasing Allah by instituting the *mawlid* of great saints (*awliyā'*), or even lesser known *awliyā'*, are committing a despicable heretical innovation and are creating an opportunity for grievous sins. In truth, the *mawlid* celebrations are the most fertile environments for manifest and hidden transgressions. In its grand gatherings, foolish actions are widespread without shame; men and women mix freely in eating and sleeping spaces and the sins of adultery and homosexuality are a common occurrence. Hashish is smoked, licentious songs and music are listened to, and the spirit of earnestness and respect is lost, replaced by nonchalance and profanity. The cleanliness of the *masjid* is also compromised and the times of the congregational prayers are disrupted. Furthermore, the people who visit these gatherings have strange beliefs. One of them may begrudgingly give his mother a few coins in charity while showing extreme generosity at these gatherings in honour of the person whose birth is being celebrated, and who—it is believed—does not disappoint those who visit him nor refuses their requests!

Some people defend the *mawlid* gatherings because they conduct *dhikr* sessions, beneficial lectures, Qur'anic recitations, or because the poor and needy are fed on these occasions. Even if the *mawlid* gatherings were free of all the sins that we have mentioned above, it would still be incumbent to abandon them as they are an expression of corrupt religious practice. The *dhikr* sessions are bewildering gatherings where various forms of movement and dance that damage the image of Islam are performed. As far the recitation of the Qur'an at these gatherings is concerned, neither the reciter nor the listener benefit therefrom. It is like a song recited in a tiresome tune that only a few listeners pretend to pay attention to, longing for it to end. The same applies to the sermons and guidance that is sometimes administered with the intention of educating the large masses that attend the *mawlid* gatherings. These are all unfruitful attempts and a compromise of the value of wise words and noble preaching.

If we were to assume that there is some good in these actions, they still cannot be regarded as a justification for the institution of *mawlid* celebrations, as we have already explained the detriment that these practices cause. The principle of the *sharī'ah* pertaining to this matter advocates that the avoiding of harm is given precedence over the attracting of benefit.

Ibn Ḥajar said: "Do you not see that the Legislator has advocated the enactment of good to the level that is easy for one, weaning us away from all forms of evil, such that the Messenger of Allah (ṣ) said: 'If I command you to undertake an action, do it to the level of your ability, and if I prohibit you from something, then avoid it altogether.'"[14] In other words, evil—even in small proportions—is not pardoned in the least, while good is pursued to the level of one's ability. How can we then open the door of certain evil for the sake of probable good? Furthermore, what is the vessel that carries this probable good: an action that was not undertaken by the Messenger of Allah (ṣ), his Companions, or those who emulated them in virtue for many centuries?

The former head of al-Azhar, Shaykh Muḥammad Muṣṭafā al-Marāghī, reached a similar conclusion. He said:

> There are certain matters that may be *bid'ah* or that may not be *bid'ah*. For example, if you were to celebrate the Prophet's birthday, the day of *hijrah* (migration to Madīnah), or pregnancy, regarding them as worship or religious expression, then this is undoubtedly a heretical innovation (*bid'ah*), because it is the creation of an act of worship that did not exist and which was not granted permissibility.

However, if it were undertaken as a cultural practice, where the celebration of the *hijrah* and the Prophet's birthday were a revival of honoured memories, it would be a pretence for good and an occasion for thankfulness that urges the person to hold steadfastly to guidance and noble character. Therefore, it would not be a heretical innovation (*bid'ah*) as it does not purport to be religious expression, nor does it intend to innovate a religious practice. However, if these innovations—which are not heretical innovations (*bid'ah*)—are encompassed by actions that are *bid'ah*, or actions that contravene the *sharī'ah*, they are prohibited due to their association with actions that are *bid'ah* and actions that are sinful.

Every commonplace sin is not *bid'ah*. Everything that happens in the marketplaces, *masjids* and communities, every constraint that people choose to ignore and which may contravene the principles of the *sharī'ah* cannot be labeled as *bid'ah*; they are sins and transgressions.

Paying attention to the defining features of *bid'ah* greatly helps in identifying it. To reiterate: the defining characteristic of *bid'ah* is the treatment of an innovated action as if it were a religious practice that one engages in as an act of worship, and where the one who performs it does so as an act of worship, religious expression, or devotion to Allah the Most High.

In my opinion, there is no doubt that those who celebrate the various birthdays, spending much upon them, carrying the burdens of traveling to distant places to participate in these proceedings, do so because they regard it as an act of devotion to Allah, an expiation for misdeeds, and as a means of elevating their religious status. As a result, I am inclined to generalize the prohibition so as to cover all such types of birthday celebrations and to characterize them all as heretical innovations that should be rejected, without offering any defensive excuses to legitimate them.

One of the methods used by autocratic leaders to detract their subjects from criticizing them was to give undue attention to insignificant events, weaving superstitions around them, and spreading them among the masses so that the people remain preoccupied for some time. When people lose interest, their attention is drawn to something else that is circulated in a similar manner, leaving the corrupt leaders to continue without any censure.

Perhaps this explains the secret behind the expanding of the story of 'Antarah ibn Shaddād in the past, such that its constitutive parts finally comprised over sixty volumes. The same applies to *A Thousand and One Nights* and similar encyclopaedias of fantasy fiction. Today, newspapers that seek to kill certain important issues do so by giving prominence to stories of passion and prohibition, capturing their reading audiences by outlining every trivial detail.

In my opinion, the rotation of the blind masses from one place of holy pilgrimage (*mazār*) to the next, the constant movement from one religious celebration to the next, turning the life of the community into a series of continuous religious amusements, was the desired objective of some of the rulers of the past and the *mawlid* was a successful means for attaining this objective. Is there any time and energy left for a community to devote itself to the truth and to noble deeds after such triviality has consumed so much of its time and effort?

Indeed, the abolishment of the *mawlid* celebrations is both a religious and a secular necessity. In addition to the innovated *mawlid* celebrations, the innovated pilgrimages should also be abolished; they are related and represent the completion of a circle of religious innovations that the common masses engage in as an expression of their own vain desires.

Islam has established only three religious celebrations: *'īd al-fiṭr*, *'īd al-aḍḥā* and the day of Jumu'ah (Friday) once a week. However, today there are many fabricated celebrations and pilgrimages, linked to just as many traditions. An example is the day of 'Āshūrā'. Muslims are divided on it into two camps: the Shī'ah, who busy themselves on this day by beating themselves with whatever is at hand, in expression of sadness for the murder of al-Ḥusayn, and the *ahl as-sunnah*, who practise exactly the opposite, holding celebratory gatherings and providing food and sweets in abundance. The actions of both—in addition to the division and craziness they give expression to—have no basis in Islam.

Similarly, celebrations have been organized for the birthday of the Prophet (ṣ), the night of *al-isrā' wa al-mi'rāj*, the night of the middle of Sha'bān (*laylah al-barā'*), the night of *al-qadr* and the new *hijrī* year. Agreed-upon dates have been identified for these celebrations and the effort put into them is regarded as an expression of religiosity. Common people and others celebrate by over-indulging in food and speech and this is seen as a service to Islam!

Muslims thereafter became even more confused and Crusader traditions started influencing their days of celebration, such that Sunday took the place of Friday. Many of the large capital cities I have visited close their shops and factories on Sunday and grant their workers the obligatory opportunity for rest and leisure once a week. This, in spite of the fact that the Messenger of Allah (ṣ) said: "The best day that the sun has risen upon is the day of Friday."[15] He also said: "This is a day of celebration that Allah has allocated for Muslims, so whoever reaches Friday should take a bath and if he has perfume, he should use it; you should also brush your teeth."[16] It is also recorded that the Messenger of Allah (ṣ) had mentioned Friday and said: "In this day there is an appointed hour wherein, if any servant of Allah's is standing in prayer and were to ask anything of Allah, it will be granted."[17]

These days the big cities show almost no movement on Sundays as most of the workplaces are closed. However, on Fridays there is no break for the worker, time for the profiteer, or rest for the fatigued. The entrenchment of the customs of the Europeans and the accompanying Crusader traditions that go along with them are becoming far more prominent. The abandonment by Muslims of the constitutive elements of their religion and of their livelihood in the face of this missionary invasion is bound to have negative consequences, especially when those who take such liberties start thinking that the flexibility of Islam in dealing with those who differ with its adherents is a reflection of respect for their false practices and tacit participation in their celebrations, even though this is strictly prohibited.

'Umar ibn al-Khaṭṭāb said: "Do not learn the gibberish of the foreigners and do not enter the churches of the disbelievers on their day of celebration as the anger [of Allah] descends upon them."[18] This prohibition does not mean that we should not learn other languages, as this is made permissible in several prophetic traditions. Nor does it mean that we should insult the practices of other faiths. There is a huge difference between participating in falsehood and leaving people freely to practise and believe what they want to. What is emphasized is that our own personality should remain clear, our practices should be firmly established, and our Islamic identity should be manifest in our private and public lives.

Indiscriminate imitation, degeneration, dependency and incapacity are the beginnings of disbelief, and suicide.

Notes

1. *At-Targhīb wa at-Tarhīb*, al-Mundharī, 4/256. See also *Ḍaʿīf at-Targhīb*, al-Albānī, ḥadīth no. 2047.
2. *Musnad Aḥmad*, ḥadīth no. 22963.
3. A very important classical text that exposes and corrects corrupt religious practices, written by the Mālikī scholar, Ibn al-Ḥājj. See: Muḥammad ibn Muḥammad ibn al-Ḥājj (1995), *al-Madkhal ilā Tanmiyyah al-ʿAmāl bi Taḥsīn an-Niyyāt wa at-Tanbīh ʿalā baʿḍ al-Bidaʿ wa al-ʿAwāʾiq allatī Intuḥilat wa Bayān Shanāʿatahā*. Edited by Tawfīq Ḥamdān (Beirut: Dār al-Kutb al-ʿIlmiyyah) [Translator].
4. *Sunan at-Tirmidhī*, Book of Funerals, ḥadīth no. 919.
5. *Musnad Aḥmad*, ḥadīth no. 12559.
6. *Ṣaḥīḥ al-Bukhārī*, Book of Adherence to the Qur'an and Prophetic Practice, ḥadīth no. 6749.
7. *Ṣaḥīḥ Muslim*, Book of Knowledge, ḥadīth no. 4823.
8. *Musnad Aḥmad*, ḥadīth no. 26199.

9. *Tanqīḥ at-Taʿlīq*, al-Mizzī, 3/173.

10. I discuss various aspects of this topic in a chapter of my book *Min Hunā Naʿlam*. [This book has been translated into English by Ismāʿīl Rājī al-Fārūqī under the title: *Our Beginning in Wisdom* (Washington: Octagon Press, 1953) [Translator].

11. *Sunan Abū Dāwūd*, Book of Rituals, ḥadīth no. 1746. See also *Ṣaḥīḥ Abī Dāwūd*, al-Albānī, ḥadīth no. 2042.

12. See note 11, above.

13. *Ṣaḥīḥ al-Bukhārī*, Book of the Friday Congregational Prayer, ḥadīth no. 1115.

14. *Ṣaḥīḥ Muslim*, Book of Pilgrimage, ḥadīth no. 2380.

15. *Ṣaḥīḥ Muslim*, Book of the Friday Congregational Prayer, ḥadīth no. 1410.

16. *Sunan Ibn Mājah*, Book of Establishing Prayer, ḥadīth no., 1088.

17. *Ṣaḥīḥ al-Bukhārī*, Book of Supplications, ḥadīth no. 5921.

18. *Iqtiḍāʾ aṣ-Ṣirāṭ al-Mustaqīm*, Ibn Taymiyyah, 1/511.

Conclusion

When seeking Allah's pleasure through righteous deeds and steadfast commitment to His commandments, perseverance becomes an obligation, even if we each must walk this path alone. I have been moved by the advice of Ibn Qayyim, which has filled my heart with joy and encouraged me to heed his words as he speaks about "those that walk the solitary path."[1] I therefore want to conclude this treatise with words of advice for those who love the truth, which will perhaps assist them to hold on to it, steadfastly and constantly. There are so many people that are ignorant of the truth and so many that turn away from it in this lifetime. Those that walk the "solitary path"—among the heedless and the resentful—are surely in need of words that are able to ease the hardships of their journey.

The virtuous, chaste young man among peers that follow their every desire; the man who prays among those that are negligent of their prayers; the Muslim who holds steadfastly onto the Prophetic tradition among those who embrace heretical innovations and superstitions; the one who perseveres to protect the teachings of his religion among those who show no consideration for the belittling of their religion or the flaunting of that which is sacred ... all of these people walk the solitary path and feel the burden of loneliness, even if they are surrounded by people. They feel isolated even if the hearts of the heedless people around them are overflowing with joy and satisfaction. However, because the truth is with them, they feel as if they are in the majority even if they are but a few. They regard the many as being in the minority because these masses follow falsehood.

This feeling of honour and self-esteem is a prerequisite for every person that walks the solitary path. It is a barrier that protects the virtues and sublime values it encompasses; it defends against the misfortunes of ignorance and crushes the arrogance of the foolish; it is able to transcend the vast distance that separates it from its intended goal without showing any concern for the traps set up along the way by highway robbers! This is not surprising, because the one who moves against the current is in need of added strength and faces a longer struggle.

The one who works for the cause of Allah among those who do nothing, and the virtuous person among those prone to vice, are both in need of unique strength to be able to remain healthy among those who are gravely ill. Just imagine what is then required from the one who aims to do away with corruption and to straighten that which is crooked. Can one imagine what is required from the one who alone seeks Allah's pleasure among those who seek only vice and who worship only dust?

Those who walk the solitary path were mentioned by the Prophet (ṣ), when he said: "Islam had begun as an isolated phenomenon and will once again become an isolated phenomenon, just as it had begun. So blessed are the Exiles."[2] It was asked: "Who are they, O Messenger of Allah?" He said: "Those who remain virtuous when others have become corrupt."[3]

Imam Aḥmad reported that 'Abd ar-Raḥmān ibn Mahdī reported from Zuhayr, from the Prophet (ṣ), who said: "Blessed are the Exiles." It was asked: "Who are they, O Messenger of Allah?" He said: "Those who increase, when others decrease." This means: those who increase in good deeds, faith and God-consciousness, when others have lost it all.[4]

Al-Aʿmash narrated a tradition from Ibn Masʿūd, who said: "The Messenger of Allah (ṣ) said: 'Islam had begun as an isolated phenomenon and will once again become an isolated phenomenon, just as it had begun, so blessed are the Exiles.' It was asked: 'Who are they, O Messenger of Allah?' He said: 'Those who stray from the tribes.'"[5]

Another narration states: "'Who are the Exiles?' The Prophet (ṣ) replied: 'A small group of pious people among a large group of corrupt people, and those who disobey the pious people are far more numerous than those who obey them.'"[6]

Another narration states: "The most beloved to Allah are the Exiles." It was asked: "Who are they?" The Prophet answered: "Those who flee, taking their religion along with them."[7] That is, those who flee from dissension.

Another narration asks: "Who are the Exiles?" The Prophet answered: "Those who revive my practices and teach them to the people."[8]

Those who walk the solitary path, even if they are alienated from people, are not harmed by the contempt of the common masses or the hostility of people in power. They may be pressured by maladies and alienation, but this does not cause them to turn to people in search of compassion.

It is narrated that when Mūsā fled from the people of the Pharaoh, in the condition that has been mentioned in the Qur'an—alone, a stranger, scared and hungry—he said: "O my Lord, I am alone, I am ill, I am a stranger!" It was said: "O Mūsā, the one who is alone is such who does not have Me for company. The one who is ill is such who does not have Me as his Healer. The stranger is one who has no interaction with Me."

The truth of the matter is that if Allah fills the heart of His servant with faith, He frequently tests him with hardship along its bitter path. If he is imprisoned, it is an opportunity for seclusion; if he is banished, it affords him the opportunity to travel; if he is killed, he becomes a martyr. As a result, he is isolated from people but has a unique relationship with Allah. In his person, he embodies an entire community.

People naturally enjoy the company of others. Coming together is a human instinct that no one doubts. But if a person's path is elevated above that of others, and his determination is far greater than that of those around him, he becomes alienated. He develops a need for companionship and for a feeling of satisfaction that can replace what he has lost. In this instance, the remembrance (*dhikr*) of Allah, the Honoured and Sublime, is his comfort in isolation, his companion in loneliness, and the oasis in which he finds rest in the expansive wasteland of the whims and caprices of the common masses and the depravity of those in authority.

The Prophetic practice (sunnah) and lessons from the life (*sīrah*) of the Prophet (ṣ) are also a consolation that brings cheer to the Exile. They are a refuge that he visits ever so often, to bask in their light and to breathe in their gardens, so that he does not feel the pain of loneliness and is not overpowered by his isolation.

The Prophet (ṣ) has equated turning towards Allah in times of trouble with keeping his companionship in his lifetime and joining his company in his city. He said: "Worship in the time of turmoil is like migration (*hijrah*) to me."[9] Why would a pious believer want to strike roots and settle in this world when he is ultimately going to leave it behind and be surrounded by thousands of wandering servants of Allah.

Ibn Qayyim said:

If Allah has granted a believer clear understanding of his religion, of the practice of his Prophet (ṣ), of the Qur'an, and Allah has shown him the heretical innovations and misguidance that people follow, their deviation from the path that Allah's Messenger and his companions had followed, and if this believer wants to follow the straight path, then he should be prepared to face the slander of ignorant people and the followers of heretical innovations, their accusations, their degradation, their incitement and their warnings against him, just as the disbelievers had done with his predecessor and leader, the Prophet (ṣ). If he invites them to the straight path and denounces their practices, they will have met their reckoning and will seek to bring down calamity upon him, attribute sorcery to him, and invoke the wrath of Satan upon him.

He is alone in upholding his religion, due to the corruption of their religious practices; alone in clinging firmly to the Prophetic example, due to their firm hold on heretical innovations; alone in his belief, due to the corruption of their belief; alone in his prayers, due to the poor quality of their prayers.

Exile can sometimes be both physical and spiritual, but spiritual exile is the basis of distinction and prestige. Being far away from one's homeland is like being isolated from people and disconnected from their reality, but people with far-reaching determination do not like to remain in their places of birth. They stretch their vision to the far ends of the earth and they like to travel to all corners; they are not tempted by any single location, only in as far as they are able to fulfil their calling there and give rest to their consciences. As a result, migration and travel has been the characteristic of all people of virtue and honour in every age. Their bold steps serve to widen the circumference that is granted to them in the gardens of bliss, on the day that they bid farewell to this world and return to Allah.

'Abdullah ibn 'Umar narrated that a man who was born in Madīnah had died in Madīnah, never having left the city. The Messenger (ṣ) prayed for him and said: "If only he had died somewhere other than the place of his birth." A man asked, "Why, O Messenger of Allah?" The Prophet said: "If a man dies in exile, he is allotted a place in *jannah* the breadth of which is measured from his place of birth to the place of his death."[10]

In another narration it is stated that Allah's Messenger (ṣ) stood at the grave of someone who had died in Madīnah and said: "If only he had died in exile."[11]

If Muslims had understood the virtue of exile, they would have preceded the Europeans in searching for unknown places and in spreading out widely over the earth, developing it and extracting its riches, in addition to fulfilling their universal message in the shadow of this expansive activity. Unfortunately, Muslims remained sitting in their homes until they were invaded and humiliated. The Europeans travelled to all continents and peoples, gaining dominance and prestige.

Exile is to stand out before one's peers and to be at the forefront of the row in which one marches. The highest level of exile is that which pushes a person forward, making him progress, until none can follow in his path, and until he disappears in the eyes of those watching from a distance. This solitary traveller who leaves behind his contemporaries in time and space sends forth for people a guiding light that illuminates their path. His exile is, therefore, not one of isolation, but of sublimity! There are many solitary figures that, by virtue of their condition, their determination, their objectives and their principles, have left a deep impression on those who knew them and on those who discovered them later.

Ibn Qayyim said: "The determination of the one who knows is focused upon that which he knows—that is, upon Allah—and he is alone even among the people of the hereafter, let alone those of this world, just as the one who seeks the hereafter is alone among the people of this world."

This solitary traveller is unique in his knowledge because his horizons are wider, his understanding is deeper and his vision is sharper. He is unique in his emotions because the illumination of divine love in his heart has excited his sentiments, deepened his emotions, and the mercy he shows to those both near and far is overwhelming. He is unique in his worship because, as worshipers and ascetics busy themselves with acts of devotion, he has work with Allah that causes him to turn his attention to his Lord, while still fulfilling the required acts of devotion. He is unique in his behaviour and his judgements because, in his solitary state, he soars above and sees that which others do not. As such, the truth of his pronouncements and actions are only grasped after some time, when those behind finally reach the lookout point he had stood on, staring at the unknown. To others it may be all the same, but he sees what they do not, and passes judgement on the basis of that which they have no insight into.

May Allah shower mercy upon those who walk the solitary path and grant them comfort in their loneliness, by leave of His Honour and Favour!

Notes
1.   This is discussed in his book *Madārij as-Sālikīn*.
2.   *Ṣaḥīḥ Muslim*, Book of Faith, ḥadīth no. 208.
3.   *Musnad Aḥmad*, ḥadīth no. 16094.
4.   *Madārij as-Sālikīn*, Ibn Qayyim, vol. 3, p. 194.
5.   *Musnad Aḥmad*, ḥadīth no. 3596.
6.   *Musnad Aḥmad*, ḥadīth no. 6775.
7.   *As-Silsilah aḍ-Ḍaʿīfah*, al-Albānī, ḥadīth no. 1859.
8.   *Sunan at-Tirmidhī*, Book of Faith, ḥadīth no. 2554.
9.   *Ṣaḥīḥ al-Jāmiʾ*, al-Albānī, ḥadīth no. 3974.
10. *Sunan Ibn Mājah*, Book of Funerals, ḥadīth no. 1603.
11. *Kitāb al-Ghurabāʾ*, al-Ājirrī, p. 36.

Index